Awakening to a World of Need

Awakening to a World of Need

The recovery of evangelical social concern

Timothy Chester

Inter-Varsity Press

INTER-VARSITY PRESS
38 De Montfort Street, Leicester LE1 7GP, England

First published 1993

British Library Cataloguing in Publication Data
A catalogue record for this book is available from the British Library.

IVP ISBN 0–85110–989–6

Set in Linotron Palatino

Photoset in Great Britain by Parker Typesetting Service, Leicester

Printed in England by Clays Ltd, St Ives plc

Inter-Varsity Press is the book-publishing division of the Universities and Colleges Christian Fellowship (formerly the Inter-Varsity Fellowship), a student movement linking Christian Unions in universities and colleges throughout the United Kingdom and the Republic of Ireland, and a member movement of the International Fellowship of Evangelical Students. For information about local and national activities write to UCCF, 38 De Montfort Street, Leicester LE1 7GP.

Contents

To my parents

Foreword
by John Stott

This book badly needed to be written, and Timothy Chester has put us in his debt by writing it with considerable skill, insight and balance. By dint of wide and careful listening he has told the story of the recovery, during the past quarter-century, of our temporarily mislaid evangelical social conscience. He has plotted the course of the various tributaries which have formed the current confluence, and he has illumined his narrative with human stories and quotations from key documents. I am glad that he has paid tribute to George Hoffman, whose leadership of Tear Fund for nearly twenty-five years contributed significantly to this whole development.

This is a story for which we may, I think, be justly thankful, but of which we have few grounds to be proud. For we are Johnny-come-latelies in this area, our steps have been faltering, and our progress sometimes hesitant, even reluctant. Our amateur excursions into the realms of politics, economics and development have often seemed to others to be decidedly simplistic. Moreover, although in general terms it is now securely established in the evangelical mind and conscience that we have an inescapable social responsibility, we have not yet attained the really influential unity of mind and action which the size of our constituency could command.

Our ongoing agenda must surely include further initiatives, not least by local churches, which could prove to be models of gospel outreach, combining good news with good works. And the movement needs further theological undergirding if our unity is to grow. We need to reassure those with continuing hesitations that we are affirming and proclaiming the Word of God, not neglecting it; that we are seeking to be faithful to the social implications of the gospel, not lapsing into the social gospel of early twentieth century theological liberalism; and that we desire to encourage people in their particular vocations, not distract missionaries from theirs.

Our evangelical tendency to polarization is always debilitating, and during the last decade of this millennium we need to seek God's grace to repent of it. Only conscientious common Bible study will help us overcome the residual tensions in our understanding between creation and kingdom, history and eschatology, evangelism, renewal and justice, Word and Spirit, power and weakness, cross and resurrection. May God lead us into a greater integration of these biblical concerns!

Most of the time Timothy Chester faithfully fulfils the role of historian. But he does not suspend his critical faculties. Every now and then he allows himself a judicious comment, and I am glad that in his conclusion he engages in a challenging reflection on the relations between faith, hope and love.

John Stott
President, Tear Fund

April 1993

Preface

In 1993 Tear Fund celebrates its twenty-fifth anniversary. This book was commissioned by Tear Fund in order to mark this anniversary and to do so in a way that would encourage reflection upon the growth of evangelical social concern over the period. I must acknowledge their generous support, and particularly the help of Stephen Rand and Dewi Hughes. Thanks must also be given to David Kingdon, theological books editor of IVP, and Stephen Williams, the deputy director of the Whitefield Institute, for their help and wisdom. The merits of this book are due largely to these people and to all those who generously allowed me to interview them. Thanks therefore are also due to Clive Calver, Gerald Coates, Martyn Eden, Tom Houston, Vinay Samuel, John Stott, and Chris Sugden who granted me interviews; to C. B. Samuel who was interviewed on my behalf by Stephen Rand; and to René Padilla for responding on tape to my questions. And finally my thanks to individuals and organizations who generously responded to my letters and questions. While the credit belongs to all these people, any shortcomings of this book are entirely mine.

My primary aim in writing this book has been to tell the story of the recent growth of evangelical social action. Although the book is broadly chronological, the diversity of material has demanded an approach which is at the same time thematic. I have not had the opportunity to reflect upon that story from a theological, sociological and historical perspective that I would have liked. My hope is that the book will pave the way for further reflection by others more capable than myself. In writing this book I have sought to give examples of the sort of social action in which evangelicals have been engaged. I have necessarily been selective and I hope readers will bear this in mind. The examples are just that, examples: they do not represent the whole, nor necessarily the best, of evangelical social action over the past thirty years.

Some, particularly from the more radical wing of evangelicalism, have argued that the term 'Third World' has pejorative overtones and prefer to speak of the 'Two Thirds World'.[1] Nevertheless I have decided to follow common usage and refer throughout the book to the 'Third World'.

Timothy Chester

Abbreviations

ACET	Aids Care and Education Trust (UK)
BGEA	Billy Graham Evangelistic Association (USA)
CWME	Commission on World Mission and Evangelism (of the WCC)
CEPAD	Council of Evangelical Churches Pro-Denominational Alliance (*Consejo de Iglesias Evangélicas Pro-Alianza Denominacional*)
CLADE	Latin American Congress on Evangelism (*Congreso Latinoamericano de Evangelización*, Bogotá 1968, Lima 1978, Quito 1992)
CONEP	National Evangelical Council of Peru
CRESR	Consultation on the Relationship between Evangelism and Social Responsibility (Grand Rapids 1982)
COWE	Congress on World Evangelization (Pattaya 1980)
EA	Evangelical Alliance (UK)
ECUM	Evangelical Coalition for Urban Mission (UK)
EFI	Evangelical Fellowship of India
EFICOR	Evangelical Fellowship of India Commission on Relief
ESSA	Evangelical Support for South Africa
ICOWE	International Congress on World Evangelization (Lausanne 1974)
IEEN	International Evangelical Environment Network
IFES	International Fellowship of Evangelical Students
IMC	International Missionary Council
INFEMIT	International Fellowship of Evangelical Mission Theologians
IRDA	Interchurch Relief and Development Alliance
IVF	Inter-Varsity Fellowship (now known in Britain as the Universities and Colleges Christian Fellowship)
LATF	Latin American Theological Fraternity

LCWE	Lausanne Committee for World Evangelization
LTEG	Lausanne Theology and Education Group
NAE	National Association of Evangelicals (USA)
NEAC	National Evangelical Anglican Congress (UK)
PIM	Partnership in Mission (USA)
PCR	Programme to Combat Racism
SCF	Save the Children Fund
TAFTEE	The Association for Theological Education by Extension
UNICEF	United Nations International Children's Emergency Fund
WCC	World Council of Churches
WDM	World Development Movement
WEF	World Evangelical Fellowship

Introduction

At the end of October 1966 nearly a thousand evangelicals gathered from across the world in Berlin for a massive congress on evangelization. Never before had evangelicals seen an event on this scale. Evangelicals, it was claimed, were taking up the mantle of world evangelization which had been discarded by the ecumenical movement. The world, many confidently believed, could be evangelized by the end of the century. At the same time a significant minority of the delegates maintained that if evangelism was to be effective it must be accompanied by social action. The condemnation of racism in the final declaration was unprecedented among evangelicals. When in July 1989 another world evangelical congress was held in Manila, a successor to Berlin, evangelization was still the main concern. Now, however, there were major sessions on 'Good News for the Poor' and 'Social Concern and Evangelism' and the final declaration, known as the Manila Manifesto, stated that 'the biblical gospel has inescapable social implications'.

In April 1967, a year after the Berlin Congress, British Anglicans met together at Keele University for the first National Evangelical Anglican Congress. Keele marked a notable change in attitudes. For two or more generations evangelicals had felt like an embattled minority trying to keep the flame of orthodoxy alive through dark times. But at Keele there was a radically different, almost euphoric, spirit. Evangelicals were now growing in numbers and in confidence. And again social involvement came high on the agenda. Today, in a way undreamed of in the years between the two great wars, evangelicals are involved in all areas of British public life from politics to the media, from the arts to the provision of social care.

In 1968 the late George Hoffman joined the Evangelical Alliance as a part-time assistant to its General Secretary Morgan Derham. On his arrival Derham handed him a number of files and told him to make what he could of them. One of them, which bore the rather odd name 'EAR Fund', contained details of small amounts of money received and paid out for work among refugees. Within three years Hoffman had dropped all his other responsibilities to concentrate on the fund, now called Tear Fund. Today Tear Fund is one of Britain's largest relief and development organizations and has a central place in the life of evangelicals.

In 1970 Peter Hill returned from missionary service in India. Arriving back in Britain he was appalled by the decline in moral standards, the suggestive advertising and permissive attitudes to sex. Finding others sympathetic to his concerns he began to organize what became known as the Festival of Light. In September 1971 rallies were held in Trafalgar Square and Hyde Park. For perhaps the first time since Wilberforce and Shaftesbury, evangelicals were re-entering the political world in a significant way. Today the Festival of Light's successor, CARE (Christian Action, Research and Education), continues to lobby government on a range of issues, and political activism by evangelicals is almost commonplace.

What was happening in these years at the end of the sixties and why? And what has happened since? In 1972 David Moberg, borrowing a phrase from the historian Timothy Smith, published a book called *The Great Reversal*. The great reversal referred to the turning away by evangelicals from their traditional commitment to social action. Towards the end of the nineteenth century and at the beginning of the twentieth, evangelicals, for a variety of reasons, lost the social activism which had characterized their predecessors. This book tells the story of how in the past twenty to thirty years evangelicals have, for the most part, rediscovered social concern, and assesses the place of social action within evangelicalism today. Any book such as this must inevitably focus on conferences, books, leaders, organizations and so on. The full story of evangelical social action, however, is the story of the many evangelical Christians, most of whose names will never be widely known, who have responded to Christ's love for them by sacrificially loving others. The apostle John says:

> This is how we know what love is: Jesus Christ laid down his life for us. And we ought to lay down our lives

for our brothers. If anyone has material possessions and sees his brother in need but has no pity on him, how can the love of God be in him? Dear children, let us not love with words or tongue but with actions and in truth. (1 John 3:16–18)

This book is about how evangelicals have sought not simply to speak of God's love but to demonstrate it with actions and in truth. It is both the story of the practical outworking of love in social action and the story of biblical and theological discovery so that love might be in truth.

I

Back into the arena

The cries of suffering humanity today are many. No evangelicalism which ignores the totality of man's condition dares respond in the name of Christianity. (Carl Henry, The Uneasy Conscience of Modern Fundamentalism)[1]

Sociologically, it could be said that evangelicals broke their isolation because they had grown and were too numerous, they had entered the world of higher education and knew too much, and by conquering a higher economic status, they had too much. Growth, knowledge and wealth are antagonistic to isolation. (Valdir Steuernagel)[2]

An American Gallup Report described 1966 as 'the year of the evangelical'.[3] For many years evangelicals had felt embattled and on the defensive, but now their numbers and influence were growing. Evangelical scholars were better equipped to articulate and defend orthodox theology. Confidence was high. Two international congresses brought evangelicals together from around the world on an unprecedented scale.

In Britain, too, according to Clive Calver, the present Director of the British Evangelical Alliance, 1966 was a 'watershed' – and 'it wasn't that we won the World Cup!'[4] Not that it was an easy year for British evangelicals. Their two most important leaders had publicly clashed at an Evangelical Alliance meeting in London. Dr Martyn Lloyd-Jones (1899–1981), minister of Westminster Chapel, London, had called upon evangelicals to leave mixed denominations. John Stott, Rector (now Rector Emeritus) of All Souls, Langham Place, London and later President of Christian Impact, who was chairing the meeting, opposed him. Yet at the same time there was a new spirit. After years of decline evangelicals were growing in numbers and confidence. Evangelicals would no longer simply focus on preserving the gospel, guarding it like a spluttering flame. Instead they would seek to infiltrate the world with it. From the late sixties there was an explosion of evangelical activity, not only in the socio-political arena, but in many other areas: in evangelism, in new forms of music, in the arts, in the media. New churches sprang up, existing churches grew. The rise in social concern was, in many ways, part of a broader evangelical renaissance. In the past two or three decades there has been not simply a rediscovery of social concern but, according to Calver, 'a whole renaissance of multi-faceted evangelicalism'.[5]

By the beginning of the twentieth century the rise of biblical criticism and challenges to traditional orthodoxy had led to the polarization of the church in the United States and, to a lesser extent, in Europe between liberalism (or modernism) and fundamentalism. In 1908 the Federal Council of Churches was formed in the United States to bring together those of a liberal persuasion who emphasized the social nature of the Christian faith. Many fundamentalists reacted to theological liberalism by affirming biblical literalism and withdrawing from the mainline denominations. Between 1910 and 1915 a series of pamphlets was published called *The Fundamentals: A Testament to the Truth*, which defended traditional orthodoxy and attacked the rising liberalism in theology. In contrast to the social gospel of many liberals, the fundamentalists were politically conservative, strongly emphasizing instead, often in a legalistic way, personal morality and a pessimistic view of history and social progress.[6] And because social action seemed to have replaced personal salvation in modernist thinking, it tended to become suspect by association in fundamentalist thinking.

In the 1940s, however, a number of American evangelicals began deliberately to distinguish themselves from fundamentalism. While wanting to remain true to traditional Protestant orthodoxy and to maintain the inspiration and authority of the Bible, they rejected what they saw as fundamentalism's anti-intellectualism and separatism. Though still largely conservative in their politics, they nevertheless deplored fundamentalism's lack of cultural involvement and its apathy over social issues. They spoke of themselves as new evangelicals or neo-evangelicals, although, as their influence grew, they were soon thought of as *the* evangelicals while fundamentalism became regarded as a subculture within orthodoxy.

A number of events helped to give the group an identity and bring it to national prominence. In 1942 the National Association of Evangelicals (NAE) was established under the presidency of Harold J. Ockenga (1905–85), pastor of Park Street Congregational Church in Boston, USA. The NAE was to express its commitment to social action in 1944 through its development arm, World Relief. Ockenga became the first President of Fuller Theological Seminary, founded in 1947 to provide evangelical scholarship of the highest standard and to encourage a more socially enlightened ministry.[7] Also the rise of the new evangelicals saw the flourishing of new para-church groups like Youth for Christ, the Navigators, Campus Crusade and Young Life.

The movement's leading spokesman was Carl F. H. Henry. A former journalist, he lectured at Fuller Seminary from its beginning, was a founder member of the NAE and supported and advised Billy Graham. In 1956 he left Fuller to become the first editor of the new fortnightly magazine *Christianity Today*, which became in many ways the mouthpiece of the new evangelicals.[8] It was avowedly scholarly, orthodox and yet also popular. Furthermore, it regularly dealt with contemporary social issues, particularly in its editorials. Indeed these were often not welcomed by some of the magazine's financial backers. In 1968 Henry was fired as editor of *Christianity Today*. He then became 'professor-at-large' at Eastern Baptist Theological Seminary and in 1974 'lecturer-at-large' for World Vision, the American based Christian relief organization, giving him more time to write and speak on a wider scale.

Of particular significance was Henry's book, published in 1947, *The Uneasy Conscience of Modern Fundamentalism*. In it he described fundamentalism as 'the modern priest and Levite, bypassing suffering humanity'.[9] Fundamentalism, claimed Henry, had lost its social conscience: 'the sin against which Fundamentalism has inveighed, almost exclusively, was individual sin rather than social evil'.[10] In contrast, Henry argued that the message of redemption affects all of life and so he called upon fundamentalism to work out the social implications of the gospel. 'How is it', he asked, 'that a world-changing message narrowed its scope to the changing of isolated individuals? . . . Whereas once the redemptive gospel was a world-changing message, now it has narrowed to a world-denying message.'[11]

Social concern, Henry argued, had been taken up by non-Christian groups and as such had become divorced from its real hope, the redemptive work of Christ. Instead of giving such groups this needed focus, fundamentalism, Henry claimed, had rejected them as unbiblical, and with them, all moves to social reform. Henry noted, too, that even this chosen non-involvement was often far from neutral. Fundamentalism, he pointed out, had been quick to condemn left wing political programmes, in, for example, the Federal Council of Churches, yet had been silent about the evils of a capitalist system. He called upon fundamentalists not to focus on those secondary issues which divide them but to speak on matters of primary importance with a united voice. Looking back on events Henry says: 'What distressed the growing evangelical mainstream about the fundamentalist far right were its personal legalisms, a suspicion of advanced education, disdain for biblical criticism *per se*, attitudes toward those in ecumenically related denominations, and an uncritical political conservatism often defined as "Christian anti-communism" and "Christian capitalism" that, while politicizing the gospel on the right, deplored politicizing it on the left.'[12]

The evangelist Billy Graham aligned himself with the new evangelicals from an early stage and it was his growing prominence and success which brought the new evangelicals to the attention of the wider public. He had been impressed by the force of *The Uneasy Conscience* and was the prime mover behind the foundation of *Christianity Today*. Graham has long accepted the importance of the social aspect of the gospel and has always been by nature generous towards those in need. Yet his passion for 'soul-winning' has meant that preaching has always been to the fore in his mind. He has been mindful, too, of the conservatism of some of his most important backers. Nevertheless he has consistently and actively supported government programmes to combat poverty.[13] Indeed, mirroring developments within evangelicalism as a whole, Graham's commitment to social action seems to have grown over the decades. In 1973 the Billy Graham Evangelistic Association started its World Emergency Relief Fund which channels money to the poor and particularly to victims of disasters. And by the early eighties

Graham was talking about God's 'special concern for the poor' – a phrase not dissimilar to the controversial claim that God has 'a preferential option for the poor'.[14]

Social involvement was by no means the only issue with which the new evangelicals were concerned or upon which they distinguished themselves from fundamentalism. Yet their emphasis on it marked a significant departure from fundamentalism. The growing confidence of the new evangelicals also marked them off from the pessimism of fundamentalists. The advent of liberalism and the questioning of orthodoxy had tended to place evangelicals on the defensive, giving them a separatist, survival mentality. Now they were growing in number and influence and were producing able scholars capable of defending the faith. With this came a new-found confidence, a confidence which enabled them to speak and act on social issues in a new way.

In Britain the conflict between the Federal Council of Churches and the fundamentalists was mirrored to some degree in the conflict between the Student Christian Movement (SCM) and the evangelical Inter-Varsity Fellowship (IVF). The Christian Union at Cambridge broke with the theologically diverse SCM in 1910, in 1919 the first annual inter-varsity conference was held by evangelical Christian Unions and the IVF was officially formed in 1929. In Britain, too, the years after the Second World War witnessed a reversal in the decline of evangelicalism. Under the leadership of Douglas Johnson, General Secretary of IVF, and Martyn Lloyd-Jones, the Inter-Varsity Fellowship grew in strength and influence. The successful university missions of the fifties, led by John Stott and others, further strengthened the evangelical cause among students. Johnson was among a group of evangelical leaders who conceived the idea behind Tyndale House in Cambridge which, by providing support and a focus for evangelical scholarship, helped to give evangelicalism a sense of intellectual credibility. The IVF also organized professional groups to encourage graduates to apply and work out their faith in their professional lives.

Then in February 1954 Billy Graham began his three month Greater London Crusade in the Harringay arena at the invitation of the Evangelical Alliance. Despite adverse publicity and organizational difficulties – Graham drove to the first meeting fearing no-one would be there and that he faced humiliating failure – the crusade was a success beyond all expectations. Extra meetings had to be arranged and telephone relays – voice only – were set up in response to the demand from around the country. Public figures, including the Prime Minister, Winston Churchill, met with Graham. All this was a revelation to British evangelicals, used as they were to being marginalized and despised. That their message could create such popular interest had a significant impact upon them. For many it was the first indication that the evangelical cause might hope for more than simply to hold its own.[15]

At the same time premillennialism was losing its influence, particularly in Britain. The premillennialism which had dominated the evangelical scene at the end of the nineteenth century and beginning of the twentieth had so emphasized the deterioration of society prior to Christ's return that it had proved a strong disincentive for social concern.[16] If things were going to get worse many felt it was best simply to wait until Christ returned and concentrate instead on eternal and personal salvation. David Bebbington cites one Baptist minister who in 1949 wrote that his (premillennialist) understanding of the second advent of Christ 'made him realise it was not the business of the church to Christianize society'.[17] By the end of the twentieth century, however, most evangelicals in Britain, particularly those who would advocate social action, were either amillennial or postmillennial. One milestone in the decline of premillennialism in Britain was the publication in 1971 of *The Puritan Hope* by Iain Murray which reasserted postmillennialism on historical grounds. 'With the fading of the gloomy opinion that the world was under imminent sentence of death,' writes Bebbington, 'effort to improve it seemed more worthwhile. A pent-up potential for social involvement was released.'[18] In the United States premillennialism remains strong and this may be one reason behind the continued resistance to social action in some quarters in the United States.

The new found confidence was also evident a decade after Harringay at the first National Evangelical Anglican Congress held at Keele University in April 1967. Keele, the first time that British Anglican evangelicals had gathered on such a national scale, has been described by David Bebbington as 'the chief landmark in a post-war evangelical renaissance'.[19] The atmosphere was exhilarating: there was a sense of history in the making. As in America so in

Britain, evangelicals had for many years been on the defensive, fighting what seemed to be a losing battle against the full tide of liberalism. Keele '67, however, gave evangelicals, particularly in the Anglican Communion, a new sense of confidence. Their numbers and influence were growing and among them were young and able men and women.

As a result Keele felt able to give support to evangelical social involvement – the first public expression of a growing social concern among British evangelicals. The modernist controversy had never been as strong in Britain as in the United States and likewise the suspicion of social action, though evident in some circles, was not as great. Now a new generation of evangelicals was coming to prominence. They had not lived through the dark days when the evangelical cause had seemed so fragile. And some of them had less affinity with the Establishment, for with improved public education, a greater number came from working-class or lower-middle-class backgrounds.[20]

Michael Saward sees Keele as the turning point in evangelical social responsibility in Britain.[21] He acknowledges that the section on social responsibility in the Keele Report was 'full of well-meaning platitudes and little else'. The important factor, however, he believes, was the note of repentance. There had been a failure in the past, the Report confessed, to be truly involved in the world. 'We believe that our evangelical doctrines have important ethical implications,' it said, and 'evangelism and compassionate service belong together in the mission of God'. The report called upon evangelical Anglicans to think more deeply and radically about social problems.

Although Keele was the first representative commitment to social involvement in Britain, it did not come out of the blue. Influential voices such as those of Sir Norman Anderson and Sir Fred Catherwood had already begun to argue for Christian involvement in the world. Both Anderson and Catherwood were prominent in the Inter-Varsity Fellowship and both were lay people. One of their concerns was that Christians should see their secular employment as part of their Christian calling and apply Christian principles to it.

Sir Norman Anderson had been a missionary, army officer, lawyer and academic. In his autobiography he acknowledges that it was his son Hugh – who died tragically in 1970 of cancer at the age of twenty-one – who first made him sensitive to the need for Christian involvement in issues of social justice. Anderson was one of the key speakers at Keele and the main contributor on the question of social action. His contribution[22] had quite an impact on the Congress and was later expanded into a book, *Into the World*[23] – in response to Keele's resolve 'to give ourselves to more study of these crucial issues in future'. In it he argued that 'the Christian must recognize man's duty to use all God's gifts, not only of redemption but also of creation – gifts direct and indirect, both personal and social – in a way which corresponds as closely as possible with the Creator's purposes as revealed in the Scriptures'.[24] Later, particularly as the influence of Third World evangelicals was felt, the theme of the kingdom of God would play a significant part in the understanding of social action by evangelicals. Indeed, as we shall see later, tension has existed between these two approaches. At this stage, however, the emphasis among British evangelicals was primarily upon the theme of creation.

Sir Fred Catherwood, a nonconformist who came from Northern Ireland and is the son-in-law of Martyn Lloyd-Jones, had a background in industry and management. At the time of writing, he is a Conservative MEP and President of the Evangelical Alliance. He is a former Vice-President of the European Parliament. Since the sixties he has written a series of books dealing with Christian responsibility in contemporary society.[25] The first of these, *The Christian in Industrial Society* (1964), arose from a series of discussions between Christians involved in commerce and industry – Catherwood acting as spokesperson for the group. Their conviction was not only that Christians had responsibilities in their daily life in the world, but also that Christian witness would only be effective when Christians lived out those responsibilities in a distinctive way, both individually and collectively. On the basis of this conviction they sought to work out the nature of Christian responsibility in industrial and commercial life.

Then, in 1971, Britain witnessed the Festival of Light.[26] Although by no means exclusively evangelical, the majority of its supporters were from the evangelical constituency. It had begun in the previous year when Peter and Janet Hill returned from missionary service in India. Arriving back in Britain, Peter Hill was struck by what he perceived to be a significant decline in moral standards, particularly in what was presented in the media and in advertising. He soon found that others felt the same. Mary Whitehouse, for example, had been an art teacher with responsibility for sex education. Concerned by the effect of television on the girls she taught, she took on the broadcasting media in a 'Clean-Up TV Campaign' which later evolved into the National Viewers and Listeners Association. In May of 1971 Lord Longford, an ex-Labour minister, announced he was forming an unofficial group, which included Sir Fred Catherwood, to investigate the rise of pornography and the general decline in moral standards in Britain. The group and its report, published in September 1972, attracted a good deal of ridicule, not least for its trip to Copenhagen in August 1971 'to study pornography and its effects', yet it represented a widespread feeling that the liberalization of moral standards had gone too far.

Encouraged by the support he received, Hill became convinced that some sort of national protest should be organized. Hill was going to call it AMP (About Moral Pollution) but Malcolm Muggeridge, the noted broadcaster and writer and one of the movement's main spokespersons, suggested the name 'Nationwide Festival of Light' in order to stress its positive message. According to Gerald Coates, Muggeridge said to Hill: 'My dear boy, we don't want people marching *against* things, we want them marching *for* things. So instead of having a march against moral pollution, why don't we have a festival of light? That is what we need in this country!'[27] Unfortunately the written word cannot convey Coates' affectionate impersonation of Muggeridge's accent!

Although anti-porn, and it was this negative aspect which the press tended to focus on, the Festival also aimed to make 'a positive stand for purity, love and family life'.

The Festival was strongly criticized from many quarters and organized attempts were made to disrupt its meetings. Nevertheless, after numerous regional rallies and the lighting of nearly three hundred beacons across the country, the Festival culminated in two rallies in London on 25 September 1971. The first, in Trafalgar Square, was the more overtly political. It was a public protest against the rise of pornography and the increasing attack on family life. The second, in Hyde Park, was intended to affirm and proclaim the positive Christian message.

The Festival of Light was yet another sign of the growing

evangelical strength and for many it was their first taste of political action and protest. While evangelicals were experiencing something of a renaissance, they were feeling at the same time a growing sense of moral decline within their nation. When the law legalizing abortion had been passed in 1967 evangelicals had raised little protest. Yet now only a few years later they were waking up to their responsibility and recognizing that they had a potential influence. The Festival of Light itself continued to hold rallies until it was replaced by CARE – Christian Action, Research and Education. CARE, established in 1983, continues to lobby government on a range of moral and social issues and also to educate and inform the public, particularly the Christian public. It has also now developed Care for the Family which is based in Cardiff and which concentrates on social issues and policy as they relate to the family.

The sixties and early seventies, as we can now see, marked a return by evangelicals to the social and public arena. This would not have been possible without growth in numbers and in confidence. But the return to the arena was to be accompanied by vigorous debate among evangelicals over the relationship between the task of world evangelization and commitment to social concern and action. This debate, the beginning of which is described in the next chapter, provides a leading theme through the seventies, eighties and into the nineties.

2

The debate begins

*Any evangelism which does not take into consideration
social problems and which does not proclaim the salvation and lordship of Christ within the context in which
those who listen live, is a deficient evangelism which is
traitor to biblical teaching and does not follow the
example set forth by Christ, who sends us forth as evan-
gels. (Samuel Escobar at CLADE I, 1969)*

In August 1960 Billy Graham and Carl Henry met together with
other evangelical leaders in Montreux, Switzerland[1] to discuss the
possibility of bringing evangelicals from across the world together
for 'fellowship, study and challenge'. Nothing happened immediately, but in early 1964 Billy Graham telephoned Carl Henry in
Washington: he was about to take a taxi from the White House to
the airport; could he pick Henry up in order to talk with him? In the
back of the taxi Graham again shared his vision of an international
congress on evangelism. He felt, however, that it should not be
held under the auspices of the Billy Graham Evangelistic Association (BGEA) because this would look like self-promotion. He also
feared the BGEA lacked the necessary intellectual credibility. Henry
suggested that it be sponsored by *Christianity Today* to celebrate its
tenth anniversary in 1966. Graham in turn suggested that Henry
should be the congress chairman and Henry agreed on condition
that Graham be the honorary chairman.[2] So it was that on 25
October 1966, more than a thousand evangelicals gathered in Berlin
under the title One Race, One Gospel, One Task.

A major impetus for this and subsequent international evangelical gatherings arose from the incorporation of the International
Missionary Council into the World Council of Churches. The IMC
was founded in 1921 as a result of the great World Missionary

Conference at Edinburgh in 1910 in order to increase co-operation between Protestant missionary bodies. With the formation of the WCC in 1948, however, it came under pressure to become the WCC's missionary arm. This eventually took place at New Delhi in 1961 when it become the Commission on World Mission and Evangelism (CWME). Since the WCC could, by its constitution, receive only churches (denominations) into membership, a number of interdenominational or unaffiliated missionary societies were effectively excluded, most of which were strongly evangelical. In 1957, for example, only 42% of all American missionaries were related to member churches of the American National Council of Churches and so, through it, to the WCC. In 1969 it was only 28%, and in 1975 only 14%.[3] Others were unhappy about involvement in the broader ecumenical movement. This created for the first time a need and opportunity for missionary fellowship and co-operation by evangelicals on an international scale. As a result, then, of these changes in the IMC and WCC, 'a new movement would be launched: the "evangelical ecumene"'.[4]

The Berlin Congress, the World Congress on Evangelism,[5] involved a total of over 1,100 carefully chosen evangelicals from over 100 countries. The speakers, however, were still predominately Western. Though it was a congress on evangelism there were signs at Berlin that social involvement was creeping up the evangelical agenda. The closing statement included a condemnation of racism and confessed the failure to love with 'a love that transcends every human barrier and prejudice'.[6]

In particular, it was becoming clear that many felt that the task of evangelizing the world could not be adequately met without facing the issue of social involvement. John Stott, one of the main speakers, spoke of the need to identify with people and to demonstrate God's love to them. We must, he argued, 'win the right to share with them the good news of Christ'.[7] In a paper entitled 'Evangelism and Social Concern', Paul Rees cited examples of the way in which racism could be a hindrance to the gospel and he claimed that the distinctions between sacred and secular and between individual and social 'are never, never completely exclusive'.[8] And in response to Rees's paper, Benjamin Moraes from Argentina spoke of a 'total evangelism' that includes the social implications of the gospel as well as personal conversion.[9]

Before the Congress Carl Henry and others at *Christianity Today* had wanted more attention to be given to the issue of social action, but in the end – not least because such an emphasis was not welcomed by the financial backers of the Congress – it did not feature greatly on the Congress agenda. Instead the focus of the Congress was on what it declared to be the 'one task' of the church: this it saw solely in terms of evangelism without reference to any form of social action.[10] In his opening address, Billy Graham, while acknowledging the need for compassionate action against social evils, argued that the church's 'main task' was that of 'proclaiming the gospel and getting people converted to Christ'. Only in this way could it have a significant impact on 'the social, moral and psychological needs of man'.[11] One Congress speaker, Josip Horak from the then Yugoslavia, went further: 'We should not', he said, 'lose our so precious time for propagating or fighting political ideas. Our job is to proclaim the gospel of salvation . . . dead men do not need this freedom [of religion] or other human rights.'[12]

The spirit of the Congress was typified by a 30ft population clock that clocked up a 1,764,216 increase in the world's population during the Congress. And it was preceded by a Billy Graham crusade in Berlin. The goal of the Congress 'was nothing short of the evangelization of the human race in this generation'[13] and it viewed this task with an almost apocalyptic urgency. Certainly there was a sense of an historical crisis, a crisis, furthermore, for which only concerted evangelism could offer any hope. Carl Henry spoke of 'a critical moment'[14] and Billy Graham spoke of 'the edge of a crisis', of 'the fuse getting shorter and shorter'.[15] Ishaya S. Auda summed up the mood of the conference when he said: 'If possible, the urgency for evangelism is greater today than at any time in history because time is running out, people are multiplying, the world situation is worsening, and distress and unrest are increasing by the minute.'[16]

If the Congress, in contrast to the generally optimistic spirit of the sixties, took a pessimistic view of history, it was supremely optimistic about what it could achieve. Carl Henry astonishingly described the Congress as 'an event unique in Christian history. Not even the Protestant Reformation . . . offered anything entirely comparable to this.'[17] It was the beginning of the space age and it seemed as if technology, in particular American technology, could achieve anything. Many at the Congress, for example, saw great potential in the use of the mass media and computer technology. This spirit represents to some extent the switch in power within evangelicalism from Europe to North America. The European missionary force was in decline while North America's was rising, and something of the American frontier spirit was present at the Congress. The official image of Berlin was that the Congress had established a common goal of evangelizing the world; the focus would now switch to the best means to this end.

Berlin was not the only international evangelical gathering in 1966. Six months before, in the April of 1966, the Congress on the Church's Worldwide Mission[18] was held in Wheaton, USA. There were over 900 participants at the Wheaton Congress from over 70 countries. *Christianity Today* called it 'the biggest and most representative meeting of evangelical missionary leaders ever held'. It was still, however, predominately a North American gathering.

In its final declaration, known as the Wheaton Declaration, the Congress confessed 'an unscriptural isolation from the world' and a failure 'to apply scriptural principles to such problems as racism, war, revolution and communism'.[19] Nevertheless preaching remained firmly to the fore. The declaration stated 'That we affirm unreservedly the primacy of preaching the gospel to every creature and we will demonstrate anew God's concern for social justice and human welfare', and 'That evangelical social action will include, wherever possible, a verbal witness to Jesus Christ.' Yet the Congress also called upon 'all evangelicals to stand openly and firmly for racial equality, human freedom and all forms of social justice throughout the world'. This latter statement, which was not in the original document, was added to it in response to conference debate. Although it could not be described as a radical document, the declaration was significant as the first international sign of a growing concern amongst evangelicals for social involvement.

The long-term significance of the Berlin Congress lay as much in the conferences it spawned as in the Congress itself. The immediate follow-up included a series of regional conferences sponsored by the Billy Graham Evangelistic Association. These culminated in Lausanne 1974, the sequel to Berlin. Like Berlin, the official focus of these follow-up conferences was the task of evangelization. Yet the issue of social responsibility regularly arose.

At the first such follow-up conference, the Asia and South Pacific Congress on Evangelism, Singapore, November 1968,[20] B. E. Fernando of Colombo, Sri Lanka, argued that evangelical biblical witness was causing a social revolution in which, tragically, evangelicals were avoiding participation. He therefore challenged evangelicals to be involved in social change.

The official face of the the US Congress on Evangelism, Minneapolis, September 1969,[21] was similar to that of Berlin. In the keynote address Dr Oswald Hoffman said: 'The church will make little or no contribution to our world if it does not "do its thing". That "thing" is to take the good news of Jesus to heart and then to tell people by every means about Jesus Christ.'[22] The focus was on the question of how to spread the good news – the question of what the good news is was assumed to have been answered at Berlin. Nevertheless a number of the black delegates present made a significant impact on the Congress, expressing their concern that evangelism should not be isolated from the question of racism and civil rights. And Leighton Ford called upon Christians to work out the social implications of the gospel and give themselves in concern for justice.[23]

In the same year, in November 1969, the Latin American Congress on Evangelism (CLADE I)[24] was held in Bogotá, Colombia. This was probably the most significant follow-up conference in terms of its stance on social issues but it was also the most tense and in some ways the most difficult. A year before, Colombia had hosted the now famous second Latin American Episcopal Conference in Medellín, Colombia's second city, at which Roman Catholic bishops had given support to the emerging theology of liberation. Ever since Fidel Castro's takeover of Cuba in 1959 the issue of revolution had been added to the political and social ferment of the continent. During the Bogotá Congress Peter Wagner, then a missionary in Bolivia, went round giving out his new book, *Latin American Theology: Radical or Evangelical?*, to all the participants he could. And the response it produced was very mixed. In it he contrasted five 'radical left' theologians with five 'evangelical alternatives' and introduced church-growth thinking.

Although organized from outside (Billy Graham asked Clyde Taylor of the American NAE to organize it), the Congress itself asserted Latin American leadership and strength. The most popular address was that of Samuel Escobar, 'The Social Responsibility of the Church'.[25] Samuel Escobar from Peru, who at the time was working for the International Fellowship of Evangelical Students (IFES), had together with his colleague René Padilla been advocating evangelical social involvement for some time. At CLADE Escobar issued a strong call for the church to follow the way of incarnation: not to stand apart from the world but to be involved in it and particularly in social change. This would involve sacrificial and costly service, but this, Escobar reminded the delegates, is our calling as disciples. Political activity and evangelism, social responsibility and evangelism, go together, they are inseparable. Escobar's paper 'brought delegates leaping to their feet in a standing ovation'.[26]

That evangelicals should be discussing social responsibility in this way Escobar saw as a sign of maturity and indicating a healthy change of attitude among Latin American evangelicals who in the past had been very influenced by North American fundamentalist missions. The final Evangelical Declaration of Bogotá called for evangelism which took seriously the many needs of people. 'The time has come', the Congress declared, 'to take seriously our social responsibility'.[27] Nor was the conference all theory, for examples of Christian involvement in health-care and education were shared.

That the Congress should be so positive towards social action probably had more to do with the concerns of its participants than with the desires of its organizers. One commentator, writing in advance of the Congress, said: 'Its announced program reflects little consciousness of the deep and vexing social problems that currently are shaking the Latin American church . . . Bogotá's carefully restricted invitations, inoffensive topics, and "safe" speakers cast a shadow very definitely to the right.'[28] That the reality proved otherwise is an indication of the extent to which social issues impinged upon the day to day discipleship of indigenous Latin American Christians.

The last of the regional follow-up conferences, the European Congress on Evangelism,[29] held in Amsterdam 28 August–4 September, 1971, was more conservative than CLADE. Social responsibility tended to be given a more minor role in relation to evangelism which was seen as the primary task of the church.

Though it was an issue, little was added to what had already been said at Berlin. Paavo Kortekangas from Finland warned that the gospel is 'misunderstood if we shut our eyes totally to the social implications of our faith'.[30] John Stott again argued that the Spirit of God can use the non-verbal witness of the Christian community to communicate the gospel. Christians, he said, need to communicate the love of God in actions even if this then needs to be interpreted by words. Jacques Blocher from France claimed after the conference: 'We are also making a frontal attack on social problems; as a result of Amsterdam, our French-speaking evangelicals are already moving against drug abuse in an unprecedented way.'[31]

It would be wrong to maintain that Wheaton, Berlin and the subsequent regional conferences led to evangelical social involvement. Rather they were the first signs on an international level of a growing concern for social involvement among a minority of evangelicals, particularly from the Third World. Looking back at them in 1974 Samuel Escobar could say: 'After Berlin, the national and regional Congresses rediscovered an articulated evangelical social concern with a surprising coincidence in contents and tone.'[32] The main thrust of these conferences was on the urgency of evangelization. Those advocating social involvement certainly did not question the need of evangelism. Nor did they simply argue that social involvement had a place alongside evangelism. Rather they argued that evangelism could not be truly effective if it was isolated from the social aspect of the gospel. At Berlin, in the reports from around the world, the so-called 'windows on the world', Benjamin Moraes from Argentina acknowledged: 'It is difficult to preach the gospel to people who are hungry, live in miserable huts and are disease-ridden. Some Christian social work must accompany the regular program of preaching.'[33] Likewise the report from southern Africa pointed out that 'the socio-economic superiority of the whites against their political background makes it increasingly difficult for a burdened white missionary to evangelize the non-white'.[34] At the US regional conference one of the black participants, Tom Skinner, said: 'The church must take a stand against racism on the grounds of the kingdom of God and the clear teaching of scripture. For the church to continue to deny biblical truths is a blow from which blacks cannot recover.'[35] They did not question statements main-

33

taining the centrality of the proclamation of the gospel, as long as it was not a gospel divorced from its social consequences. What they feared was an entrepreneurial evangelism with a message of believism in which the demands of repentance and the social outworking of the gospel were forgotten.

Furthermore, at Wheaton and at Berlin Christians from the First World began to encounter their counterparts from the Third World. 'Berlin was the first evangelical congress', believes Valdir Steuernagel, 'that was affected by its own internationality . . . at Berlin the Third World began to speak out and offer criticism of the West and the West began to listen.'[36] During this period Third World theology and practice were coming of age and asserting their independence from First World theology. Third World theology was finding First World models inadequate to deal with the reality of its own missionary experience. On the immediate issues that they faced, the issues of poverty and injustice, First World theology had little to say. Vinay Samuel, for example, describes working on the synoptic gospels at Cambridge and realizing how much they have to say about the poor and how little had been written on this by Western theologians.[37] The final declaration of CLADE said that Jesus Christ should be incarnate in the life of the church 'in the critical Latin American reality of underdevelopment, injustice, hunger, violence and hopelessness'. These were issues which the Western church did not have to face as a daily reality and to which therefore it gave little prominence. Through this contact First World Christians began to be confronted with the fact that their theological presuppositions might to some degree be culturally determined and that their received understanding of theology might be inadequate for the issues facing their Third World brothers and sisters.

If it is to be relevent to Third World situations, it has been argued, evangelical theology must address such issues as poverty, injustice and underdevelopment. It cannot simply be imported, unchanged in expression and emphasis, from the First to the Third World. To use a word which over the last twenty years has become something of a slogan, our theology must be *contextualized*. Our understanding of the Bible must arise in response, and speak, to the particular situation in which we serve and the particular needs which we face. From Berlin onwards, as First and

Third World evangelicals increasingly found each other, contextualization, in one form or another, became a key concept in the on-going theological debate. At the same time the growing social concern of many arose as they came face to face with need.

3

Face to face with need

We've been visiting a hospital in a refugee camp outside Calcutta. As a result, one of those horrible silences has settled over us as we drive out of the camp now. As we stood by one ward a man collapsed in front of us as he was being brought in by his relatives. He was in the advanced stages of cholera. Five people died yesterday in that ward alone, of cholera. In the same place five babies were born.

The mothers held up before us their little babies that looked as though they were dying. The tears were streaming down their faces as they reached over the barbed wire to where we stood. They desperately asked [if there was] anything that we could do to help. All we could do was turn our backs and walk away.

I wondered all of sudden why I couldn't move my legs. I found there was a woman wrapped around them, holding my feet and kissing them, refusing to let them go. Tears ran down her face ... It is very hard on such occasions not to weep also, and throw every penny you've got down.

It's strange. When we left Calcutta this morning the conversation in this truck was animated. Ever since we left the camp there has been hardly a word spoken. We are just sitting, strong, grown men, with watery eyes, finding it very difficult to talk ... (From a record distributed by Tear Fund of George Hoffman's first-hand account of the refugee crisis in Calcutta after the 1971 civil war in Pakistan)[1]

At the conferences described in the previous chapter social issues for the first time were becoming part of the evangelical agenda. The conferences, however, did not create this interest. If they influenced people's thinking it was not so much in convincing them of the biblical case for social action, but rather in giving confidence to those already involved in it. They also showed those who were dubious about social involvement that advocates of social action were not isolated extremists but part of a growing movement.

During this period many evangelicals discovered that the Bible has much to say on social issues. For some this discovery arose from theological debates. At the beginning of this century two New Testament scholars, Albert Schweitzer (1875–1965) and Johannes Weiss (1863–1914), sought to demonstrate that at the heart of Jesus' message was the coming of the kingdom of God and that this was nothing less than a new apocalyptic order. Their work sparked off a long debate about the nature and timing of the kingdom of God. The most important evangelical contributor to this debate was George Eldon Ladd (1911–82) whose book *Jesus and the Kingdom*[2] has proved extremely influential. Vinay Samuel and Chris Sugden among others point to the crucial role which *Jesus and the Kingdom* played in their own thinking.[3] Ladd argued that the kingdom of God is the rule or reign of God over all of life and that it is present as well as future. That the kingdom is central to the message of Jesus was a revelation to many evangelicals brought up on a theology which focused on the individual's relationship with God brought about through justification by faith in Christ. This personal relationship was in no way denied but was now seen within the wider theme of the kingdom of God, God's rule over all of life. With this recognition came the realization of the importance of the kingdom community, the community in which the blessings and demands of the kingdom are lived out. At the same time, as we have seen, others, such as Norman Anderson, were advocating social involvement on the basis of the doctrine of creation rather than on an understanding of the kingdom of God.

But this was not the only route along which evangelicals came to a rediscovery of what the Bible said about the social implications of the gospel. For many the important factor was not so much a changed understanding of theology but a straightforward response to need.[4] For them theology followed practice: as they faced various needs and sought to respond to them so they were forced to examine afresh what the Bible had to say. The practice itself was not initially prompted by a new theology but by a response of love and compassion. Organizations like the Evangelical Fellowship of India Commission on Relief (EFICOR) and Tear Fund in Britain arose in order to provide some means for evangelicals to channel money to those in need. It was only as these organizations began to grow that they themselves began to deepen and develop the response of evangelicals to social needs.

These needs confronted evangelicals in a number of different ways. Many engaged in evangelism in the Third World found that the poor responded more readily than the better-off to the gospel. Not only was this in itself significant (especially in India) but also evangelism resulted in churches whose members were in great economic need. This meant that those involved in this work were faced with their responsibility to their brothers and sisters. For others the famines and day to day suffering of the poor prompted them to compassionate action. As we shall see, in the West this response was closely linked with the advent of television news pictures.

The major evangelical relief agency already around in the early sixties was World Vision. In 1948 Bob Pierce, a young American evangelist, was preaching in China even as the Communist revolution was taking place. At Amoy he was asked by Tena, a missionary of the Dutch Reformed Church, to speak at a local mission school. After explaining the gospel he called upon the children to commit themselves to Christ and go home and tell their parents of their new faith. The next day he called back at the school. He was met by an angry and distraught Tena. In her arms was a little girl, White Jade, sobbing and showing signs of having been beaten and whipped. For doing what Bob Pierce had asked she had been beaten by her father for dishonouring her ancestors and thrown out of her home. Tena thrust the traumatized girl into Pierce's arms and demanded to know what he was going to do; she already had six other children to care for. Holding the young child in his arms Pierce was profoundly moved. He gave Tena five dollars, all he had with him, and promised to send money regularly, which he did until he lost contact with White Jade in 1949 after the Communist takeover. The confident evengelist had been deeply humbled by the plight of that young child and saw for the first time something of the social implications of the gospel.

In 1950 Bob Pierce preached in Korea. When he returned to the United States he began to tell people of the tremendous needs of the Korean church and, as money started to come in, World Vision was officially formed on 22 September. In the same year Pierce made World Vision's first publicity film, *38th Parallel*. Money was used to care for Korean orphans, many the result of liaisons between American troops and Korean women, and for medical work. In 1953 World Vision began a child sponsorship scheme. On a return visit to Korea Bob Pierce wrote inside his Bible: 'Let my heart be broken by the things that break the heart of God.'

Since its beginnings, when Bob Pierce's heart was moved by the plight of White Jade, World Vision has grown into a multi-million dollar organization with offices in every part of the world. World Vision seeks support not only from the evangelical community but also from the general public. Its sheer size and power have tended in the past to make it somewhat controversial. In reality it has tended to vary from country to country, particularly in the extent to which it seeks to integrate evangelism and social concern.

In 1967 famine hit the Bihar region of India. The church in Bihar wrote to the Evangelical Fellowship of India asking for help. Dr Ben Wati included a report in *Aim*, the monthly magazine of EFI, of which he was the editor, simply asking for prayer. Money, however, began to come in even though in the first place it had not been asked for, and so a target was set of Rs. 25,000. In the end Rs. 115,000 came in with additional money coming from overseas. In order to distribute this money EFI established a committee for emergency relief (EFICER). When the crisis in Bihar was over the committee remained in being in order to provide further emergency relief for those suffering as a result of natural disasters. As EFICER became an established part of the work of EFI it dropped the term 'emergency' and became the Evangelical Fellowship of India Committee on Relief (EFICOR) and later the Commission on Relief.

Two years later, in 1970, speaking at the All India Congress on Evangelism,[5] Dr Ben Wati defended this renewed involvement in social action. He pointed to the record of both Western missionaries and Indian nationals in social care and reform in the past. William

Carey (1761–1834), for example, and his colleagues at Serampore had campaigned against suttee, the practice of burning widows with the corpses of their husbands. Ben Wati acknowledged that most Indian Christians were themselves poor but called upon the churches in India to share what they had rather than simply look to Western help. He gave the example of one rural pastor and pioneer evangelist. Ben Wati had visited him and found him and his family suffering from malnutrition. Ben Wati arranged for money to be sent so that he could buy rice. The sum of just Rs. 190 overwhelmed the pastor who nevertheless gave a tenth to the village church. When a further sum was sent he first of all bought twenty blankets for the needy of the village before looking to his own family's needs. When, later, he discovered a baby abandoned because it was deformed, he cared for it alongside his own eleven children. Seeing that pastor's love and concern for the poor, Ben Wati went on, several people from the village had been converted.[6]

During the following year, 1968, Tear Fund was launched in Britain. George Hoffman (1933–92), the first Director of Tear Fund, had been profoundly influenced by Keele and as such Tear Fund owes its origins in some measure to that Congress. The story of Tear Fund, however, does not begin with Keele but with World Refugee Year. World Refugee Year, launched in June 1959, brought into focus the needs of refugees, and a number of the members of the Evangelical Alliance sent money for it to use for refugee work through its contacts with overseas missionaries. As with EFICOR, this money was initially unsolicited. The EA decided to set up a fund under the title Evangelical Alliance Refugee Fund (EAR Fund).

Over the next few years money continued to come in – still with hardly any publicity. When Morgan Derham became the new General Secretary of the EA in 1966 he decided that the fund should be broadened to include relief work in general. The name was changed accordingly to the Evangelical Alliance Relief Fund and assigned a new temporary member of staff, Mary Jean Duffield, to examine and develop its potential. Mary Jean had planned to find a well paid job before going up to university. Instead, concerned to do something in the light of the predicted famine in Bihar, she accepted the post at the EA in January 1967. It was not an easy task for a young twenty-one-year-old and she often felt a lone voice. Nevertheless Morgan Derham was convinced that the fund had potential. Evangelicals, he felt, were waking up to their social responsibilities. At the same time, he was concerned to remove what he called the evangelical alibi, namely that there were no evangelical bodies through whom money could be given and care expressed.[7] Tear Fund would always channel money from evangelicals to those in need through evangelicals.

By the time Mary Jean left, George Hoffman had joined the EA staff on a part-time basis while remaining assistant editor of *Crusade* magazine. When he arrived Morgan Derham handed him twelve files on EA projects. One was the EAR fund file. Hoffman immediately felt a proper committee should be formed of people with expertise and experience and Glyn Macaulay was asked to be its first chairman. To her surprise Mary Jean was also asked to join and served for a while as a welcome thorn in the committee's side by pressing for a more radical and political approach to Third World issues. Concerned not to alienate its supporters, Tear Fund continued to be very cautious about political involvement, although in 1970 it did send a letter for publication to most of the Christian press urging voters in the coming election to make overseas aid an election issue. Peter Meadows, founder of *Buzz*, a monthly magazine for young Christians, was also included on the committee and was responsible for most of the fund's early publicity material. It was Meadows who suggested the name TEAR Fund – as an improvement on 'EAR Fund'! – and who designed the distinctive tear-shaped lettering of its logo.

The first official committee meeting was held on 29 May 1968, although the public launch was not until November. At the press conference a simple meal of crisped rice, powdered milk and fruit contrasted sharply with the silver candelabra on the table: the diet of millions served in the splendour accorded to only a few. In January 1969 the first Tear Fund concerts were held with Cliff Richard performing in the Albert Hall in order to raise money and publicize the fund.

As Tear Fund grew it was able to realize one of the early aims, that of informing and educating the evangelical constituency. In late 1969 George Hoffman persuaded John Capon to include a four-page supplement on the work of Tear Fund in the two papers of which Capon was then editor, the *Church of England Newspaper* and the *Christian Record*. Later the supplement was produced independently and became *Tear Times*, Tear Fund's own quarterly magazine. During the following year the first summer work camps were organized. These were followed by the launch of Tear Fund Sunday, the first Tear Fund soundstrip, *Down to Earth*, and the first harvest thanksgiving packs. In 1971 Tear Fund produced a record of George Hoffman's moving first-hand account of the refugee crisis in Calcutta.

Tear Fund's income grew from £34,000 in its first year to £208,000 by 1971 when George Hoffman finally dropped his other commitments and became the full-time Director of Tear Fund. During the previous year Tear Fund had become effectively independent of the Evangelical Alliance – a move which was later recognized in the change of name from 'The Evangelical Alliance Relief Fund' (TEAR Fund) to simply 'Tear Fund'. Since its launch in 1968 Tear Fund had been able to make grants across the world, the first to a development programme in Argentina.

Although Tear Fund has not sought to become an international organization in any way, other national evangelical alliances have set up corresponding 'Tear Funds'. Each national Tear Fund, however, is autonomous and has developed distinctive working practices. Tear Australia and Tear Fund Holland, for example, do not support individual child sponsorship on principle. In 1980, during its seventh General Assembly, the World Evangelical Fellowship arranged a meeting of development agencies linked to national evangelical fellowships. This meeting led to the formation of IRDA, the Interchurch Relief and Development Alliance, which exists to encourage co-operation and dialogue between evangelical relief and development organizations from both the First and Third Worlds.[8]

During the year before Tear Fund's launch the eastern region of Nigeria attempted to secede and form the independent nation of Biafra. In 1968 the resulting civil war led to widespread famine. What was significant about this for evangelicals in the UK was, first, the fact that for the first time they had a recognized evangelical agency through which to channel their response. And second, the famine received widespread coverage on the television news. Pictures of emaciated children, all too familiar now, were shown for the first time. And with them the reality of hunger and starvation was evident as never before to the growing proportion of the population who had television sets.

During the late fifties and early sixties television had become a mass medium. In 1950 only 10% of households in Britain possessed a television; by 1963 only 10% did not.[9] In 1954 commercial television was launched prompting the BBC to give a greater priority to the new medium.

After its achievements during the Second World War, BBC Radio News became somewhat élitist and conservative in approach and initially television news followed a similar pattern. No personalities were allowed to intrude, the approach was always serious with little attempt to focus on 'human interest' and accuracy was more important than speed – there was no desire for 'scoops'. Indeed originally, apart from a regular newsreel style programme, television news consisted of a ten-minute summary at the end of transmission read over the BBC logo – most people turned off![10]

The coming of Independent Television News, however, brought great changes to television news reporting. ITN sought to be impartial but also entertaining, to speak with the same authority as the BBC but without the BBC's 'solemn ritual'.[11] It was more personality orientated and aimed to develop an approach to the news specifically geared to the television medium, one which recognized the importance of pictures. The success of ITN inevitably meant changes to BBC news. Television news finally was given its own department and started its own news bulletins. By the end of the fifties most people received their news from the television rather than the radio.

Another important development was the recognition, first made by Richard Dimbleby, of the distinction between the 'immediate news' of the news bulletin and the 'permanent news' which demanded its own approach – in other words, current affairs programming. In 1955 the BBC launched *Panorama* which centred on Richard Dimbleby as its anchorman. The current affairs output was immediately more adventurous than the news bulletins. It allowed more scope for location reports, for reporters' personalities, and gave more opportunity to deal with controversial subjects. Soon the two approaches were being combined in magazine style programmes which mixed news bulletin with interviews and analysis:

Tonight on the television and *Today*, *Ten O'Clock* and *The World at One* on the radio.

Of great significance, too, was the Pilkington Report, published in 1962. Commercial television had had a difficult beginning and had only survived through cheap, popular programming. By the sixties, however, it was a financial success; indeed Roy Thompson, the media baron and owner of Scottish Television, described it in 1959 as 'a licence to print money'.[12] The Pilkington Report strongly attacked the standard of ITV companies' programming and the size of their profits. This led the government to levy a tax on their revenue in 1964. With less incentive to maximize profits and under the pressure created by the Pilkington Report, ITV companies began to introduce a greater number of serious programmes. It also meant that the Independent Television Authority (which became the Independent Broadcasting Authority in 1972 when independent radio was added to its orbit) had more muscle.

The combination of these factors lay behind the introduction of *News at Ten* in July 1967. Research in 1966 showed that 83% of viewers were content with a fifteen-minute news summary at 8.55 p.m.,[13] but the pressure created by the Pilkington Report led to Britain's first half-hour news slot. As it turned out, *New at Ten* soon became so popular that the ITV companies built their evening schedules around it and the BBC extended their nine o'clock news programme. It is also meant that news coverage was deepened. No longer was it simply an illustrated supplement to the radio and newspapers. Newscasters no longer just read the news, they became journalists and interviewers. Location reports and foreign correspondents became the norm. And later the development of satellite transmission created the possibility of immediate contact with foreign news stories.

In short, within a decade television had become the dominant medium in Britain, and television news had moved from being short, read summaries to a popular, visually orientated format with interviews and location reports backed up by documentaries and detailed analysis.

These developments were to have a profound effect on perceptions of Third World need. Whereas poverty and starvation had been far removed from Western evangelicals, suddenly it was in their homes providing a dramatic contrast to their own lifestyles. If action in India was prompted by the needs on people's doorsteps, in Britain it was the proximity of those needs through the medium of television that produced a response. Indeed it may be this factor as much as any other which has led to involvement by British evangelicals in Third World poverty.

Since its inception Tear Fund's annual income has three times all but doubled in one year. In each case the jump in income can be related to the reporting on television of a particular crisis. The first time was in 1971 when it rose from £88,000 to £208,000 – in 1971 the civil war in Pakistan which led to the creation of Bangladesh unleashed an immense refugee crisis. The second time was in 1973 when it rose from £271,000 to £542,000 – in 1973 drought hit India and twenty million people faced starvation. The third time was in 1984 when income rose from £6,402,000 to £11,178,000 – in 1984 ten million people faced starvation as a result of drought in Ethiopia.

Evangelicals in Britain clearly respond to need when confronted by it. Yet at the same time for many their involvement is not simply confined to disaster relief in this way. Although Tear Fund's income has risen dramatically as a response to immediate need, the increased level of giving has always been maintained. Only in 1985, the year after the greatest ever increase, did income fall (from £11,178,000 to £10,289,000). Even so this still represented a more than 60% increase on the 1983 figure of £6,402,000. Stephen Rand, the Communications Director of Tear Fund, likens the response to media coverage of poverty to waves coming in: 'while that wave of giving goes back, the tide has come a bit further in'. In other words, people do respond in a special way to the coverage of need, perhaps for the first time, but many of those people carry on giving in a committed way even when the coverage goes away.[14]

4

The turbulent sixties

If I thought that being an evangelical automatically involved accepting male domination, corporal punishment, bourgeois prejudices, trivial views, poor taste, a hankering after organising other people's lives, a refusal to look facts in the face, and a persecution complex, I should drop evangelicalism like a hot brick. But I do not believe that these commonly occurring features are indispensable components of an evangelical faith. Indeed, I think they are dangerous and objectionable and more than ripe for repudiation. An increasing number of evangelicals are gradually doing the repudiating. When the process is well in hand, we shall see evangelicalism in a fairer light. (John King, until 1968 editor of the Church of England Newspaper, *in 1969[1])*

To say that there is a generation gap between the post-thirty establishment evangelicals and their pre-thirty offspring is not only to state the obvious but to border on understatement . . . While the establishment debates concepts of organic evolution with scholastic precision, we face the challenges of social revolution. While the establishment continues to split hairs as to how we are to separate from the world, we wonder how we can become meaningfully involved. (Paul Henry, the son of Carl Henry, in 1970[2])

In 1948 India gained its independence and the dismantling of the British empire began. Throughout the fifties and sixties former colonies followed India's lead. Back in Britain prosperity grew and there was virtually full employment. 'You've never had it so good', the Prime Minister, Harold Macmillan, told the nation. When the oil crisis of the early seventies created world recession people became more insecure; they looked to their personal interests and the primary concern of students was getting a job. But the sixties were heady days when no-one feared unemployment. It was 'the decade of protest, when young people were rebelling against the materialism, superficiality and hypocrisy of the adult world they had inherited'.[3] In America, Britain, France and Czechoslovakia there were calls for radical social change. In America the Vietnam war and racism were the focus of much of the protest. The civil rights movement, and Martin Luther King Jr in particular, forced many hard questions upon evangelicals. On an academic level James Cone provided a critique, from a black perspective, of American society and theology. All this ferment was bound to have an effect on evangelicals. 'The civil rights movement of the 1960s gave great impetus to evangelical reflection on social involvement.'[4]

In the 1940s Billy Graham was, like most from his background, a segregationist. By 1953, however, when he noticed rope divides at a crusade in Chattanooga, Tennessee, he began pulling them down to the embarrassment of the ushers. Although critical of the civil rights movement's defiance of authority, Graham insisted on mixed crusades and increasingly he took a strong line in condemning segregation. In 1960 he refused to include South Africa in an African tour, describing segregation in both South Africa and North America as immoral and unchristian. It was not until 1973, when Michael Cassidy managed to arrange an historic unsegregated crusade, that Graham finally went to South Africa. Cassidy was, so to speak, a spiritual grandchild of Graham – he had been converted by a Harringay convert – and was a great admirer of Graham. In South Africa he established a multi-racial evangelistic team and has gone on to play a major role among those white evangelicals who have stood against apartheid.

It was as a result of the civil rights movement that Graham could confess: 'My belief in the social implications of the gospel has deepened and broadened. It is my conviction that the evangelist must not hedge on social issues.'[5] Although their approach was very different, Graham and Martin Luther King had a mutual respect. In fact the issue that really divided them was not race but the Vietnam war. King opposed the war from an early stage.

Graham's approach, although somewhat ambiguous, was generally supportive of the government – he was certainly critical of the anti-war protests.

It was among a younger generation of evangelicals, however, that the civil rights movement and the anti-Vietnam protests made the greatest impact. Most of the church stood by the political establishment, worried by what they perceived to be the forces of anarchy.[6] Indeed in some ways, because the liberal churches whole-heartedly supported the civil rights movement, such social concern was suspect by association. As such the civil rights movement prolonged the modernist/social gospel controversy in North America in a way that did not happen in Britain.[7]

Nevertheless, for many, and especially for students, the issues of racism and the Vietnam war raised questions which they could not ignore and that went to the heart of the gospel message they had been brought up to believe. Had things not begun to change it is possible that some with a radical social conscience would have lost contact with the church. In Britain, for example, the emergence of Tear Fund provided a channel for social concern that was not as yet common in the churches.

Yet only a few were actually involved in student unrest. Christian Unions in Britain and America continued to focus on evangelism. At one national IVF conference at Swanwick, CU representatives signed a document on student protest which pointed to sin as the underlying problem and Christ as the only solution: the implication was that the solution did not lie in political unrest. In 1972 Inter-Varsity Press published a collection of essays edited by Brian Griffiths entitled *Is Revolution Change?* 'The basic thesis of this book', concluded Griffiths, 'is that the Christian approach to the problems of modern society is totally different from that of contemporary revolutionary culture.'[8] At the same time the contributors were not defending non-involvement by Christians but instead were concerned to work out a Christian approach to social problems. The book included, for example, Samuel Escobar's address to the CLADE.

Although there were politically active evangelical students they were rarely active members of the Christian Unions which by and large remained immune from radical student protest. The spirit of the sixties was an important influence[9] but not in any simplistic way. The evangelical social activitists of the seventies were not simply copying or baptizing the radicalism of the sixties. 'That really wasn't how it was at all', says Chris Sugden. Sugden is currently the Director of the Oxford Centre for Mission Studies, but in 1968 he was the President of the Christian Union in Oxford. He says: 'None of us were involved in any student demonstrations . . . It is a caricature to say that, it certainly would be unrecognizable as a description of the people who were in the evangelical Christian groups at that time.'[10] Nevertheless as they reached out to their fellow students Christians were forced to face the challenge of the issues being raised. Was Christianity 'the pie in the sky' Marxists and others accused it of being or did it in fact have a relevance to social issues? Christian students were being confronted with alternative worldviews which forced them to reassess the Christian view of the world in all its dimensions. They could not remain entirely free from the spirit of the times.

The evangelicals most affected by the radical protests of the sixties were those closely involved in them who then became Christians. When radical protestors were converted they brought with them a social conscience that sat uneasily with the suspicion of social action still held by most evangelicals. 'For me', says Clive Calver, 'the radical protesting wasn't "they", it was "we" – five rows from the front as we stormed the American Embassy – that was where I come from'. He was later converted through contact with Roger Forster and seeing a social conscience worked out in his life. 'I was converted . . . having rejected the words but then seeing the life', a life which 'demonstrated for me an evangelicalism that worked in practice which I had never seen'.[11]

One of the most prominent evangelicals to emerge from the radical student movement was Jim Wallis, founder of the Sojourners community in Washington, USA. In his autobiography, *The New Radical*, he describes his rejection of his white American, conservative evangelical upbringing and his discovery of the 'other' America – the America of poverty, injustice and discrimination. As a student Wallis was heavily involved in the radical protest movement and its campaigns against racism and the Vietnam war. As disillusionment with the movement grew he began to discover a powerful mandate for social action in the Bible. Looking back he wrote:

I finally knew that I wanted to be a follower of this Jesus. Contrary to the message I had received from the church, Jesus' message was as political as it was personal, as economic as it was spiritual, having as much to do with public life as individual devotion. Jesus had lived and preached and died to begin a new order that would turn the world upside down and change lives and history in every way.[12]

Wallis decided to go to Trinity Evangelical Divinity School, Illinois and there he and a group of other like-minded students began to meet and work together. Wallis recalls how their anti-war protests were met by vehement opposition from most evangelicals. Nevertheless, to a minority they brought a sense of relief, for people were glad to know they were not alone in their beliefs. The group later evolved into a community committed to work among the marginalized in American society and it brought out a magazine, *Post-American*, which would later become *Sojourners*. Although the magazine was produced on a shoestring budget and had no means for large-scale publicity or circulation, it attracted a wide and enthusiastic response. Wallis likens its publication to the raising of a flag up a flagpole:

Many people on the ground, at grass roots level, were longing for an alternative to the narrow versions of Christian faith they were experiencing in their churches, but they didn't know one another. Many of the earliest letters to us expressed people's long-held feelings of being alone in their beliefs, wondering if any other Christians like them existed. People from many places saw the flag and met one another around the flagpole.[13]

The magazine provided a focus for those with convictions like Jim Wallis's, born of the radical movements of the sixties but rooted in their understanding of the Bible. In Britain, too, the writings of Wallis proved popular among some. The radicalism of the sixties was forcing many Christians to turn afresh to their Bibles and to place themselves and their culture under the word of God.

An equally significant example from the black community in the

United States is that of John Perkins, founder of Voice of Calvary Ministries. Perkins grew up among the violence, racism and poverty of Mississippi before 'escaping' to California. After a period in the army he left and with a good job began to 'make it'. Then, through the influence of one of his children, he came to know Christ. Soon he felt called to return to Mississippi to work among the black community there and so in 1960 he left California with his wife and family and moved to Simpson County, Mississippi.

Initially he began preaching and teaching wherever he could, though soon this began to be combined with social action. There were two factors which led to this development. First was the terrible poverty which he and his wife encountered day by day as their evangelism involved them in people's lives. Perkins writes: 'We began to discover that real evangelism brings a person face to face with *all* the needs of a person. We had to see people not just as souls, but as whole people.'[14] It was the need they saw around them which initially prompted them to act and so they began with a day-care centre for young children. Older children often could not go to school because they had to look after their younger brothers and sisters. The day centre gave them the opportunity to go to school and ensured that the younger children had a nutritious meal. The Perkinses came to realize that effective evangelism would require them to be involved not only with people's spiritual needs but also with their physical needs.

The second factor was the civil rights movement. Just as involvement in evangelism led to social action, so social action led to a realization that much poverty had its roots in structural injustice.[15] They began to pray that the growing civil rights movement would come to Mississippi. And when it did Perkins was involved from the start, even though involvement would mean being imprisoned and being hospitalized. This involved not only campaigning for equal rights but also working towards economic independence through the establishment of co-operatives. 'As we got deeper and deeper in the community through evangelism,' Perkins writes, 'and as the civil rights movement got closer and closer to Simpson County, we saw the struggle of our ministry taking place on three different levels at once – spiritual, social and justice.'[16]

The influence of the civil rights movement was certainly evident at the Berlin Congress, where racism was the only issue of social concern addressed in the final statement.[17] It recognized 'the failure of many of us in the recent past to speak with sufficient clarity and force upon the biblical unity of the human race'.[18] The issue of racism was significant, too, at the US Congress on Evangelism (1969). Tom Skinner, whose contribution was described by one commentator as 'the highpoint' of the Congress,[19] asked the delegates: 'When I move to your community and buy a home and I'm being given a rough time, will you take a stand? If my daughter falls in love with your son and they decide to get married, will you allow them to marry in peace? Will you reciprocate by accepting me as a brother? This is what black Christian brethren are crying out for, a genuine relationship.'[20] Ralph Abernathy – who a year previously had succeeded Martin Luther King as President of the Southern Christian Leadership Conference after King's assassination – likewise called upon the Congress to defend the rights of everyone regardless of their race. He challenged 'the church to be the church': not just a middle-class social club but a dynamic and prophetic influence in society taking its message to all. 'Evangelize', he exhorted the conference, 'until men live together as brothers.'[21] The Congress declaration included a commitment 'to challenge the powers of darkness, spurring the churches to stimulate believers everywhere to mount a vigorous attack upon the forces producing misery, inequality, emptiness, discrimination, and other evils in our society, and to lift, wherever possible, the spiritual and temporal burdens of man'.[22]

The impact of the black delegates was such that Tom Skinner felt it necessary to write to *Decision* magazine (December 1969) denying press reports that there had been a black revolt at the Congress and calls for reparation. They had issued a sheet of 'recommendations' – presented by nearly fifty of the black delegates – but these had included no demands for money. He also denied any opposition to the position of Billy Graham. He concluded by saying: 'this Congress has gone far beyond our expectations in terms of the movement of the Spirit of God'.[23] As a result of the Congress, Billy Graham used his contacts to arrange a meeting between black church leaders and the American President.[24]

Another contributor at the US Congress on Evangelism was the prominent evangelical politician, Mark Hatfield, the Republican Senator and former Governor of Oregon. At the National

Governors' Conference in 1965, of the fifty Governors he had been the sole dissenter to Lyndon Johnston's Gulf of Tonkin Resolution, already overwhelmingly passed by the Senate and Congress, which paved the way for the Vietnam war. For his stand against the war Hatfield received piles of angry letters from American evangelicals, some beginning 'Dear former brother in Christ'.[25]

At the US Congress on Evangelism Hatfield, in his paper 'Evangelism and World Peace', said: In our mission of peace 'we must not be bound by rigid categories of what is a spiritual message and what is a social action ... For too long the artificial polarization between those who preach the truth of individual conversion and the activists who proclaim some form of "social gospel" has prohibited a full understanding of the gospel's meaning in our world'. He spoke of peace as 'an holistic concept ... with both a political and spiritual dimension'. He also called upon evangelicals to examine the values guiding their culture and when they do not accord with God's purpose to challenge them with a prophetic voice.[26]

In 1972, while still at Trinity Seminary, Jim Wallis and others went to Explo '72, a massive Campus Crusade conference for Christian young people. The organizers had turned down suggestions for a greater social emphasis in the programme. Campus Crusade was started by Henrietta Mears, a wealthy Californian, and Bill Bright, a Californian Presbyterian: both were dispensationalists, both vehemently anti-Communist and both saw the American way of life as the true Christian alternative. One of the evening celebrations included a Flag Day ceremony and testimonies by military officers of their faith and patriotism. Wallis and those with him unfurled banners saying 'Cross or Flag', 'Christ or Country' and shouted 'Stop the war!' The crowd responded with loud booing. Wallis writes: 'The nose was frightening, and I was scared that we might be attacked.'[27] In fact they were removed by the police. In the aftermath of this experience Wallis, along with Wes Michaelson, an aide to Mark Hatfield, pushed for an evangelical forum on social concern. A committee was formed under the co-ordinating hand of Ron Sider.

Ron Sider had grown up on a farm in Ontario, Canada where his father served as a pastor in a church in the Anabaptist tradition. Sider had graduated from Yale with a PhD in Reformation history and anticipated a career defending the evangelical faith in a secular, academic context. In the event he had at that time recently accepted an appointment to work in a small inner-city college in Philadelphia and increasingly he found himself writing and speaking on social issues for a Christian audience. In 1974 Sider was to launch Evangelicals for Social Action, which, with relatively small support (around three to four thousand members) focuses on analysing congressional bills.

The forum, the Thanksgiving Workshop on Evangelicals and Social Action,[28] met in Chicago in 1973. It brought together both the new radicals, such as Jim Wallis and John Perkins, and those like Carl Henry who were concerned for social action yet whose politics remained relatively conservative. Henry chaired the gathering. The resulting Chicago Declaration of Evangelical Social Concern[29] was a clear sign that social action was beginning to be taken seriously by American evangelicals.[30] It stressed God's claim on all of people's lives, repentance that is social as well as personal and discipleship that is concerned to see justice where there is injustice. It called on evangelical Christians 'to demonstrate repentance in a Christian discipleship that confronts the social and political injustice of our nation'. It also acknowledged 'that we have encouraged men to prideful domination and women to irresponsible passivity. So we call both men and women to mutual submission and active discipleship.' This stance led to the bulletin *Daughters of Sarah* and, a year later, to the formation of the Evangelical Women's Caucus.

The declaration was not as strong as it might have been. Some wanted, in the light of the growing Watergate scandal, a condemnation of Nixon's 'lust for and abuse of power'. An original document of over 1,000 words was eventually replaced by the 473-word declaration. The argument which prevailed was that if the statement was too radical its impact upon the broader evangelical constituency would be blunted.

Nevertheless, a few participants at the Chicago forum, including John Howard Yoder, declined to sign the final document believing it had not gone far enough. Yoder's book, *The Politics of Jesus* (1972),[31] has been highly influential among evangelicals and has been described as 'seminal'[32] and as 'a landmark in biblical social ethics'.[33] Yoder, who is a Mennonite, argues in *The Politics of Jesus* that we have read the New Testament assuming 'that Jesus is simply not relevant in any immediate sense to the questions of social ethics'.[34] Instead we have largely based our ethics upon natural theology and the natural order of things. In contrast Yoder argues that our understanding of the example and teaching of Christ should be the basis of our social ethics. As such he began to explore the social implications of New Testament themes such as kingdom, jubilee and reconciliation.

In 1970 Oliver Barclay, the then General Secretary of the British Inter-Varsity Fellowship (now the Universities and Colleges Christian Fellowship), published *Whose World?*[35] In this he argued that we should give due importance to the material world and due care to physical well-being, and not just as a means to evangelism – for the Christian, love is sufficient motivation. This will involve the Christian in political action as well as philanthropy and the development of a Christian mind in all areas of life, that is, a specifically Christian approach, for example, to culture, education, science, marriage and money. In contrast to Yoder's approach, Barclay maintained throughout that a proper approach to social action arises, not so much from our understanding of redemption, but from our understanding of creation.

In part the book was a reflection upon the debate created by Anderson and Catherwood. In part, too, it was a response to the student movements of the late sixties. As head of IVF, Barclay knew the issues that Christian Unions were having to deal with as they faced the questions raised by the student movements. The book has been described as 'crucial' in the development of social involvement in Britain.[36] To an extent it was an indication of an openness to social issues on the part of IVF. Nevertheless it was a sign of the times that Barclay, in order not to draw IVF into controversy, felt it necessary to write under the psuedonym, A. N. Triton. It is a sign of how far evangelicals have moved since that whereas at the time Barclay himself called the book 'very controversial', it now seems somewhat tame and conservative.

In 1967 Samuel Escobar came to speak at the IVF Swanwick conference and had a profound influence on many there. At the end of 1970 the American equivalent of IVF, the Inter-Varsity Christian Fellowship, held its ninth and largest ever triennial missionary conference at the University of Illinois, Urbana, Illinois.[37] On the opening day Escobar gave voice to 'a dominant emphasis that was to reverberate throughout Urbana '70'.[38] He said: 'The gospel of Jesus Christ is for the whole man and cannot be sliced up into social and spiritual pieces.'[39] The students were warned to distinguish beliefs and practices which were Christian from those that were simply derived from Western culture. In the keynote address David Howard said that the student movement faced a similar situation to that of fifty years ago. He warned them not to make the same mistake again and polarize between social concern and evangelism.[40] And Tom Skinner called upon them to prove 'that is it possible for the invisible God to make himself visible in a man'.[41] While the spirit of Urbana '70 was very different from that of the radical student protests (a small civil rights protest went largely unnoticed), the emphasis on the social dimension at Urbana '70 showed that Christian students were being influenced by what was happening around them. 'It became apparent', writes David Moberg, 'that the 12,000 students who attended were much less concerned about formal missions subjects than with the relationship between evangelism and social concern.'[42]

In the wider church, too, the Vietnam war and the civil rights movement politicized many fundamentalists, particularly in the United States. It has been said that Vietnam was the first television war. At that time American television generally carried few location reports and even fewer reports of an unpleasant nature: Vietnam was the exception.[43] Night after night American viewers were able to watch the war unfold in all its horror. The war was a continual source of debate in churches and youth groups around the country. Faced with the possibility of losing their children in a war which was proving increasingly unpopular, people were forced to question seriously the 'my country right or wrong' mentality. Across Europe, too, demonstrations were held against the war. In Britain in 1968 protests against the war led to riots in Grosvenor Square.

Then in 1974 the Watergate scandal shook the United States and threw into question once again the moral righteousness of the American establishment and system. People working for President Nixon's re-election committee attempted to burgle the Democratic Party's national offices in the Watergate buildings. The administration's efforts to hide the connection provoked Senate and Justice Department investigations which ultimately implicated the President. Ordered by the Supreme Court to surrender tapes showing his involvement, President Nixon resigned in August 1974. American evangelicals' belief in the establishment and in the morality of American culture received a severe blow. 'The ... Watergate scandal', says Athol Gill, 'dampened the confidence of American evangelicals and led to a more realistic understanding of the Christian's responsibility in the world.'[44]

It was not just that the American political establishment was shown to be corrupt; evangelicals, particularly in the person of Billy Graham, were seen to be naïvely complicit in this. Billy Graham had been associated with Presidents Eisenhower and Johnson but it was Nixon with whom he was particularly close. It had always been Graham's desire to see a God-fearing, family man in the White House and no-one seemed to fit the bill in Graham's eyes like Nixon. He once described Nixon as 'the best-trained man for President in American history, and he is certainly every inch a Christian gentleman.[45] Although he frequently claimed to keep out of politics, Graham made no secret of the regard in which he held Nixon, both in 1960 when Nixon lost to Kennedy and in 1968 when Nixon was finally elected President. Indeed in the 1968 election he publicly endorsed Nixon four days before polling day. And with Nixon in the White House Graham became effectively a pastor to the President.

When the Watergate scandal broke it was not only Nixon's involvement in the cover-up which was revealed but also that his charitable giving was very low and that he was a frequent swearer; in other words he was not the God-fearer he had been thought to be. Although Graham has remained essentially loyal to Nixon, it was clear to many that he had been used by the administration.[46] His total lack of guile, his openness and sincerity – so important to his success as a preacher[47] – seemed to have a corresponding political naïvety.[48]

There can be no doubt that Watergate had a profound effect upon Billy Graham – and with him many other American evangelicals – and not only on his political involvement but on his whole perception of the relationship between American culture and the gospel. At the Lausanne Congress, held at the height of the Watergate scandal, Graham warned that evangelists must be careful not 'to identify the gospel with any one political program or culture', adding 'this has been my own danger'.[49] And in 1980 he said: 'In my earlier days . . . I tended to identify the kingdom of God with the American way of life. I don't think like that now.'[50] Nevertheless, at the time Graham's support of Nixon was a sign of what a younger generation of evangelicals perceived to be a 'de facto alliance with privileged interests and conservative socio-political forces'.[51]

In Britain the Vietnam war and civil rights were never issues in the same way as they were in North America. Nevertheless, the same spirit of change was in the air. If Vietnam and Watergate dented America's belief in herself, Britain was coming to terms with losing the empire and no longer being a world power. It was working out afresh its relationship with the rest of the world, especially its former colonies. In the field of mission this meant a new emphasis upon indigenous training and leadership. Although it would take time, gradually Third World evangelicals were able to express their particular concerns and to share with the First World the insights they had gained from mission among the poor. With new political relationships being formed, Third World evangelicals began to experience a more genuine partnership with their brothers and sisters in the West. Although the financial importance of the West, especially North America, in international evangelical organizations meant they would largely retain control of such bodies, the growth of the Third World church would in time lead to a shift in power and to significant new ways of thinking about mission.

5

Mission in the melting pot

One significant factor in developments among evangelicals was the developments taking place within the World Council of Churches (WCC), particularly the proposal to integrate the International Missionary Council (IMC) into the WCC.[1] The IMC had been formed in 1921 from the continuation committee of the first great ecumenical missionary conference in Edinburgh in 1910. Its purpose was to encourage and co-ordinate the churches and mission societies in the task of worldwide mission. The incorporation of the IMC into the WCC in 1961 was a controversial, but almost inevitable, move. Many expressed strong reservations about the effect of integration upon the IMC and the missionary movement as a whole. Others, however, hoped its presence would place the task of evangelization once again at the heart of the ecumenical movement. The decision for integration was eventually taken at the IMC conference in Ghana in 1958. And so in 1961, at the Third Assembly of the WCC in New Delhi, India, the IMC became the Commission on World Mission and Evangelism (CWME) of the WCC. Its aim was stated to be: 'To further proclamation to the whole world of the gospel of Jesus Christ, to the end that all men may believe and be saved.'

In the years following its formation the CWME lost many of its key staff and a number of posts were vacant for some time. Without this leadership the CWME failed to make evangelization the heart of the WCC; instead it was the WCC which influenced the CWME and its understanding of mission. A number of factors were involved in this. Many evangelical mission societies which had been part of the IMC left either because they were non-denominational (the WCC could receive only churches as members) or because they felt unable to participate in the broader ecumenical movement. With the decline of colonialism it was felt by many that a new, less imperialist, missionary model was needed. Indeed the WCC was at times highly, and somewhat indiscriminately, critical of its missionary forebears. And all too often ecumenical co-operation in mission meant missionary no-go areas. The Orthodox churches, for example, which joined the WCC in 1961, feared that Western Protestant churches would seek to evangelize their many nominal members.

The first meeting of the CWME was at Mexico City in 1963. With churches now determining delegates, delegates tended to be denominational representatives who were not necessarily directly involved in mission. They met under the slogan 'Mission to Six Continents'. It was chosen to underline the fact that the church is always in a missionary situation – mission is needed in the First World as well as the Third World. In emphasizing the church's responsibility to its own locality, however, it had the effect of turning attention away from the vast majority of people outside the sphere of any church. The central issues at Mexico City revolved round the relationship between God's activity in the church and in the world. It was a question which was largely unresolved.

In 1968 the Fourth Assembly of the WCC met at Uppsala, Sweden. Its thinking here was influenced by the World Conference on Church and Society, Geneva 1966, and by its own reports, *The Church for Others* and *The Church for the World*. At Uppsala the talk was of New Mission: whereas turning people to God had been the goal of traditional mission (Christianization), today the concern was with enabling people to be truly human (humanization). Also challenged was the belief that God related to the world through the church; the pattern God–church–world now became God–world–church. In other words the emphasis shifted from God speaking to the world through the church to God speaking to the church through what he was doing in the world. Mission was still understood as a participation in the *missio Dei*, the mission of God, but now this was understood as 'entering into partnership with God in history'. The *missio Dei* was seen in terms of secular movements and the task of the church was to encourage these. One consequence of this was that the experience of the Spirit in the world and in secular movements claimed authoritative status along with the Bible in determining the mission of the church today.

If at Uppsala (a conference of the WCC as a whole) this new conception of mission arrived – despite the strenuous resistance of a number of evangelicals who had been present – then at the next CWME conference in Bangkok its position within the missionary arm of the ecumenical movement (the CWME) was consolidated. Originally planned for 1969 or 1970, Bangkok was put off until 1973 because the CWME were not ready. Indeed intensive planning was involved to ensure that the ideas of Uppsala were not only re-affirmed but would begin to be implemented. The aim was to begin a new era in missionary activity. The conference met under the title 'Salvation Today'. It was evident from the preparatory material, however, that salvation today was to be determined by what we perceive God to be doing in the world today, whether within the church or not. Although evangelism was affirmed in the final state-ments it received very little attention and no mention was made of the unreached. Instead the goal of mission was seen as the bringing about of a just socio-economic order.

Of the various programmes set up to implement this new under-standing of mission, the one which attracted most attention was the Programme to Combat Racism,[2] set up in 1969 as a result of the Uppsala conference. Part of the programme was a special fund for oppressed racial groups and it was this that the press highlighted when it was decided to make grants to guerrilla groups in Zimbabwe. The bulk of the programme was largely ignored so that many perceived the PCR to be simply the special fund. Many, even within the WCC, especially in the West, reacted to these press reports with alarm.

Most evangelicals reacted strongly against these changes in the understanding of mission. Even before the Uppsala Assembly Donald McGavran had written an article asking 'Will Uppsala Betray the Two Billion?' in which he expressed his fear that the Assembly would not give attention to the needs of mission to those who have not heard the gospel.[3] At the Assembly itself a number of evangelicals led by John Stott complained that they did not see in the report a concern for the spiritual hunger of people comparable to that which had been expressed regarding physical hunger and poverty.[4] In the light of their intervention the Report was revised but the original thrust remained.

In Germany Peter Beyerhaus of the University of Tübingen and a former missionary in South Africa issued a challenge to the ecumenical view of mission in the form of a book entitled *Humanisierung – Einzige Hoffnung der Welt*? (Humanization – the only hope of the world?). When this received no response from the German Missionary Council, a group of German theologians led by Peter Beyerhaus adopted a declaration in March 1970 on the 'Fundamental Crisis in Christian Missions'. The Frankfurt Declaration, as it became known, was modelled on the Barmen Declaration, the statement made in response to Nazism by the so-called 'Confessing Church' in Germany. Beyerhaus believes it to be a German equivalent to the Wheaton Declaration (1966).[5] It speaks of an 'inner decay' in contemporary ecumenical mission and 'the displacement of their primary tasks by means of an insidious falsification of their motives and goals.'[6] The Declaration encouraged people to indicate their support for it. It was reprinted, for example, in *Christianity Today* and commended to American evangelicals in an introduction by Donald McGavran. Beyerhaus' original book was also translated into English under the title *Missions: Which Way? Humanization or Redemption.*[7] Although the aim of the Frankfurt Declaration was to bring about change within the ecumenical movement, its effect in Germany was to contribute to a split between ecumenical and evangelical mission societies.

The affirmation at Bangkok of the emphases of Uppsala on new mission and humanization served only to polarize further most ecumenicals and evangelicals. At Lausanne Stott said: 'During the last few years, especially between Uppsala and Bangkok, ecumenical–evangelical relations hardened into something like a confrontation.'[8] In his contribution to Lausanne, Stott sought to show some of the common ground between the two groups, confessing that evangelicals can learn from ecumenicals. Ultimately, however, he remained critical of the mission emphases and the conception of salvation at Uppsala and Bangkok.[9]

The Berlin Declaration on Ecumenism, drawn up between Bangkok '73 and Lausanne '74, attacked the WCC for its acceptance of 'an ungodly humanism'. Like the Frankfurt Declaration, the Berlin Declaration emanated from the Theological Convention of Confessing Fellowships, a conservative movement within the Lutheran church, with Peter Beyerhaus heavily involved again. The Berlin Declaration was a response to Bangkok just as the Frankfurt

Declaration had been a response to Uppsala. It spoke of an 'unavoidable division', an 'antithesis', between 'the biblical profession of Jesus Christ and a secularist ecumenical movement' and it accused the WCC of forsaking the gospel for 'an anti-Christian ideology'. Berlin and Lausanne were in part an attempt to take up the mantle of the early ecumenical commitment to evangelization which evangelicals believed had been forsaken by the WCC.

Nor were the accusations one-way. Just prior to the Berlin Congress, for example, a letter was sent by one spokesman of the ecumenical American National Council of Churches to Berlin churches. The letter accused the evangelical delegates to the Berlin Congress of being like those German Christians who did not oppose Hitler, who stuck to 'business as usual' so that the rise of Nazism would not interfere with traditional church priorities.[10] If those behind the Frankfurt and Berlin Declarations saw themselves as being in the same tradition as those Christians who opposed Hitler, others chose to see them in a totally opposite way.

The impact of these developments upon evangelical thinking should not be underestimated even though that impact is complex. Many who were involved through their denominations either welcomed or were challenged by the emphasis on the horizontal aspect of mission. The All India Congress on Evangelism, for example, which met in 1970, discussed ecumenical developments, particularly the Uppsala conference. It called for more involvement in social action while at the same time affirming the priority of evangelism.

Yet, as the Frankfurt and Berlin Declarations reveal, the majority of evangelicals were highly critical of what they perceived to be the total betrayal of evangelism and mission to the unreached. This made many of them very suspicious of any advocacy of social action. Words like 'humanization' and 'liberation' immediately implied for many the 'evils' of ecumenism and an abandonment of the true gospel. As we shall see in the next chapter, in 1974 evangelicals from around the world gathered for the Lausanne Congress on World Evangelization and a number of the key speakers were signatories of the Frankfurt and Berlin Declarations. In the light of the conflict between evangelicals and ecumenicals at this time it is perhaps all the more remarkable that the Lausanne Congress would declare in its final statement, the Lausanne Covenant, that we should share God's concern '... for the liberation of men from every kind of oppression' and call for 'socio-political involvement' by Christians. On the other hand, the perceived failings of ecumenical theology may well lie behind the clear distinction which was made at Lausanne between evangelism and social action and the priority given to evangelism. It is often the case, as it was with the very earliest of Christian creeds, that the definition of a position is shaped by external factors. The Lausanne Covenant was no exception.

Clear evidence that social and cultural involvement need not imply the compromising of evangelical orthodoxy was to be found in the person and stance of Francis Schaeffer (1912–84). Schaeffer was a constant opponent of ecumenism and his stand in later years on biblical inerrancy made even some evangelicals uncomfortable. As a young student Schaeffer himself had lived through eccesiastical divisions. Although he regretted the harshness of spirit created by church splits, throughout his life the authority of Scripture remained for him what he called the 'watershed'. Yet it is for his thought on contemporary culture and society that Schaeffer is best known.

In 1947 Schaeffer was given a three-month sabbatical by his church in the United States to travel round war-torn Europe to assess its spiritual needs. As a result, in the following year the Schaeffer family moved to Lausanne, Switzerland, as missionaries. In 1951 Schaeffer went through a spiritual crisis. He was deeply concerned for the cause of historic Christianity yet also aware of the lack of reality in so much of the church and indeed in his own life. Out of these struggles came Schaeffer's characteristic emphasis upon the lordship of Christ in all areas of life. 'True spirituality', he was to say later, 'covers all of reality ... the lordship of Christ covers *all* of life and *all* of life equally.'[11] Coming to a different culture he was able to realize that true spirituality did not consist in the traditional taboos about drinking, dancing, and cinema- and theatre-going. Instead Schaeffer sought to approach and analyse drama, music, literature and contemporary thought from a Christian perspective.[12] Spirituality was not withdrawing from the world but living in the world in a Christian way and with a Christian mind. Christianity, Schaeffer argued, was not an option for our spiritual lives, but it was the Truth upon which all of life should be built.[13]

It was out of this experience that the L'Abri community was conceived.[14] L'Abri was founded in 1954 when the Schaeffers opened their chalet to any who came searching for answers or seeking to apply their faith to contemporary life and thought. Schaeffer encouraged people to recognize the presuppositions of contemporary thought and to show where these led, before pointing them to the gospel.[15]

In the 1970s Schaeffer's teaching became more sociological and political as he 'carried the lordship of Christ in the whole spectrum of life further'.[16] He was a fierce critic of the values of modern society. Modern men and women, Schaeffer argued, were alienated from God, from themselves, from their neighbours and from material creation. In his A Christian Manifesto (1981),[17] one of his last books, Schaeffer argued that a moral decline was occurring in society because its foundations were no longer rooted in a Judaeo-Christian worldview but were now based upon a humanistic worldview. People were no longer seen as being made in the image of God and there was no sense of responsibility towards our Creator. This analysis lay behind his concern about pollution and his assessment of the ecological crisis[18] and his attack on abortion and euthanasia, most famously in the film and book Whatever Happened to the Human Race?[19] 'We who are Christians', Schaeffer concluded, 'must, on the one hand, fight with determination and sacrifice for the individual in society, and on the other, provide the loving care of people as individuals. Thus the world will truly feel our presence in its midst as the true salt of the earth.'[20] In pursuit of these aims, argued Schaeffer, we must if necessary work together with non-evangelicals.

In A Christian Manifesto Schaeffer argued that if a government contravenes God's word Christians should resort to civil disobedience and, if necessary, force. A Christian Manifesto was heavily influenced by Lex Rex, the reply by the seventeenth-century Scottish Puritan Samuel Rutherford (1600–61) to the theory of the divine right of kings. Schaeffer's own influence is clear in, for example, the American campaign Operation Rescue, started in 1988, which seeks to picket abortion clinics. A Christian Manifesto, with its attack on humanistic values, and on abortion in particular, and its call for Christian political action, was eagerly received by the

New Christian Right in America. Jerry Falwell, the founder of Moral Majority, described it as the most important piece of literature in America today[21] and it has been called 'a manifesto for the politics of Moral Majority'.[22] Schaeffer has also been described as proposing 'an evangelical civil religion'.[23]

Yet it is for his apologetic and cultural thought that Schaeffer is best known and his influence upon evangelicalism as a whole has been considerable. He was able to show many that their evangelical faith could be both faithful to the authority of the Bible and intellectually rigorous at the same time. And he was able to convince many that artistic and cultural involvement was legitimate and even desirable for Christians. If his later thought influenced the Right, his emphasis on the lordship of Christ in all of life and his demonstration of the relevance of Christianity to modern thought had a significant impact on a much wider circle of people.[24] Indeed some of the radicals of the sixties and seventies might not have remained evangelicals had it not been for his influence. Many young Christians, challenged by modern worldviews, found in Schaeffer a critique of these and a Christian alternative which was intellectually and sociologically credible.

If Schaeffer's apologetic proved influential it should not be forgotten that he was essentially a compassionate evangelist driven to wrestle with the questions being raised by students and others. In his own unique way he combined a passionate commitment to evangelism with a constant listening to people for whom the traditional evangelical churches had no answers.

Lausanne: congress,
covenant, movement

We affirm that God is both the Creator and the Judge of all men. We therefore should share his concern for justice and reconciliation throughout human society and for the liberation of men from every kind of oppression. Because mankind is made in the image of God, every person, regardless of race, religion, colour, culture, class, sex, or age, has an intrinsic dignity because of which he should be respected and served, not exploited. Here too we express penitence both for our neglect and for having sometimes regarded evangelism and social concern as mutually exclusive. Although reconciliation with man is not reconciliation with God, nor is social action evangelism, nor is political liberation salvation, nevertheless we affirm that evangelism and sociopolitical involvement are both part of our Christian duty. For both are necessary expressions of our doctrine of God and man, our love for our neighbour and our obedience to Jesus Christ. The message of salvation implies also a message of judgment upon every form of alienation, oppression and discrimination, and we should not be afraid to denounce evil and injustice wherever they exist. When people receive Christ they are born again into his kingdom and must seek not only to exhibit but also to spread its righteousness in the midst of an unrighteous world. The salvation we claim should be transforming us in the totality of our personal and social responsibilities. Faith without works is dead. (Paragraph 5 of the Lausanne Covenant, 'Christian Social Responsibility')

Conferences are not always as significant at grassroots level as the organizers and participants like to think. More often they are a sign of changes which have taken place independently. The Lausanne Congress was certainly such a sign: it was the clearest indication yet that social action had been accepted as a legitimate concern among many evangelicals. Yet it was also an exception to the rule, for it in turn was a significant influence on the thinking of others. No previous conference could have claimed to speak for evangelicals in such a way and it spoke in favour of social action, providing 'international sanction for evangelical social commitment'.[1] For many it was a challenge to rethink their position. For others it gave them confidence in their convictions.

The success of Lausanne, believes Tom Houston, the current International Director of the Lausanne Committee, was due to process and timing. All the papers were circulated six months before 'and it was almost a condition of getting there that you commented on [them]'. The resulting Covenant was drafted on the basis of the papers, the responses to them and comments made during the Congress. It was also a matter of timing. 'The evangelical world', Tom Houston believes, 'was uncomfortable in 1974 on a series of issues and finding that the fundamentalist/modernist controversy had left it not well equipped for the modern world.' The Covenant provided 'a wider umbrella under which evangelicals could shelter'.[2] It brought people together and provided a basis for co-operation even where differences persisted. Peter Beyerhaus puts it somewhat more poetically: 'What made Lausanne '74 a unique event was that small rivers, some of which had gone unnoted before, became confluent and formed one mighty stream, deep enough to carry a fleet of evangelical fishing boats and spiritually fertilize the dried soil of latter twentieth century Christianity.'[3]

The Lausanne Congress, officially the International Congress on World Evangelization, met in July 1974.[4] In December 1969 a group of around one hundred Christian leaders had been consulted by Billy Graham on the advisability of another international congress. They had felt that the time was not yet right. Meeting again in March 1972 in Florida a similar body gave the go-ahead and planning for the Congress was set in motion. With nearly 2,500 participants – well over half of them under the age of forty-five – and 1,000 observers from 150 countries (a wider representation than the

United Nations, was the organizers' boast) and representing 135 denominations, *Time* magazine described it as 'possibly the widest ranging meeting of Christians ever held'.[5]

If the Berlin Congress met during the heady optimism and turmoil of the sixties, Lausanne gathered against a more sombre background. The United States was undergoing its greatest political crisis for many years with President Nixon resigning just two weeks after the end of the Congress. In September/October 1973 the Organization of Petroleum Exporting Countries (OPEC) raised the price of oil by 70%. Dominated as it was by Middle-Eastern countries, OPEC also used the price of oil as a political weapon against Western support of Israel in the war of October 1973. This led to a further 130% rise in December. The oil crisis severely affected economies throughout the world. Furthermore, many of the radicals of the sixties were turning their attention to environmental issues, highlighting for the first time the ecological problems facing the planet.

In addition the needs of the poor were as great as ever – at least half the Lausanne participants were from the Third World – and increasingly apparent to the wider world. During the year before the Lausanne Congress, 20 million people had faced starvation in India as a result of drought – a fact made immediate in Western homes by television. In the autumn of 1973 Jonathan Dimbleby presented a programme in the Thames Television's *This Week* series entitled *The Unknown Famine*. It was a powerful account of the suffering and death in northern Ethiopia as a result of a famine, reports of which had been consistently denied by the administration of Emperor Haile Selassie – a speaker at the Berlin Congress! Indeed, although it did not itself have a strong political message, the programme has been credited with a significant part in his downfall in 1974.[6] On the day of his deposition the film was shown on Ethiopian television and the Emperor was forced by his captors to watch it.

Thus it was that Lausanne met in a more sombre atmosphere. There was a realism about the needs of the world and about what could be achieved as a result of the Congress. There was perhaps also less triumphalism. John Stott told the conference: 'I hope in my paper to strike a note of evangelical repentance, and indeed I hope we shall continue to hear this note throughout the Congress.'[7]

Those professing to live under the authority of Scripture, he explained, have very often been selective in their submission to it and their traditions in fact often owe more to culture than to Scripture.

At the same time, however, there was a very real sense of excitement at Lausanne. In fact in many ways there was a more optimistic view of history at Lausanne than there had been at the Berlin Congress. Instead of talking of historic crisis, Waldron Scott and Billy Graham began their opening addresses by pointing to 'the amazing expansion of Christianity'. Even the great needs of the world were seen as exciting opportunities for mission.

The Congress had been convened 'to arouse all believers to a new obedience to Christ in world evangelism'. Indeed many felt that Berlin had dealt with the theology of mission and evangelism and as such Lausanne would address itself to more strategic issues. The question of 'what' would become the question of 'how'. Prior to the Congress, Donald Hoke, the Congress Director, shared the Planning Committee's goals for Lausanne. The Congress aimed (i) to impart a vision and sense of responsibility for evangelism, both locally and cross-culturally, (ii) to inform people of successful methods and tools, (iii) to facilitate evangelical co-operation in evangelism and (iv) to identify unevangelized areas. There were three resources, he said, which the evangelical community had as never before: tools (*i.e.* technology), manpower and money.[8] Berlin had been a congress on evangelism, Lausanne would be a congress on evangelization – its aim was the proclamation of the gospel throughout the world within a generation. This was certainly the dominant theme of the Congress and it was at Lausanne that the concept of 'unreached peoples' first gained prominence.[9] But the theme which captured the most attention and created the most debate was the role of social action.[10] Throughout the Congress it 'surfaced again and again'.[11]

In his opening address Billy Graham spoke of his hope that the Congress would state conclusively the relationship between evangelism and social responsibility. In the opening plenary session John Stott, in a very significant step, said that instead of equating mission simply with evangelism, we should speak of the total mission of the church to the world. This, he argued, includes both evangelism and social action.[12] At Berlin Stott's addresses had focused on the Great Commission as recorded in each of the synoptic gospels and, to his later embarrassment, he had denied that social action was part of the Great Commission.[13] At Lausanne, by his own admission, he expressed himself differently.[14] He focused now on the Johannine Commission (John 20:21) in order to stress that the pattern for mission laid down by Jesus is one of service and incarnation. In such mission both evangelism and social action are 'authentic expressions of the love that serves'.[15] He also emphasized the importance of the 'Great Commandment' of love as a necessary parallel to the Great Commission to make disciples.[16]

Major seminars were also given by George Hoffman and Carl Henry. Hoffman said 'a Christianity which would use the vertical dimension as a means of escape from responsibility for and in the common life of men is a denial of the incarnation of God's life for the world manifested in Christ'. Henry argued that political involvement had a biblical mandate. 'The church', he said, 'under Christ's lordship, is sent into the world to proclaim personal and social redemption.' A spontaneously arranged strategy group produced the Social Responsibilities of Evangelization Report which stated that 'social service must be part of our evangelization, being in itself an essential expression of the love of God for his world'.[17]

But it was the younger, Third World theologians, René Padilla and Samuel Escobar, who 'set the cat among the pigeons', according to John Stott,[18] by placing the issue of social action and its relationship to the gospel at the centre of Congress discussion. Chris Sugden goes further: 'The blue touch-paper for evangelical social responsibility this century was lit at the Lausanne Congress in 1974 by ... René Padilla and Samuel Escobar. Their papers on evangelism triggered an explosion ... of evangelical involvement in relief and development ... [and] evangelical missiology.'[19]

At the heart of Padilla's and Escobar's concern was the fear that the Congress would endorse an evangelistic strategy in which, for the sake of numerical success, the claims of the gospel would be replaced by a gospel of 'cheap grace'. They firmly maintained that any true proclamation of the gospel must include the call to repentance in its social as well as individual dimensions. Said Escobar:

> The temptation for evangelicals today is to reduce the Gospel, to mutilate it, to eliminate any demands for the

fruit of repentance and any aspect that would make it unpalatable ... it must stress the need for the whole Gospel of Jesus Christ as Saviour and Lord whose demands cannot be cheapened. No eagerness for the quantitative growth of the church should render us silent about the whole counsel of God.[20]

In his paper, 'Evangelism and the World',[21] Padilla argued that the gospel is a cosmic message: 'the only true evangelism is that which is orientated toward that final goal of "the restoration of all things" in Christ Jesus'.[22] Such true evangelism proclaims Christ as Lord of all and as such calls people to live according to his rule and not according to the way of the world. Padilla identified two ways in which the world had entered the church. The first was what he called 'secular Christianity' which excludes the supernatural. The second, what he called 'culture Christianity', was closer to home and it was this which he chose to focus on in the presentation of his paper at Lausanne. 'Culture Christianity', he argued, arises when the Christian faith confuses aspects of Christianity with, for example, 'the American way of life' with its political conservatism and its tendency to treat the gospel as a product to be marketed as efficiently as possible. Although he did not mean to imply that other Christians were not affected by their cultures detrimentally, Padilla focused on this particular form of culturally compromised Christianity because of its dominance, not least at the Congress. He feared that a concentration on technology and efficiency and a tendency to measure success in numerical terms would undermine the integrity of the gospel.

The same concerns were shared by Samuel Escobar in his paper, 'Evangelism and Man's Search for Freedom, Justice and Fulfilment'.[23] He criticized those who wish to concentrate on evangelization while denying the importance of acts of service and the search for justice. As with Padilla, this concern arose not because Escobar was not committed to world evangelization, but because he was. True evangelism is compromised, he believed, when people, usually speaking from a position of personal affluence, undermine the very message of the gospel as they seek to make it palatable by playing down its ethical demands. 'A spirituality without discipleship in the daily social, economic and political aspects of life is religiosity and not Christianity.'[24] In response to Billy Graham's contention that concentrating on social issues would lead to an abandonment of evangelism, Escobar declared: 'I would like to affirm that I do not believe in that statement. I think the social gospel . . . deteriorated because of poor theology. The sad thing is that those who have the right theology have not applied it to social issues.'[25]

Going into the Congress many would have concurred with the assessment of Gilbert Kirby of the London Bible College at the European Congress on Evangelism in 1971 when he said: 'We stand on common ground. We will be discussing not the content of the gospel, but how to communicate that content.'[26] Yet the response to the centrality given to repentance in the proclamation of the gospel by Padilla in his paper circulated before the Congress exploded the idea that the content of the message could be assumed by the Congress. 'There is no use assuming', Padilla asserted, 'that we all agree on the gospel that has been entrusted to us and that all we need now is more efficient methods to communicate it. If we think so, we deceive ourselves. The gospel of repentance is one thing, the gospel of cheap grace is something else.'[27]

What emerges from the contributions of Padilla and Escobar is not a concern that social action should be given a place alongside evangelism. Rather the issue as they saw it was whether repentance in all its facets was to have a primary place in evangelism. Their protest was against an easy gospel which was prepared to sacrifice the kind of discipleship demanded by the cross for the sake of numerical results. The need, they believed, was for the church to be faithful to the ethical demands of the gospel, in particular in its social dimensions. The affluence of the West in contrast to the poverty of the Third World coupled with a culturally conditioned view of the gospel and of evangelism threatened to undermine the very cause their detractors sought to espouse – the evangelization of the world. The issue was not whether social action was part of mission but whether the church would proclaim and adhere to a gospel that included the call to repent and to produce the fruit of good works, particularly action against poverty, racism and injustice. At Lausanne Padilla concluded: 'The future of the church does not depend on our ability to persuade people to give intellectual assent to a truncated gospel but on our faithfulness to the full gospel of our Lord Jesus Christ and God's faithfulness to his Word.'[28]

The contributions of Padilla and Escobar had a profound effect on the Lausanne Congress.[29] 'They both had the courage to be critical of the evangelical West', says John Stott, 'and, of course, the Americans were stung by it.'[30] Their papers were the subject of much informal discussion among the delegates. Coming in the midst of the Watergate scandal and Billy Graham's own acknowledgment of the dangers of confusing a particular culture with the gospel,[31] Padilla's attack on 'culture Christianity' was particularly pertinent. In a symposium on Lausanne published two years later, Escobar wrote: 'The fear that Lausanne 1974 would opt for the imposition of a triumphalistic, Western gospel through North American sales techniques was dispelled by the reality of the event.'[32] It was evident that as he and Padilla looked back, they viewed the outcome of Lausanne with a sense of relief. Padilla wrote:

> The Lausanne Congress might have been nothing more than an enormous (and expensive) launching platform for a vast programme of world-wide evangelization which avoided the theological problems posed by evangelization for the church today ... Fortunately, as this vast gathering developed the theological problems imposed themselves upon the discussions and resulted in the Lausanne Covenant, a document which questions positions traditionally entrenched in the evangelical churches.[33]

Instead of such fears being realized, Lausanne in fact proved significant for its note of repentance and its endorsement of social action. The Congress has been variously described as 'a turning point in evangelical thinking' (both Athol Gill and John Stott), 'a definitive step' (René Padilla), 'a watershed' (both Edward Dayton and Samuel and Sugden), and 'a catalyst for a whole movement' (Vinay Samuel and Chris Sugden).[34]

The Lausanne Covenant had been prepared before the Congress in draft form on the basis of speakers' papers. Already it contained an affirmation of social action. Yet as a result of the way the

Congress developed, the drafting committee, under the chairmanship of John Stott, strengthened its position. The reference to *social action* was replaced by one to *socio-political involvement* and the call to denounce injustice was added.[35] These changes made it clear that the Covenant was affirming not only social care or philanthropy but also social reform, the attempt to challenge or change society.

The Covenant has had a tremendous impact. In formulating its theology of mission, Valdir Steuernagel believes,[36] the Congress had struggled with two issues: (i) Is the mission of the church more than evangelism or is evangelism all that mission is? (ii) If mission is more than evangelism, that is, if it includes social action, what is the relationship between evangelism and social action? The response enshrined in the Covenant was that mission was indeed broader than evangelism, but that evangelism was the primary task of the church. That the Congress could agree to this was remarkable. Lausanne represented 'a rare and delicate moment of consensus'.[37]

At Lausanne II in Manila in 1989 Michael Cassidy said that the most important feature of Lausanne was the Covenant. He went on to say that it has been

> unbelievably helpful to be able to say to many evangelicals who had castigated us for having social and justice concerns, who had said we were mistaken and were betraying the gospel, that we were not as out of step as you think. We have been taking this posture, many of us for ten or fifteen years before Lausanne I, and now 4,000 world evangelicals have actually said what we've been saying all along. So to an extent a lot of people in the South African church in the evangelical world began to face this issue.[38]

For those involved in EFICOR, for example, it was evidence to its detractors that it could be involved in social action and still legitimately claim to be authentically evangelical. As René Padilla puts it: 'social involvement had finally been granted full citizenship in evangelical missiology'.[39] With Lausanne evangelical social concern became official.

As a result of Lausanne, 'evangelical relief and development agencies around the world received fresh energy because they could appeal to the evangelical constituency as "family" without the fear of either being rebuked for preaching the "social gospel" or being charged with compromising on evangelism'.[40] At least one magazine, *Third Way*, was established on the basis of the Lausanne Covenant.[41] Aiming to look at social and cultural issues from a Christian perspective, *Third Way* has, in the estimation of Michael Saward, not been without significance in the development of evangelical social responsibility in Britain.[42] Billy Graham's own son, Franklin, who was going through a rebellious period, attended the Congress. Meeting Third World Christians and understanding something of their sufferings moved him tremendously. As a result he committed himself wholeheartedly to Christian service and is now head of the relief arm of the BGEA.[43]

The Lausanne movement has received comparatively little coverage in Britain, due mainly to the fact that it has had no office in this country. Nevertheless among those who attended it had a profound impact. And the thinking reflected at Lausanne has filtered down, particularly through the writings of John Stott, even if people are rarely aware of where it comes from.[44]

7

After Lausanne

We confess that . . . We have been failing in our obedience to the lordship of Christ and have been refusing to submit to his word and be led by his Spirit. We have failed to incarnate the gospel and to come to men as servants for Christ's sake. Our testimony has often been marred by triumphalism and arrogance, by lack of faith in God and by diminished love for his people. We have often been in bondage to a particular culture and sought to spread it in the name of Jesus. We have not been aware of when we have debased and distorted the gospel by acceptance of a contrary value system. We have been partisan in our condemnation of totalitarianism and violence and have failed to condemn societal and institutionalized sin, especially that of racism. We have sometimes so identified ourselves with particular political systems that the Gospel has been compromised and the prophetic voice muted. We have frequently denied the rights and neglected the cries of the underprivileged and those struggling for freedom and justice. We have often separated Jesus Christ the Saviour from Jesus Christ the Lord. We have sometimes distorted the biblical understanding of man as a total being and have courted an unbiblical dualism. We have insulated new Christians from life in the world and given simplistic responses to complex problems. We have sometimes manipulated our message, used pressure techniques and been unduly preoccupied with statistics. We have allowed eagerness for quantitative growth to render us silent about the whole counsel of God. We have been usurping God's Holy Spirit of love and power . . .

> *We resolve to . . . submit ourselves afresh to the Word*
> *of God and to the leading of his Spirit, to pray and work*
> *together for the renewal of his community as the expres-*
> *sion of his reign, to participate in God's mission to his*
> *world in our generation, showing forth Jesus as Lord*
> *and Saviour, and calling on all men everywhere to*
> *repent, to submit to his lordship, to know his salvation,*
> *to identify in him with the oppressed and work for the*
> *liberation of all men and women in his name.* (From A
> Response to Lausanne: The Statement on Radical
> Discipleship)

Despite the significant step forward for evangelical social concern
made at the Lausanne Congress and in the Lausanne Covenant, for
many it did not go far enough. In 1970 Partnership in Mission
(PIM), a Philadelphia-based body, contacted Vinay Samuel, now
Executive Director of INFEMIT, in India. PIM was led by Steve
Knapp who, according to Samuel, was ahead of almost everyone
else in defining the gospel in terms of the kingdom of God.[1] With
the backing of the de Moss Foundation[2] they were exploring new
forms of theological education and Samuel became a consultant for
them. He suggested that since the Third World did not have access
to many books they should produce booklets containing summaries
of the latest literature on a particular theme. One of the first was
upon the kingdom of God and included a summary of George
Eldon Ladd's *Jesus and the Kingdom*.

When Samuel moved to Cambridge the team at PIM continued to
meet with him regularly and through PIM a wider network was
created which included René Padilla, Samuel Escobar and John
Perkins. During the week before Lausanne five of the PIM team
gathered together in Cambridge: Vinay Samuel, Steve Knapp,
Robert de Moss, Matt Bradshore and Peter Savage (who had helped
to found the Latin American Theological Fraternity). Together they
thrashed out the agenda which they wanted to see discussed at
Lausanne. Samuel did not go to the Congress but the others met
together daily along with René Padilla, Samuel Escobar, Don Jacobs
(from a Mennonite background) and Harold Fenton (who gave
them some respectability in NAE circles). Over the previous few
months they had done a lot of preparation on the kingdom of God,

on the gospel and culture and on social issues and they were determined that this thinking be made part of the evangelical agenda. 'There was a definite attempt', claims Samuel, 'not to subvert, but an attempt to demonstrate that there was another position.'[3]

At the same time others, unaware of the PIM network, felt they would like to discuss further with Samuel Escobar and René Padilla the issues they had raised in their papers. Asking around they found that others were interested and so a meeting was organized simply by word of mouth. On the Sunday night of the Congress itself around two hundred of the Congress participants met together. It was agreed that a small group should draw up a response to Lausanne, which the group entitled *Theology and Implications of Radical Discipleship*.[4] This statement, largely made up of quotes from various Congress papers, went significantly further than the first drafts of the Lausanne Covenant. It defined the gospel as 'the Good News of liberation, of restoration, of wholeness, and of salvation that is personal, social, global and cosmic'. The Christian community, they stated, must make known this gospel not only through proclamation, but through its life as the new society, through the prophetic denouncement of evil, through the pursuit of justice and through the care of creation. While affirming that salvation is by grace alone, they emphasized the need for radical repentance in every area of a person's life. The statement also confessed that often evangelicals have confused the gospel with a particular culture and have failed properly to proclaim the gospel, to emphasize repentance, and to seek justice.

Because this group made the kingdom of God central to social action they were more inclined to advocate radical change (in line with the radical nature of the kingdom) than those who made the doctrine of creation central and who thereby tended to be more politically conservative (inclined to preserve the created order). In the Covenant itself the paragraph on social responsibility began with an affirmation of God as Creator and Judge of all people but it also said that Christians must seek to exhibit and spread the righteousness of God's kingdom. But what really alarmed their critics was the way the advocates of radical discipleship defined the gospel as 'Good News of liberation, of restoration, of wholeness, and of salvation that is personal, social, global and cosmic'.

This made social action, or rather corporate salvation, not only part of mission but part of the gospel. It is this factor which above all others distinguishes the social thinking of the radical evangelicals from that of the evangelical social activists of the nineteenth century. The year after Lausanne, for example, Chris Sugden wrote *Social Gospel or No Gospel*[5] in which he argued that a gospel without this social aspect is not the true gospel.

The statement was signed by over five hundred people before the end of the Congress. During the Congress John Stott met with a group involved in framing the alternative statement led by John Howard Yoder. He tried unsuccessfully to persuade them that their concerns could be, and indeed were being, expressed within the Covenant itself. As it was, Stott sought to defuse the issue by welcoming the Statement on Radical Discipleship as an addendum to the Lausanne Covenant and saying publicly that he would be the first to sign it. Commenting later Stott says: 'I felt so much in sympathy . . . and in agreement with what they were saying that I begged them not to produce an alternative . . . I didn't want there to be an unnecessary polarization.'[6]

René Padilla himself has described the Response to Lausanne as 'the strongest statement on the basis for wholistic mission ever formulated by an evangelical conference up to that date'.[7] It has provided a focal point for those within evangelicalism who are particularly concerned for social justice, for the contextualization of the gospel and for repentance that is both social and individual. Indeed, there are those who speak of the 'radical evangelicals' or the 'radical discipleship group' as a specific group or movement within contemporary evangelicalism.[8]

In order to explain the radical discipleship statement and introduce its thinking to a wider audience Scripture Union invited Chris Sugden to write the book which became *Radical Discipleship* (1981).[9] In the event it proved too hot for Scripture Union to handle and they declined to publish it. It was eventually published by Marshalls on the strong advice of Michael Eastman of the Evangelical Coalition for Urban Mission. ECUM were concerned to have a theological basis for what they were doing.[10]

In contrast to those who thought Lausanne had not gone far enough, there were those who, perhaps inevitably, believed it had gone far too far. Some were deeply concerned about Lausanne's 'holistic evangelism' whose roots they felt lay in a social gospel and in universalism. The most notable of these critics was Arthur P. Johnston, Professor of Mission at Trinity Evangelical Divinity School, Deerfield, Illinois and a participant at the Berlin and Lausanne Congresses. Initially Johnston welcomed Lausanne, comparing it favourably with Edinburgh 1910, the first great ecumenical missionary conference of this century.[11]

In 1978, however, he published *The Battle for World Evangelism*.[12] The book charts the developments within the WCC and within the evangelical ecumene: the implication is that by including social action within mission evangelicalism is in danger of going the same way as the WCC. Although Johnston does not oppose social action in itself,[13] he argues that too much emphasis upon it inevitably leads to an abandonment of evangelism.[14] Johnston decries Lausanne's 'holistic' view of mission: mission for Johnston is evangelism and evangelism alone.[15] It was not enough for Johnston for the Lausanne Covenant to maintain that 'evangelism is primary' (Section 6); it should 'have retained not only its priority and primacy, but also the unique status it held from the nineteenth century to Berlin'.[16] If socio-political action is included as part of mission, argues Johnston, evangelism will inevitably be edged out. Indeed Johnston argues that Christian social action will not be possible if evangelism is not accorded this unique status since there will be no socially active Christians.[17]

Johnston was particularly critical of the position taken by John Stott. Because Stott had described social action as the partner of evangelism, Johnston accused him of having 'dethroned evangelism as *the* only historical aim of mission'.[18] As Johnston saw it, Stott was saying that mission *must* include social action and this he could not accept. 'The principle of the complete self-authentication of the word of the gospel in mission through the ministry of the Holy Spirit in evangelism', Johnston argued, 'is modified by the necessity of some incarnational socio-political actions.'[19] He also attacked Stott's acceptance of the Response to Lausanne as an addendum to the Covenant.[20] He accuses Stott, Padilla and Escobar of supporting an unrepresentative and 'ecumenical theology of evangelism'.[21]

Christianity Today allowed John Stott to write an open letter in reply to Johnston's criticism.[22] Stott points out that the distinction between evangelism and social action is often artificial. The words and works of Jesus 'belonged indissolubly to one another', the works making the words visible. In this way service can not only precede and follow evangelism, as Johnston acknowledges, but the two can also be in partnership. Individual Christians may have specialist ministries but 'the Christian community as a whole should not have to choose, any more than Jesus did'. He agrees with Johnston that the gospel is self-authenticating but asks, 'Does not the gospel lack credibility whenever Christians contradict it by their lives?' Citing 1 John 3:17, Stott concludes by claiming that rather than dethroning evangelism as the only historical aim of mission, he has sought to 'enthrone love as the essential historical motivation for mission'.

Johnston, however, was not alone in his concerns. Peter Wagner wrote in *Christianity Today* a year after Lausanne: 'Not only did the Lausanne program build in what I consider a disproportionate emphasis on social aspects of the Christian mission for a congress "on World Evangelization", but many influential media reports even exaggerated this, thereby diluting the evangelistic component.'[23] Likewise Peter Beyerhaus said that he believed the broader definition of mission to be 'incompatible with the concept of evangelism as normatively laid down in God's inspired Word'.[24] There was clearly a feeling in some quarters that the emphasis on social action was getting out of hand. Writing to John Stott, Jack Dain, Chairman of the Lausanne Committee, said:

> I have a very real concern over the problem of the attitude of some of our American brethren to sections of the Lausanne programme and the Covenant which they do not like. There seems to be in certain quarters a total inability to see behind the cultural and political outlook of the typical well-to-do American Christian.

And Samuel Escobar, this time in a letter to Jack Dain, said: 'I think that there is a concerted effort on the part of the conservative elements that are in charge of *Christianity Today* to change the meaning and the direction of Lausanne.'[25]

The important thing to realize is that both the advocates of radical discipleship, on the one hand, and those like Arthur Johnston, on the other, were concerned for evangelism. The one believed that evangelism could not truly take place if it was divorced from social action,[26] the other believed that evangelism would not take place if social action was emphasized. At Lausanne Padilla and Escobar argued for *true* evangelism, evangelism that did not compromise on the demands of the gospel for the sake of 'success'. Johnston argued that if social action was emphasized it would necessarily deflect attention from the one, *true* task of mission, namely evangelism. The debate was to continue, with the relationship between evangelism and social action the key issue at the Grand Rapids Consultation in June 1982, as we shall see in Chapter 11.

During the Lausanne Congress a poll was conducted in which of the thousand-plus participants who responded, 86% favoured an on-going 'fellowship' of some sort and 79% supported the specific proposal for a continuation committee. On this basis a continuation committee, the Lausanne Committee for World Evangelization (LCWE), was established – against the wishes of Billy Graham. 'Lausanne', says Steuernagel, 'was a congress that became a movement, an event that became a symbol.'[27]

The first meeting of the LCWE, in Mexico City,[28] was a tense one. At the meeting a number of those present, led by John Stott, lobbied hard for a broad remit to the LCWE with a greater emphasis on social action. Stott and Graham clashed over whether the Congress mandate to the committee had been simply to promote world evangelization or to promote the implementation of the Lausanne Covenant as a whole. Graham feared that any focus other than on evangelism would not be able to unite evangelicals worldwide. Stott believed they had a duty to implement the whole Covenant. He felt, too, 'that the framers of the alternative, the Radical Statement, were all the younger, rising evangelical leadership and that if we didn't find room for their concerns Lausanne was doomed because they were the leaders of the future'.[29] Along with this issue there was intense debate as to what Graham's role should now be in the Lausanne movement. In the end he was made honorary chairman but, very graciously by all accounts,[30] did not make his view on the on-going role of the committee a condition of acceptance.

The question of the committee's focus was not so easily settled and in the end John Stott and Peter Wagner were, in Stott's own words, 'locked up in a room by ourselves and told not to come out until we had formed an agreed statement or clause'.[31] What they came up with was the following statement of purpose: 'The aim of the committee is to further the total Biblical mission of the church, recognizing that in this mission of sacrificial service, evangelism is primary, and that our particular concern must be the evangelization of the 2,700 million unreached people of the world.' The reference to the 'total mission' of the church satisfied those taking Stott's position and the mention of a particular concern for the evangelization of the unreached pleased those who supported a narrower concept of mission. At the same time the committee agreed the following as their basis of coming together: 'We recognize that we are coming together on the basis of our common commitment to biblical doctrine and duty, especially as expressed in the Lausanne Covenant, and we desire to communicate and interpret these to the church throughout the world.'[32]

If there was disagreement at the meeting, then there was disagreement too as to what its outcome had been! Arthur Johnston believed that there had been 'a circumvention of Graham's . . . counsel'.[33] Yet Peter Wagner, who took the same narrower view of mission as Johnston, believed the battle for a focus on evangelism alone had been won.[34] Likewise Graham's official biographer, William Martin, clearly believes that Graham's position won the day.[35] Tom Houston, the current International Director of the Lausanne Committee, when asked if Graham's position had been defeated, said that it had been.[36] In reality the committee had agreed to the broader concept of mission (as proposed by Stott) as its official basis but also agreed to focus in its work upon the narrower concept of mission (as proposed by Graham). Such a compromise was open to varying interpretations. By including the Christian's duty, a duty which the Lausanne Covenant said included social responsibility, within its frame of reference the Committee made its commitment to social action clear. At the same time, however, it reaffirmed the primacy of evangelism and decided that its particular concern would be the evangelization of the unreached. Both sides of the debate could be, and indeed were, happy or disappointed with the outcome depending on how they chose to see it. 'To a broader definition of the church's mission Mexico said "yes" as long as the Continuation Committee could concentrate on evangelism.'[37] As such, while 'technically' the Committee was concerned for the whole Covenant, 'the shop window of Lausanne erred on the proclamation side rather than the demonstration side'.[38] Over time, however, it would be fair to say that, at least until recently, there has been a growing realization within the Lausanne movement worldwide – and this was largely reflected at Lausanne II in 1989 in Manila – that evangelization cannot be looked at in isolation from social issues.

If the Lausanne Congress gave social involvement its official status within evangelicalism, it was Ron Sider's book, *Rich Christians in an Age of Hunger*,[39] which really brought it to popular attention in the West. Sider had published an article on the Christian response to Third World poverty in the American Inter-Varsity magazine, *His*. This created significant interest and the InterVarsity Press of America asked him to expand his ideas into the book which became *Rich Christians*, published in the USA in 1977. In Britain there were difficulties finding a publisher who would handle it and it was published, by Hodder and Stoughton, only after the Shaftesbury Project and its overseas aid group stepped in to help. It came out first in November 1978 but quickly sold out and had to be reprinted in April of the following year. In the book Sider draws the contrast between Western wealth and Third World poverty, likening it to the situation in the parable of the rich man and Lazarus (Luke 16:19–31).

In exploring the biblical teaching on wealth and poverty, Sider emphasized God's special concern for the poor. It is not that God is biased but rather 'the God of the Bible is on the side of the poor just because he is *not* biased, for he is a God of impartial justice'.[40] As such, argues Sider, the people of God are to be concerned for social justice and to help in practical ways all who are in need. He also emphasized that participation in institutionalized evil or social sin is just as wrong as engaging in personal sin and immorality. He argued too, as Padilla had done at Lausanne, that we have allowed the values of our materialistic society to shape our understanding of the Bible. He ended by calling for repentance and for changed lifestyles, for Christians to be models to the world of a better way.

It would be hard to overstate the impact of *Rich Christians*. Donald Hay says that among evangelicals it 'probably has done more than any other single book to stimulate discussion [on the relationship between rich and poor nations]'.[41] Although Sider's analysis of the economics of world poverty is open to the criticism of over-simplification, the challenge of the book is unmistakable. Hardly surprisingly the book has not been without its critics. In the United States David Chilton has 'honoured' it by writing a highly critical response entitled *Productive Christians in an Age of Guilt Manipulators*.[42] Equally vehement is Lloyd Billingsley who, in *A Generation That Knew Not Josef*, compares Sider to those who supported Josef Stalin! In Britain more measured criticisms were made, for example, by Brian Griffiths, a strong supporter of market economics who was involved in the beginnings of the London Institute for Contemporary Christianity.[43] Yet despite its critics *Rich Christians* has been extremely influential among evangelicals on both sides of the Atlantic, not least because it was so thoroughly grounded in the Bible. For many it opened up the Scriptures in a new and deeply challenging way. In his foreword David Watson (1933–1984), the international evangelist and leader of the church of St Michael-le-Belfrey in York, wrote:

> I profoundly believe that *this book contains the most vital challenge which faces the church of today* . . . I am convinced that this practical expression of God's love for people, especially for the afflicted and oppressed, will bring about the greatest impact for Christ that the church could ever make in this present world.[44]

8

Theological developments

If Lausanne answered the question of whether social action should be part of the church's mission, it only served to raise a host of other questions. How is social action to relate to evangelism? How is it to relate to salvation, to God's work as Redeemer? What is the form of the kingdom of God in history and how does this relate to social action and to the church? What does it mean to talk of redemption at a social and cosmic level? How is the church to argue for biblical values in a pluralistic society? Evangelical theology needed now to catch up with the new evangelical practice. A theology of social action and social change needed to be developed and incorporated into the broader sweep of evangelical theology. In the years following the Lausanne Congress this theological discussion unfolded in a number of books, articles and conferences.

Two related themes have, on the whole, predominated. The first is an emphasis on the lordship of Christ over all of life: those who follow Christ must work out the implications of their discipleship in every aspect of life, whether physical or spiritual, individual or social. The second is the kingdom of God. New Testament scholarship has over this century come to see the kingdom as both a present and future reality. Some have argued that what we do now for the sake of the kingdom is in some way included in the consummation of the kingdom when Christ returns. Most have stressed that, in the power of the kingdom, we are to seek its justice and to live by its values. Some have argued that the kingdom of God is present outside the church. Nearly all are agreed that the values and reconciliation of the kingdom should, and already do, take shape in the Christian community. In this way the church as an alternative society gives witness to its Lord.

In the early sixties John Stott had been asked by Jim Houston to speak at Regent College in Vancouver, Canada. Stott returned on a number of occasions and was impressed by their attempts to develop a Christian attitude to a range of secular issues and to train lay-people.[1] He also read Harry Blamires' *The Christian Mind*[2] which called for a Christian mind to be developed in response to secularism and this proved influential in his thinking. This concern to develop Christian approaches to social and secular issues found expression in Stott's 1972 Presidential Address to the IVF conference which was later published as *Your Mind Matters*.[3]

Then in 1974 Stott helped to initiate the London Lectures in Contemporary Christianity, an annual series in which Christian specialists reflected upon contemporary issues. Back in 1960, when he had been asked to give the Payton Lectures at Fuller Seminary, he had been struck by the usefulness of an endowed lectureship. The first London Lectures were given by Sir Norman Anderson who looked at a number of key issues surrounding birth (genetic engineering, birth control, abortion, *etc.*) and death (euthanasia, suicide, capital punishment, war).[4]

From the London Lectures arose the London Institute for Contemporary Christianity which was founded in 1982. Stott had retired as Rector of All Souls, Langham Place, London and Jim Houston suggested that something similar to Regent College might be established in Britain. At the same time Andrew Kirk, then based in Buenos Aires, was thinking along similar lines. Behind the project were the likes of Os Guinness, noted for his writings on contemporary culture, Brian Griffiths, the evangelical economist, Oliver Barclay, the former head of IVF, Ranald Macaulay of the L'Abri fellowship and the son-in-law of Francis Schaeffer, and Roy Clements, pastor of Eden Baptist Church, Cambridge, and a formative influence on the Jubilee Centre – a broad spectrum of people but all committed to the working out of the evangelical faith in all aspects of life. Brian Griffiths was later an advisor to Margaret Thatcher and is a strong advocate of market economics, while one of the earlier contributors to the London lectures was José Míguez Bonino, a Methodist from Latin America who advocates liberation theology and who spoke on Christianity and Marxism.[5]

A year after its foundation, the Institute was offered the use of St Peter's Church in Vere Street, just off Oxford Street in the heart of

London. Money for the transformation of St Peter's came in part from the sale of a Burne-Jones painting which had remained unnoticed on a staircase! The Institute runs courses from its base in Vere Street, as well as conferences and study days around the country and overseas with the aim of encouraging Christians to think through contemporary issues from a Christian point of view. In 1988 the Institute merged with the Shaftesbury Project to form Christian Impact. The Shaftesbury Project, founded in 1969 and based in Nottingham, had already had a major role in promoting research and education on contemporary social issues from an evangelical point of view. John Stott expressed his own reflections on contemporary issues in his seminal book *Issues Facing Christians Today* and more recently in *The Contemporary Christian.*[6]

The Institute has had a significant impact on evangelicals around the world. Its main ten-week course usually attracts people from over a dozen cultures and a number of people in leadership positions around the world have been through the Institute. In Hungary, for example, the student work is led almost exclusively by Institute graduates. A disappointment has been the disproportionately small number of people from Britain on the ten-week courses. 'It is very difficult', Stott complains, 'to persuade Brits to invest in their own education.'[7] Martyn Eden, the Institute's first Dean, puts it more strongly. The reason, he believes, is 'the dilettante attitudes of many Christians in this country towards their faith – faith is not something you have to take that seriously, it's not something you have to work at'.[8] Not many have been prepared to take the financial risk of a ten-week sabbatical, although when people have done so God has remarkably provided. Nevertheless Christian Impact and its Institute does attract large numbers to its weekend conferences of which there are currently around ten a year throughout the country. Stott would also like to see it fulfil more the role of a forum in which evangelical thinkers can come together and work through a common evangelical response to particular issues.

Two years before the publication of *Rich Christians in an Age of Hunger*, Ron Sider published an article which was later republished in booklet form as *Evangelism, Salvation and Social Justice* with a response by John Stott.[9] The debate between them was not whether evangelicals should be involved in social action, for they were both

happy to affirm that. Instead it concerned the theological background to social action and its relationship to evangelism. Sider
surveyed the alternatives before concluding that 'evangelism and
social action are equally important, but quite distinct, aspects of
the total mission of the church'.[10] In response John Stott stated his
'full agreement . . . about the partnership of evangelism and social
action'.[11] He added, however, that if pushed he would still say
that evangelism was primary, although 'one should not normally
have to choose'.[12]

They also disagreed over the extent of the kingdom prior to the
return of Christ. Sider said: 'The kingdom comes wherever Jesus
overcomes the power of evil. That happens most visibly in the
church. But it also happens in society at large because Jesus is
Lord of the world as well as the church.'[13] This argument has
proved influential,[14] although Sider himself later distanced himself
from it.[15] In response Stott insisted that the kingdom of God in the
New Testament is always centred on Christ; 'it may be said to
exist only where Jesus Christ is consciously acknowledged as
Lord',[16] although, Stott added, the righteous standards of the
kingdom 'will spill over into the world'.[17]

Ever since René Padilla's attack on 'culture Christianity', the role
of culture in our understanding of the gospel and of mission has
been a theme parallel to that of social action. This is because, as
Padilla argued, our view of social action seems particularly affected by our cultural background.[18] The Lausanne Covenant itself
says:

> The gospel does not presuppose the superiority of any
> culture to another, but evaluates all cultures according
> to its own criteria of truth and righteousness . . . Mis-
> sions have all too frequently exported with the gospel
> an alien culture, and churches have sometimes been in
> bondage to culture rather than to the Scripture.'[19]

In order to discuss these issues, the LCWE (in co-operation
with WEF) convened the Consultation on Gospel and Culture[20]
at Willowbank, Bermuda in 1978. The conference recognized the
complexity of the relationship between the gospel and culture;
culture is a gift from God but is also marred by sin. As such,

Bishop Stephen Neill said, 'the gospel can serve as the destroyer, preserver and the creator of cultures'.[21] In his contribution René Padilla called upon those who tend to see the gospel simply in individual and spiritual terms and who view mission merely in numerical terms to recognize the effect of their cultures in shaping this thinking. The Willowbank Report concluded: 'The writing and the reading of the Bible, the presentation of the gospel, conversion, church, and conduct – all these are influenced by culture. It is essential, therefore, that all churches contextualize the gospel in order to share it effectively in their own culture.'[22]

In Britain in the same year, 1978, the National Evangelical Conference on Social Ethics[23] was held at Hoddesdon with the help of the Shaftesbury Project. This provided an opportunity for academics to meet with activists and for serious reflection to be given to the theology underlying social involvement. The level of discussion was high and the conference papers, published as *Essays in Evangelical Social Ethics* (1979),[24] have proved an important contribution to the understanding of social action among British evangelicals. At this conference, too, Bruce Nicholls, Executive Secretary of the Theological Commission of WEF, met with Wayne Bragg, John Robinson, Vinay Samuel and Ronald Sider and together they proposed a process of study on the nature of development. The Theological Commission of WEF, and particularly its Unit on Ethics and Society with Ron Sider as its convenor, was to become a leading force in promoting debate on social and development issues.

At a meeting in the April of the following year the proposed programme of study took shape and it was decided to hold a consultation on the theology of development. This took place a year later in March 1980, also at Hoddesdon.[25] The consultation examined issues involved in development such as the relationship between Western donors and Third World recipients. It also began to explore, in a paper given by Vinay Samuel and Chris Sugden, an integrated theology of social change.[26] In the resulting Statement of Intent the conference participants expressed how deeply disturbed they were by poverty and injustice in the world and recognized the church's need to be involved in social change. As such they resolved to study, educate, build and work that they might 'encourage, by all peaceful and constructive means available to us, the poor and oppressed who are seeking to establish a position of dignity and self-worth'.

The participants of the conference also decided to continue the process of study envisaged by Bruce Nicholls and instigated a three-year programme: Christian Involvement in Human Development: A Programme of Evangelical Study and Action. Meeting on 31 January and 1 February 1981, the steering committee set out the following goals: '(i) We seek to promote theological reflection on attempts to meet human need in concrete local development situations. (ii) We seek further clarifications of theological issues related to development.' To this end the committee instituted a framework of study and consultation culminating in a conference in 1983.

This conference became in fact the Consultation on the Church in Response to Human Need[27] which was held in Wheaton, Illinois, USA, as the third part of a broader conference on the church sponsored by the WEF. The resultant 53-paragraph statement[28] is a comprehensive document dealing not only with development issues but with various other aspects of social involvement including the need for a stewardship of creation, the role of culture and the need for mercy and social justice to accompany one another. It stressed the centrality of the local church in social action and set social action in the context of the presence and coming of the kingdom of God.

The consultation summed up all these various concerns under the term *transformation*. This, the statement suggested, may be a word preferable to 'development' since it can include change at all levels of human existence (physical and spiritual, social and personal) and also because it can embrace change in First World societies as well as Third World societies. The statement defined transformation as 'the change from a condition of human existence contrary to God's purposes to one in which people are able to enjoy fulness of life in harmony with God' (Paragraph 11). And its goal, the statement suggested, 'is best described by the biblical vision of the kingdom of God' (Paragraph 13).

It should be remembered that conference statements rarely give the full picture of a conference. Behind the official face of conferences – represented by the statements – there has often been an unofficial jockeying for position and defending of personal attitudes. Yet at the same time it is only through the personal contact which a conference provides that misconceptions are corrected, cultural perspectives recognized and true partnership facilitated. That many of these conferences have gone largely unnoticed in the West does not necessarily reflect their true significance for the church as whole.

One of the continuing issues in evangelical theology is the use made of the Bible, particularly the Old Testament, in social ethics. Two starkly opposing answers have been proposed, largely in America, by dispensationalists on the one hand and theonomists or reconstructionists on the other.[29] Chris Wright helpfully summarizes their contrasting positions:

> At the very simplest ... dispensationalists hold that *none* of the Old Testament law applies to the Christian (or to any society in the present era) unless specifically *re-endorsed* by a New Testament imperative; theonomists hold that *the whole* Old Testament law continues to be valid both for Christians and as God's law for all human society, unless specifically *abrogated* in the New Testament.[30]

Dispensationalism is basically a variant of premillennialism and is strong mainly in North America or where there is a North American influence. Likewise reconstructionism has made little impact outside the United States although there is now a British organization, the Foundation for Christian Reconstruction, led by Stephen Perks in Whitby. Neither viewpoint has convinced many evangelicals outside the United States.[31] Most evangelicals have sought to develop a way of understanding of the Old Testament which makes it relevant for today without seeking to apply it literally or directly.

Early editions of *Transformation*, a journal for evangelical dialogue on social ethics set up following the Wheaton Consultation, contained some important contributions on the use of the Bible in social ethics. Indeed the first edition had an article with just that name, 'The Use of the Bible in Social Ethics',[32] by Chris Wright. Wright was then a lecturer at the Union Biblical Seminary, Pune, India, and is now Principal of All Nations Christian College in the UK. He argued for a paradigmatic approach. In the Bible we find the developing story of the relationships between God, humankind and the earth. These relationships in the Old Testament can be viewed as paradigms, particular cases illustrating general principles. Recognizing the change in history and culture and the development in the history of redemption, we can apply these principles to society today. Wright developed this approach in his book, *Living as the People of God* (published in the USA under the title *An Eye for an Eye*).[33] Chris Wright's article was followed up in *Transformation* by two articles on 'The Use of the New Testament'[34] by Stephen Mott, Professor of Christian Social Ethics at Gordon-Conwell Theological Seminary, Massachusetts. Like Wright's article these were also published in the Grove Ethics Series. And, according to Wright, Mott 'shattered the idea that Jesus was uninterested in politics and has nothing to offer to contemporary social conflicts'.[35]

In Britain the Jubilee Centre has also sought to develop an approach to the Old Testament which avoids the extremes of reconstructionism and dispensationalism and has sought to apply it to a range of contemporary social issues. The Jubilee Centre has its origins in Nairobi, Kenya. Roy Clements was the pastor of Nairobi Baptist Church and Michael Schluter was working in Kenya for the family business and later with the World Bank. Responding to the issues raised by life in East Africa they began to work towards an ethical framework within which the church could formulate an alternative Christian response. With his background in economics Schluter began to look at the Old Testament law and relate it to contemporary issues. This proved to be the beginnings of what Schluter and Clements call Jubilee Ethics.[36]

Although the Old Testament is central to their approach Clements and Schluter firmly reject theonomism. The law, they argue, must be seen through Christ and the principle of love must be applied to the interpretation of the law. The Christian lives now in the age to come and the loyalties of this new age (for example, to the Christian family) take precedence over the loyalties of the old (to the natural family). Nevertheless until Christ returns the old age continues in overlap. Clements and Schluter believe that what they call Jubilee institutional norms, norms based on what the Old Testament law teaches, provide a fruitful way forward for evangelical social action.

When Schluter returned to England in 1982 he set up the Jubilee Centre in Cambridge as a research and campaigning organization which aims to apply biblical principles in practical ways to various contemporary social issues. Although best known for its key role in the Keep Sunday Special Campaign, the Centre has campaigned on issues relating to family, to debt and to prison reform. In 1990 the Jubilee Policy Group was formed as the main research unit at the Centre, producing reports and briefing papers primarily for MPs, peers and policy makers. The Policy Group, it should be noted, is eclectic in its theological stance, drawing on insights from a range of approaches.

More recently the Centre has been concerned to develop an alternative approach to social and economic policy based not upon the materialism of capitalism and socialism but upon 'relationism'. Michael Schluter and David Lee have published a book entitled *The R Factor*.[37] All individuals and societies, the book argues, require both choice and obligation. Because historically there has been a link between obligation and oppression, modern Western liberalism has emphasized the importance of protecting choice from obligation. But choice without obligation leads to social breakdown. The choice, for example, to leave a marriage creates disruption which is likely to be damaging, especially where children are involved. For obligations to be effective there needs to be a commitment to them and some sense of constraint arising from the disapproval of others. But commitment and constraint, Schluter and Lee argue, are to a significant extent dependent upon closeness in human relationships – 'the R factor'. Industrialization, however, has brought a shift in the scale of the community to which an individual feels a sense of belonging. Government, business and the entertainment industry now operate on a national or even international scale. At the same time social mobility constantly interrupts relationships and the consumer economy creates the expectation of choice without a corresponding sense of obligation. These factors all militate against the relationships necessary for a sense of obligation to others.

Schluter and Lee propose a process of what they call 'convergence': policies designed to create and improve relationships. For example, they propose more local decision-making in both government and business and the encouragement of smaller businesses in which owners, managers and workers are in direct relationship. The Jubilee Centre is also concerned to develop 'relational justice' as a basis for penal reform. Crime should be seen primarily as a violation of people, relationships and communities and only secondarily as an offence against the state. As such there should be, for example, greater involvement by the community in various aspects of the criminal justice process and a shift towards sentences which maintain and restore community links rather than destroy them as custodial sentences tend to do.

Relationism arises from biblical reflection: at the heart of creation, redemption and Christian ethics are the relationships of humanity and God and of people one with another. At the same time *The R Factor* is not explicitly Christian in its presentation because it seeks to commend relationism to society as a whole. Relationism may represent a 'third way' between capitalism and socialism. It may also prove less culture-bound than classic Western liberalism, being less open to the unchecked individualism which so often characterizes liberalism. Only time will tell whether this is the case or not, and, indeed, whether relationism will have any significant impact upon the church or upon society at large.

Living more simply and trading more fairly

All of us are shocked by the poverty of millions and disturbed by the injustices which cause it. Those of us who live in affluent circumstances accept our duty to develop a simple lifestyle in order to contribute more generously to both relief and evangelism. (The Lausanne Covenant, Paragraph 9: 'The Urgency of the Evangelistic Task', 1974)

So then, having been freed by the sacrifice of our Lord Jesus Christ, in obedience to his call, in heartfelt compassion for the poor, in concern for evangelism, development and justice, and in solemn anticipation of the Day of Judgement, we humbly commit ourselves to develop a just and simple lifestyle, to support one another in it and to encourage others to join us in this commitment. (An Evangelical Commitment to Simple Lifestyle, 1980)

The Lausanne Covenant committed those who signed it to 'develop a simple lifestyle'. Although not originally his suggestion, John Stott insisted on its inclusion despite opposition from some quarters. Indeed Ruth Graham, Billy Graham's wife, refused to sign the Covenant because of it, arguing that it was too confining and too vague.[1] Through his travels in the Third World, Stott himself was already convinced of the need for a simple lifestyle. The problem was that 'simple lifestyle' meant very little in practice to most people. What is it? Who is it for? How does one live it? What is its biblical basis?

Those moved by description of the social and economic imbalance in the world in *Rich Christians in an Age of Hunger* and challenged by the biblical teaching on poverty inevitably wanted some guidance on how they as individuals could respond. At the end of *Rich Christians* Sider outlined his vision of a simpler lifestyle. Sider spoke of how we in the West persuade ourselves that we 'need' our relatively high incomes to live 'comfortably'. The sin of materialism is reason enough to commit ourselves to a simpler lifestyle quite apart from the needs of the poor. Sider suggested a graduated tithe as one, admittedly rather modest, possible model. With a graduated tithe the more you earn the higher the percentage you give. You decide on a basic figure which you tithe at 10%. The first £1,000 earned over this figure is tithed at 15%, the next at 20% and so on. Sider also suggested that Christians engage in various levels of community living. Quite apart from the other benefits, such sharing together enables Christians to live on less and so releases resources for the work of the gospel. He also gave suggestions for cutting our expenditure and consumption.[2]

It was not an entirely new idea,[3] for people had already been suggesting that Christians needed to live simply for the sake of the poor and for the vast needs of world mission. Indeed Sider points to the example of John Wesley (1703–91) who believed that since Christians should not store up for themselves treasure on earth (Matthew 6:19–23) they should give away all but what was needed for the plain necessities of life. Wesley himself lived on £28 a year despite earning up to £1,400 annually from the sale of his books.[4] And in 1973 the Chicago Declaration had attacked the materialism of Western culture and called upon evangelicals to 'rethink our values regarding our present standard of living and promote more just acquisition and distribution of the world's resources'. The key question, however, was what did living simply mean in practice? At a consultation, called by Billy Graham and Hudson Armeding in 1977, on future evangelical concerns, the question of simple lifestyle kept arising. Finally Loren Cunningham, President of Youth With A Mission, commented that evangelicals would begin to practise simple lifestyle if evangelical leaders were prepared to model it.[5] He recognized that the concept of simple lifestyle needed to be fleshed out, both theologically and with concrete models.

Furthermore, as John Stott met with Third World Christians he was asked by them whether Western Christians were really serious about the commitment they had made to simple lifestyle in the

Lausanne Covenant. During the first Lausanne consultation, he and Ron Sider had breakfast together in a Los Angeles hotel and agreed on the need for a consultation on simple lifestyle. The consultation would be co-sponsored by the Lausanne Theology and Education Group of which Stott was chairman – the Lausanne Committee agreed with hesitation and only if simple lifestyle was looked at in relation to evangelization – and by the Unit on Ethics and Society of the Theological Commission of WEF of which Ron Sider was the convenor.

In the event the Consultation on Simple Lifestyle[6] was held in March 1980 at Hoddesdon, England, a few days after the Consultation on the Theology of Development, allowing a number of people to stay on and attend both conferences. The consultation itself was the culmination of a two-year process involving local groups in fifteen countries and regional conferences in India, Ireland and the United States.

The conference crammed a lot into just four days. It looked at the biblical basis for simple lifestyle, the perspective of church history, its corporate dimensions and its relationship to evangelism and social justice. The resulting Evangelical Commitment to Simple Lifestyle, steered through by John Stott, is a comprehensive document dealing not only with simple lifestyle but with a wide range of related issues. In this way it placed simple lifestyle in its wider context so that it was not divorced from the issue of justice. At its heart, however, remains a commitment 'to develop a just and simple lifestyle'. 'Our Christian obedience demands a simple lifestyle', the statement says, 'irrespective of the needs of others. Nevertheless, the facts that 800 million people are destitute and that about 10,000 die of starvation every day make any other lifestyle indefensible.' Despite the best efforts of the organizers, the participants were biased somewhat in favour of the radical wing[7] and tensions arose between First and Third World representatives.[8] Nevertheless Stott maintained that the statement itself was not imbalanced and feels it has not had the publicity it deserves.[9]

Of equal importance were the practical testimonies of individuals and groups who had begun to implement simple lifestyles. The consultation heard of Vishal Mangalwadi. He and his wife had sacrificed the well-paid jobs open to them in order to work as evangelists among the poor in Madhya Pradesh, India. By sharing their resources they had been able to support fellow-workers and to provide, for example, for converted criminals who could not find employment. They had had to live by trusting God for their needs. In fact Mangalwadi rejected the economic description 'simple lifestyle', because what they sought to live was a cross-bearing lifestyle.[10]

They also heard from Dolphus Weary who, though able to escape from the poverty and injustice he faced as a black person in Mississippi, had turned his back on upward mobility to work with John Perkins among the black community,[11] and from Vinay and Colleen Samuel who from their privileged backgrounds had begun to reach out to the slum areas of Bangalore and to share their lives with the poor.[12] They heard too from Ralph and Roberta Winter who described how they had sought always to live according to their needs and not the pressures of their culture or the expectations of others. In this way they had been able to give themselves more fully to the work of mission, although they also stressed that it is easier to live simply when you covenant to do so with others.[13]

Nor need simple lifestyle necessarily mean living among the poor. It is not possible for all to take such a step. The challenge of the Lausanne Covenant and the Evangelical Commitment to Simple Lifestyle is directed primarily to those living in an affluent Western culture. The challenge is to take seriously the Bible's teachings on the dangers of wealth and to free ourselves from the materialism of Western culture, trusting in God rather than in what we own. In his foreword to *Rich Christians* David Watson said: 'We have accepted a lifestyle which is so similar to that of the covetous world around us as to be indistinguishable from it.'[14] The gospel will not make an impact upon our society while it has no impact upon our own lifestyles. The challenge presented by advocates of a simpler lifestyle is to respond to the needs of the poor – and also environmental problems – not just through *ad hoc* charity, but through a commitment to a just and sustainable lifestyle. This does not mean a harsh asceticism; quite the opposite. It is to learn to be truly content, to celebrate all that God has given us rather than be preoccupied with gaining more. It is to appreciate the beauty of creation and creativity and to learn to enjoy things without having to own them.

The Consultation on Simple Lifestyle heard of how David Watson and his wife Anne had set up extended households.[15] The vision originated with Anne and indeed David was initially reluctant. There were three aims involved. The first was to work out in a greater way what it meant to be the Body of Christ and to be really committed to one another as members of that one Body. Previously Watson had always put a strong emphasis upon practical care and support within the church. Second, by living communally, sharing many things in common and by living simply they sought to release people and money for the work of the kingdom. After resources were pooled each person received 'pocket money'. Students in the United States asking about his salary were amazed to discover that Watson received £3 a week and depended on buying secondhand clothes. And third, they sought to provide a loving family environment for those with particular problems or facing the loneliness increasingly common in our society.

Community life was certainly no bed of roses, for they faced many difficulties and there was a constant need for forgiveness. Eventually the households disbanded, partly because they overstretched themselves in caring for people with problems and partly because they had served their purpose.[16] Nevertheless at one time there were seven such households and others operating on a lesser scale. In this way as many as thirty lay workers were supported in the church, including all of Watson's evangelistic team, and a lot of money was released for relief work as they sought to identify with the poor. Watson also felt that the households were a catalyst encouraging the rest of the church to give and share more freely.[17]

Many examples of what a commitment to simple lifestyle had involved for people living in a Western culture were also shared at the US pre-Hoddesdon consultation. Arbutus Sider, for example, Ron Sider's wife, shared something of the experience of the Jubilee Fellowship. The Jubilee Fellowship is a small church in one of the poorer neighbourhoods of Philadelphia. It meets in a local recreation centre which, although rather run down, means that money is not tied up in property. The community stresses simple lifestyle: family budgets are discussed openly, cars are shared, as is child care allowing parents time for other activities. Through their commitment to a simpler lifestyle the community is able to run various projects including a magazine.[18]

For a while simple lifestyle was very much part of the evangelical agenda. After *Rich Christians* came out, for example, *Crusade* magazine and *Third Way* produced supplements called 'That's the Style' and 'Hard Questions for Rich Christians' respectively. Yet during the eighties it declined as an issue although there are signs that it is again resurfacing, this time in response to environmental issues. Many found it all but impossible to practise a simple lifestyle in any meaningful way on their own with a tide of Western consumerism flowing against them. Others, however, have faithfully and quietly lived simply as an expression of their commitment to Christ and to the poor.

Not only has the amount of income we need to live on been questioned but also how we spend that amount. Is it spent in a way that promotes justice or in a way that encourages injustice? These issues were raised at the Simple Lifestyle Consultation. Vinay Samuel and Chris Sugden chose to speak of 'a just and responsible lifestyle'[19] and the final statement spoke of 'a just and simple lifestyle'. As Christians have become more involved with the relief of poverty, so they have become more aware of some of its underlying causes. There has been, for example, a net flow of money from the Third World to the First as debt repayments outweigh overseas aid and new loans. Christians have begun to realize that simply sending money overseas would not in itself provide a secure and just future for those affected by poverty.

In order to address some of the underlying factors behind world poverty some evangelicals have begun to be involved in political lobbying. In 1974 Bread for the World[20] was founded in the USA with the aim of affecting US government policy on the issues of hunger and poverty and raising the issues surrounding Third World debt and trade. It is not a professional Washington lobbying body but instead seeks to be an expression of the concern of Christians and churches throughout the United States. It has a specifically Christian character and its local congressional groups make worship a central part of their meetings. A number of well-known evangelicals are actively involved. The original Board of Directors included Stan Mooneyham of World Vision, Frank Gaebelein, Myron Augsburger, John Perkins and Senator Mark Hatfield.

In Britain a similar lobbying function is carried out by the World Development Movement (WDM). Although not a specifically

Christian organization it has a Churches Committee which organizes the annual 'One World Week'. Like Bread for the World the WDM also receives significant support from evangelicals. Tear Fund, for example, arranged for a special WDM membership leaflet with an endorsement of the WDM by John Stott to be distributed in *Tear Times*. Tear Fund itself only has observer status on the WDM Churches Committee, which is responsible for One World Week, a development education week held in October every year. Tear Fund feels it cannot commit funds to an event that is based on a broad ecumenical theology, with many local groups encouraging multi-faith worship as part of the week's events. John Mitchell, the former director of the WDM, is an evangelical. When Tear Fund began Mitchell was involved, despite some criticism, in organizing student support for Tear Fund in Oxford; he was a key member of the Aid and Development Group of the Shaftesbury Project (now part of Christian Impact) and he was involved in anglicizing *Rich Christians in an Age of Hunger*. Both Bread for the World and the WDM can claim some success in affecting the policy of their respective governments.

One of the main factors behind Third World poverty is the system of international trade which favours the richer nations. Uganda – one of the world's poorest countries – used to earn 97% of its foreign exchange from coffee. In 1989, however, the international price of coffee fell by a third in one week. As a result it was not worth the while of most of Uganda's small farmers even to harvest their crop. Yet while the price of coffee has fallen, the prices of tractors and other manufactured goods have risen. Coffee produced in, for example, Brazil or Nicaragua currently buys only one fifth the quantity of manufactured goods it did in 1977. Meanwhile the richer countries impose higher tariffs on processed products forcing the poorer countries to continue producing raw materials even though these equate to ever decreasing purchasing power. In Brazil cutters of sisal, which is used to make string and ropes, earn the equivalent of just 60p for a ten-hour day. Year by year what they produce has been worth less. Today a kilo of sisal is worth a fifth of what it fetched in 1983.[21]

Richard Adams, the founder of Tearcraft and Traidcraft, stresses that our bargain is somebody else's raw deal. Adams tells of a conversation he had with Sujoy Srimal, the General Secretary of the

Equitable Marketing Association in Calcutta. 'I had commented', Adams writes, 'that some of the brushes being produced by a nearby co-operative seemed a bargain. "No," he said, "they are not a bargain. They are cheap because the people are desperate to make a sale." "For us, though", I insisted, "that means they are a bargain." "What a peculiar idea of a bargain you have in England", Sujoy replied, "For me, a bargain is an agreement when both parties are happy that they have got the best deal."'[22]

In 1972 Richard Adams left his job as industrial officer for East Lothian County Council to become a greengrocer. Since leaving college he had been concerned about the needs of Third World farmers. The aim was to import surplus produce from local farmers and sell it in this country for a greater return than the farmers could expect in their own over-supplied markets. Adams and his wife, together with his co-worker Tim McClure and his wife and their child, moved into the two-bedroom flat over the shop. Their diet, however, was exotic – even their dogs occasionally dined on asparagus. Despite eighteen-hour days and one occasion when they had to dispose of fifteen tonnes of rotting green peppers, the project proved successful.

Then in 1974, when the rise in transport costs as a result of the oil crisis was placing the business's future in question, Adams received a call from Ian Prior, an old college friend. Prior, who was working for Tear Fund, wanted Adams to meet Peter McNee, a New Zealand Baptist missionary working in Bangladesh. McNee was trying to sell jute handicrafts from Bangladesh – a country recovering from civil war and a recent cyclone. Adams ordered £1,000's worth. McNee told him later: 'I thought you were mad, a greengrocer buying jute, but I certainly was not going to complain. I should know by now that God's world is full of surprises.'[23] A friend of Adams, Ray Skinner, a curate in Newcastle, suggested that the handicrafts could be sold by mail order from his basement.

Soon after the goods arrived Adams received another call from Ian Prior. He was invited to meet George Hoffman who told him that Tear Fund was planning to charter a relief flight to Bangladesh. Could he, Hoffman wondered, go on ahead and get together enough community goods to fill the plane for the return flight? Tear Fund would cover the expenses which Adams estimated would be £10,000. There was, however, one problem – the plane was booked for two weeks' time. A cheque arrived the next day – only then did Chris, Adams' wife, believe that they were being entrusted with £10,000 by someone they hardly knew – and so in a mad rush Adams postponed their intended catalogue, flew out and bought as many handicrafts as he could. The goods ended up under the floorboards of the gym in the school over the road from Ray Skinner's house. Two days before Christmas 1974 Tearcraft became a registered business. It was not the first alternative trading organization. This was probably Self Help, the trading arm of the Mennonite Central Committee, which began in the United States in 1947.[24] In Britain it was Oxfam which in 1967 first began importing Third World goods.

With Tear Fund's supporters as a base clientele and a growing number of voluntary representatives and interested shops, the business grew. Before long it moved into a proper warehouse and Richard Adams found himself making a number of trips overseas in search of new producer partners. Many needed marketing and design advice to sell effectively to a Western market although this created its own anomalies. One Canadian volunteer was asked by a group of women in Dhaka why Westerners sat on the table to eat their dinner – they were making table mats!

Tensions, however, soon surfaced between Tear Fund and Adams. Tear Fund was committed to working with and through evangelicals. Adams and others at Tearcraft wanted to buy from non-evangelical projects and sell to non-evangelical consumers. Tear Fund received complaints when in one instance, to make up an order, goods were bought from Communist China. At the same time Tearcraft was not proving commercially successful and Tear Fund was having to commit considerable sums of money to keeping the company afloat. Writing later, Adams said: 'More than ten years have brought a dramatic change in attitudes, and it is hard to see why these issues were so divisive.'[25] Nevertheless at the time it was decided that there should be a parting of the ways. After protracted negotiations Tearcraft was split and Adams launched Traidcraft in October 1977 amid considerable controversy and a certain amount of bitterness. Traidcraft started trading from the same address as Tearcraft and sought to recruit Tearcraft reps. Looking back on events – at the time Tear Fund declined to comment – Stephen Rand, the Communications Director of Tear Fund, says:

There was, amidst all the turmoil and confusion of this split, a theological issue involved. Tear Fund's view was that the outworking of an holistic view of the gospel required that each producer group should have some key input from evangelicals, so that the gospel could be articulated within the group, as well as demonstrated in a Christian concern to provide much-needed employment.'[26]

Traidcraft, in contrast, was based on the premise that justice in trade was in itself a witness to the truth of the gospel.

Traidcraft soon outgrew Tearcraft and has expanded into wholefoods and clothing. Although its support to begin with was predominately evangelical, increasingly Traidcraft began to look to Christian Aid and CAFOD for backing. Then in 1984 it was successfully launched as a public company, offering potential shareholders not great profits but the chance to share in the company's work for justice and equity. Meanwhile Tearcraft Ltd itself officially ceased to trade in 1991, although its work continues as before, once again under the auspices of Tear Fund in conjunction with Send the Light (STL). In 1989 Richard Adams left Traidcraft to become the first director of the magazine *New Consumer* which aims to inform consumers so that they can use their purchasing power to promote just and sustainable trade.

Alternative trading organizations have undoubtedly provided an important outlet for small scale producer groups from the Third World and they do so in a way that seeks to move from dependency to proper economic development. Yet the advocacy of 'trade rather than aid' has been controversial. In reality alternative trading organizations usually involve a substantial aid element. Help and capital are often needed for product development and a charitable impulse is usually an important factor in the purchase of goods. The organizations often need external funds to remain commercially viable. Furthermore the goods have tended to be fairly costly 'gift' items creating a conflict between a commitment to simple lifestyle and a commitment to fair trade. Traidcraft was only able to move into providing more basic items such as food and clothing when it was no longer bound to buy from evangelical sources. Tearcraft in contrast has only succeeded in providing tea from a source where a witness to the gospel was part of the project – a tea estate in Assam run by a Lutheran mission organization. In reality many involved in both trade and aid see them as complementary approaches, both aiming at independence and sustainability.

In the Third World evangelicals have been increasingly involved in local, commercially viable business enterprises. Attention has turned from simply providing for the poor to enpowering them, enabling them to provide for themselves and to be economically productive. This fact was recognized at the important Oxford Conference on Faith and Economics in 1990. A previous conference had commissioned a study of income generation among the poor.[27] The report condemned 'trickle down' strategies of development as having little effect upon the lives of the poorest. Instead it urged a move towards development projects which work directly with the poor. 'It is critical', the report said, 'that the contribution of non-governmental organisations to development is not merely an exercise in welfare or charity, but a deliberate contribution to sustainable self-reliance and self-determination by the poor.'[28] The report found that where small loans – averaging less than a hundred dollars – had been given to enable the poor to become productive, repayment rates were on average better than those expected in commercial finance markets and default rates were minimal. Yet the poor were often being denied access to the formal credit market.[29] And a similar study by Norm Ewert of Wheaton College concluded: 'small scale enterprises are one means of directly addressing poverty in a way which respects individual dignity, is sustainable ecologically and economically, and protects individuals from economic mismanagement elsewhere'.[30]

The first Oxford Conference on Faith and Economics (1987)[31] had proposed a process of study, and as this developed it incorporated a very wide spectrum of economic and theological approaches. Between the first and second conferences a number of free-market economists decided to get involved. Their presence made the second conference (1990)[32] all the more significant for, through a remarkable degree of mutual openness, a comprehensive statement, the Oxford Declaration on Faith and Economics, was agreed upon. In it 'liberation orientated theologians affirmed free-market strategies and conservative market economists demanded a special focus on justice for the poor'.[33] The Report recognizes 'that poverty results from and is sustained by both constraints on the production of wealth and on the inequitable distribution of wealth and income. We acknowledge the tendency we have had to reduce the causes of poverty to one at the expense of the other.'[34] The 65-paragraph document is a remarkable testimony to the degree of unanimity which Christians can reach on social issues when they come together in openness to one another and to the Word of God.

Stirring voices from the Third World

*We acknowledge that central to God's nature is his love
and justice. God revealed himself in historical acts of
deliverance of his people from slavery, in destroying the
unjust kingdoms of Samaria and Judah, and supremely
in Jesus, his Son. Jesus' commitment to liberate men
from unjust relationships and create right relationships
between God and man, and man and man, climaxed in
his rejection and death. His resurrection confirms that
the cross establishes God's justice and that his return will
usher in full and final justice.*

*We acknowledge that God called out a people to be the
community of his kingdom. They are called to model his
love and justice in their economic, social and political
relationships, and to be instruments of his action in
society. (From* the Madras Declaration, 1979)

The role of Third World theologians in shaping evangelical social
ethics and missiology from the sixties onwards should not be underestimated. Certainly it is René Padilla's contention that the contribution of Third World evangelicals has been of central importance in
this process. Speaking of the effect of Lausanne, he says that 'social
involvement had finally been granted full citizenship in evangelical
missiology, mainly under the influence of people from the Two
Thirds World'.[1] And he concludes that in the process of shaping
evangelical social ethics over this period, 'people from the Two
Thirds World played a decisive role'.[2] Nor has their influence been
felt simply at conferences. Much of the current thinking on social
action derives, either directly or indirectly, from their writings. John
Stott, too, points to the rising generation of Third World leadership
as being 'the key influence' in the growth of evangelical social action.

The 'intellectual quality and spiritual power' of this leadership surprised those at Lausanne who had had little contact with the Third World churches. Added to which 'the Third World leadership never had the problem of the dichotomy between evangelism and social action ... to them one without the other is inconceivable'.[3] Speaking from his perspective as International Director of the Lausanne Committee, Tom Houston can say: 'Today it's not a question in any Third World country that I know that the gospel needs to be two-handed and that [the church] must face up to social and political things.'[4]

René Padilla himself was born in Ecuador and brought up in Colombia in a tradition which devalued social action although, particularly in his mother, he saw the practical outworking of Christian compassion. At high school some of his teachers were Marxists and so he was challenged to relate his faith to social issues. After graduating from Wheaton College, USA, he joined the International Fellowship of Evangelical Students (IFES). Returning to Latin America he found that a large percentage of students were interested in Marxism and saw the Cuban revolution as a model for the rest of Latin America. Working among students forced Padilla, together with Samuel Escobar and other colleagues in IFES, to rethink the gospel in terms of its social implications. They found themselves reading the Bible with new eyes as they sought to find answers to the questions raised by students and began to challenge Christians to think about social issues from a Christian perspective and to use their professions in the service of humanity.

As Padilla, Escobar and others began to write articles and give talks on these questions, so things became difficult for them because of the negative attitudes towards social action held by many church leaders and foreign missionaries. Yet, says Padilla, God was gracious and as a result of their work they saw many professionals choosing to serve the poor. In 1987 Padilla was encouraged to find that a high percentage of participants at a Latin American conference on social transformation had been through IFES-related movements.

It was student work, then, which provided the initial motivation for such reflection in Latin America. But other factors also contributed to the acceptance of the importance of the social implications of the gospel there. The most important of these is the continent's impoverishment. Many churches are deeply affected by this. Some 75% of Protestants are Pentecostal and the large majority of Pentecostal churches are among the poor.

Also important has been the influence of liberation theology and it is perhaps this factor above all others which has made the Latin American radicals suspect in the eyes of many North Americans. It is probably true to say, however, that liberation theology has not so much provided Latin American evangelicals with a set of answers as raised a set of questions. How does the gospel relate to social injustice and poverty and how are we to understand the reasons behind such injustice and poverty? If liberation theology is to be rejected as unbiblical or insufficiently biblical, what is the biblical response to poverty and injustice?

While evangelicals have not necessarily followed liberation theology's understanding of revolution, they have gained from its understanding of theology. Liberation theology has emphasized that theology and mission must be shaped by the context in which they are conducted. The questions you face and your understanding of the Bible are shaped by the situation in which you are trying to live out your Christian faith. If Latin American evangelicals have continued to stress the objective authority of the Bible, they have also been in the forefront of the recognition that our understanding of that objective authority is shaped by the relative situations in which we live and work. The influence of liberation theology can also be seen among British evangelicals, particularly, for example, in Michael Paget-Wilkes' book *Poverty, Revolution and the Church*.[5]

Another important factor has been the Latin American Theological Fraternity (LATF)– the only organizational structure to come out of CLADE I, the Latin American follow-up conference to the Berlin Congress. Little by little this has affected the social attitudes of the churches, and a number of its members are involved in theological teaching so that successive students and pastors have been influenced in this way.

In November 1979 over 250 people gathered for the Second Latin American Congress on Evangelization (CLADE II)[6] in Lima, Peru. After CLADE I Latin American evangelicals did not want any more foreign-mission initiated congresses. CLADE II was organized by the LATF, only 10% of those present were non-Latin missionaries and the majority of the finance came from within Latin America. At the Congress Orlando Costas from Puerto Rico defined evangelism as the proclamation of the gospel calling individuals to repentance and faith in Jesus Christ and incorporating them into the struggles of the kingdom against the forces of evil. The demand of faith, he argued, must always be contextualized.

CLADE II issued a pastoral letter known as the Lima Letter. It saw signs of hope amidst the 'dark picture of the Latin American situation' and was a commitment to mission in response to 'the cry of those who hunger and thirst after righteousness, of those whose most basic needs are not being met, of the marginalized ethnic groups, of broken families, of women denied the exercise of their natural rights, of youth dedicated to vice or forced into violence, of children who suffer from hunger, abandonment, ignorance and exploitation'. The concerns expressed at CLADE I, that a programme of evangelization might compromise the wholeness of repentance for the sake of numerical results, were laid to rest at CLADE II, in Latin America at least. When CLADE III[7] was held in Quito, Ecuador, in 1992 one of its aims was 'to encourage the development of a missionary vision and a wholistic evangelization all over the Latin American continent and beyond it'. Not only did the Quito Document commend an holistic approach to evangelism, it also called upon the church 'to practise justice', to prepare leaders for 'responsible participation in civil life' and to 'assume its prophetic role'.

In India in 1975 EFICOR became independent of EFI and Vinay Samuel became its first General Secretary. At the same time EFICOR began to be involved in long-term development as well as relief work and began a comprehensive training programme. Through a series of conferences it began to teach a holistic approach to mission. 'We had the edge in some ways', says Vinay Samuel, 'because we were better trained, were capable of writing and we were given resources as well. It was a very deliberate attempt to change the [situation in India].'[8]

At the number of Indian conferences following Lausanne the issue of social action regularly arose. These conferences also facilitated the growth of a network of Indian social activists. Chris Wigglesworth, now General Secretary of the Church of Scotland Board of World Mission and Unity, had been pioneering evangelical social involvement in Bombay.[9] At one particular conference on evangelization at Deveali in 1977 it was felt that a conference specifically on social action was needed and the decision was made to hold such a gathering.

The All India Conference on Evangelical Social Action[10] met in Madras in October 1979, a month before CLADE II. The conference was chaired by Samuel Kamalesan with Vinay Samuel as co-ordinator. Speaking against the context of 'the increasing oppression of the underprivileged classes', the Madras Declaration affirms the global scope of God's renewal, the importance of human dignity, the prophetic role of the church and its role as model of true humanity, the social aspects of God's judgment and of his kingdom, the need for identification with the poor and the way of the cross and non-violence.

With the Madras Declaration as a focus, EFICOR established its Educational and Training Unit in Bangalore in 1979. Under the leadership of Vinay Samuel the unit has been an important factor in the growth of evangelical social involvement in India and through-out Asia. It offers a thorough grounding in the theology of social action and development in addition to training in practical skills and community organization. The basic training involves three months' course work followed by two years' supervised field work. Also based in Bangalore, The Association for Theological Extension Edu-cation (TAFTEE) has offered a variety of degree-courses, primarily for part-time students. With courses like 'Jesus the Liberator' and 'Poverty and Development', TAFTEE has emphasized through its courses discipleship in the whole of life.

Initially EFICOR was opposed by a number of traditional Indian missionary societies who would not accept social action as part of mission. Church planting among the poor meant that many of these groups were involved in social care but, with no understanding of social involvement as part of mission, their care was largely among church members. The training programme proved its worth, how-ever, in the quality of fieldworkers it produced, not only in respect of social action but in evangelism as well. Now EFICOR trains, for example, most of the workers of the Friends Missionary Prayer Band, one of the largest indigenous missionary organizations in India. Indeed the EFICOR training programme currently trains workers from throughout Asia and the world. While, for example, it has received support from World Vision, it has also in turn had a significant impact on World Vision itself. Many of World Vision's workers are now trained by EFICOR and EFICOR has contributed to a growing emphasis on the integration of evangelism and social action within World Vision. 'The most important thing really', explains Vinay Samuel, 'is to integrate, to see people come to Christ ... There should be something Christian about the way we do development. Christian involvement in development opens people up to Christ. It has to, otherwise it's not Christian. That was our theme.'[11]

The first major follow-up to Lausanne organized by the LCWE was the Consultation on World Evangelization (COWE)[12] in Pattaya, Thailand, in 1980. The resultant Thailand Statement reaffirmed Lausanne's commitment to evangelism and social action. Yet to those concerned to emphasize the need for evangelical social involvement COWE was undoubtedly a disappointment. René Padilla said afterwards: 'It would not be difficult to prove that the organizers ... made a special effort to ensure that the task of world evangelism was dealt with in isolation from social responsibility.'[13] The emphasis was very much upon the strategy of verbal communication and the leadership seemed at pains to steer the conference clear of social aspects.[14] As a result, COWE was regarded as being 'prepackaged' and as a 'backlash' against the new understanding of the social dimension of the gospel.[15]

Instead the dominant theme of COWE was that of *people-groups*. The focus of the task of proclamation switched from isolated individuals to people-groups, people with a cultural and ethnic affinity. Although this involved a recognition of the importance of context and culture in the way people hear the gospel, a number of the participants, particularly from the Third World, felt that the concept should be widened to include the social, economic and political contexts of people. By excluding these contexts the task of reaching unreached people was being seen in terms of evangelism alone. Furthermore, a number feared that behind the emphasis on people-groups was the controversial homogeneous unit principle of church growth which has been particularly associated with Fuller Seminary's School of World Mission. This is a mission strategy which seeks to concentrate mission activity on homogeneous groups. Advocates argue that people will respond best to the gospel in a context and among people with whom they are comfortable.

Opponents fear that this leads to the creation of churches seg-regated along ethnic or racial grounds and that the costly reconcilia-tion of the gospel is sacrificed for superficial results.[16] In June 1977 the LTEG had organized a consultation of both advocates and opponents to examine the homogenous unit principle at Pasadena, USA. Although able to state broad areas of agreement, the final report also confessed remaining points of tension and disagree-ment.[17]

During the COWE a group of African delegates led by Bishop David Gitari drew up a statement expressing concern at the damage done to world evangelization when evangelicals support political and economic policies which deny the gospel. They were also concerned that this conference on evangelization was only present-ing one model of evangelism. At the same time the Latin Americans and Asians were working on a response, as they had done at the Lausanne Congress. As word got around, the two groups came together and a meeting of about two hundred people was held. The fear was expressed that by excluding social concerns the LCWE was going back on what had been achieved at Lausanne.[18] The meeting agreed that a more general document should be drawn up: the Statement of Concerns on the Future of the LCWE.[19] A small team drafted the statement. Around midnight a typewriter was found and by four o'clock in the morning the document had been typed and copied. Then between four and six it was put under all the doors of the main conference hotel so that all the participants could see it – a few unsuspecting tourists got a copy too! The idea was that if they agreed with it the participants should sign it and hand it to the drafters. This idea floundered somewhat since many supporters wanted to keep their copy. Nevertheless within twenty-four hours the Statement of Concerns was assented to by nearly one third of the participants despite a lack of official publicity.[20]

The Statement of Concerns criticized the LCWE for not having been 'seriously concerned with the social, political and economic issues in many parts of the world that are a great stumbling block to the proclamation of the gospel'.[21] It spoke of the need to 'identify not only people-groups but also the social, economic and political institutions that determine their lives and the structures behind them that hinder evangelism'. The statement was particularly con-cerned about situations where Christians, perhaps for strategic reasons, explicitly or tacitly support unjust structures or regimes and in so doing 'are a great scandal to the evangelical witness in general and to the evangelization of the poor people of the earth in particular'. Once again the concern was not only with social involvement, but with true evangelism, with the proclamation and implementation of the gospel in all its dimensions. The statement also included some recommendations including a call for the LCWE to convene a World Congress on Social Responsibility.[22]

The issues raised by COWE and the Statement of Concerns persuaded many from the Third World of the need for Third World evangelicals to reflect together on these issues 'without strings attached, whether organizational, financial or ideological'.[23] Out of these convictions came the Fellowship of Evangelical Mission Theologians from the Two Thirds World. Late one night at the COWE itself a decision was made to meet again as a Third World consultation.[24] 'They did not reject', explains Chris Sugden, 'partnership with Western Christians, as others had done before them. But they wanted to build that partnership on a proper basis of equality and mutuality.'[25]

The fellowship met for the first time in 1982 in Bangkok[26] to discuss 'evangelical christologies from the contexts of poverty, powerlessness and religious pluralism'. A second consultation was held in Cuernavaca, Mexico, in 1984. At this the Africa Theological Fraternity was formed. In 1987 this formed, along with the already established Partnership in Mission Asia and the Latin American Theological Fraternity, the International Fellowship of Evangelical Mission Theologians (INFEMIT). INFEMIT runs the Oxford Centre for Mission Studies which hosts conferences, facilitates post-graduate work for Third World students and is the base for the journal *Transformation*. There are plans too to set up regional centres in the Third World.

A further feature of these Third World mission theologians is their 'ecumenical breadth of sympathies'.[27] In part this arises from a perceived connection between a lack of social action and the anti-ecumenical stance of many Western mission leaders. It is not surprising, too, if one contrasts COWE held in June 1980 with the CWME of the WCC's conference, 'Your Kingdom Come', held a month before in Melbourne, Australia. At this, in contrast to

COWE, 'the cries of the poor, the hungry and the oppressed pre-dominated'.[28] In fact the Melbourne conference was somewhat selective in its advocacy of the oppressed. It watered down a motion from David Bosch lamenting the failure of the WCC to speak out on behalf of the oppressed peoples of the Eastern bloc. Michael Nazir-Ali, the current General Secretary of the Church Missionary Society and a former bishop in Pakistan, moved an amendment mentioning the Soviet invasion of Afganistan. This created uproar, with the Russian delegates threatening to with-draw from the WCC.

In March 1987 an international conference of evangelicals and ecumenicals, the Stuttgart Consultation on Evangelism,[29] was held under the auspices of the CWME of the WCC in Stuttgart, Ger-many. Seven out of the thirteen conference contributors[30] had been contributors to the Bangkok '82 conference of Third World mission theologians.

In fact, although the antithesis between Bangkok '73 and Lausanne '74 appeared just as great in 1980 between Melbourne and Pattaya, the period after Lausanne has seen not only a renewed interest on social action among evangelicals but also within the WCC a renewed interest in evangelism. The late David Bosch believed that since the beginning of the seventies there has been 'a growing rediscovery of the "evangelistic mandate" in WCC circles'. Lausanne in particular, he thought, 'has had a far-reaching influence on ecumenical thinking and action'.[31] John Stott says that 'an increasing number of us belong to the overlap [between "evangelical" and "ecumenical" Christians]'.[32]

With many evangelicals continuing to be suspicious of ecumen-ism, evangelical relationships with non-evangelicals are likely to remain a thorny issue. On the one hand, the theology of ecumeni-cals makes it hard for many evangelicals to contemplate fellowship with them. On the other, some of the evangelical radicals find themselves having more in common on some issues with ecu-menicals than with some of their more conservative fellow evan-gelicals. At the same time relationships within evangelicalism between the First and Third World churches are also changing. The last twenty to thirty years have seen a dramatic numerical growth in the Third World church while the Western church has been in decline. Because of its historic position and financial resources the evangelical church in the West has for most of the twentieth century set the evangelical agenda. As we approach the next millennium, however, Third World evangelicals with their growing strength and maturity look set to make an increasing contribution to international evangelicalism.

Converted to wholeness

First, social activity is a consequence *of evangelism.
That is, evangelism is the means by which God brings
people to new birth, and their new life manifests itself in
the service of others . . . Social responsibility is more
than the consequence of evangelism; it is also one of its
aims . . . (Titus 2:14, Ephesians 2:10) . . .*

Secondly, social activity can be a bridge *to evangelism. It can break down prejudice, open closed doors
and gain a hearing for the Gospel . . . We are aware of the
dangers of . . . securing converts only because of the
physical benefits we offer. But we have to take this risk,
so long as we retain our own integrity and serve people
out of genuine love and not with an ulterior motive.
Then our actions will be 'not bribes but bridges – bridges
of love to the world' . . .*

*Thirdly, social activity not only follows evangelism as
its consequence and aim, and precedes it as its bridge,
but also accompanies it as its* partner *. . . In [Jesus']
ministry,* kerygma *(proclamation) and* diakonia *(service) went hand in hand . . . Both were expressions of his
compassion for people, and both should be of ours . . .
Thus, evangelism and social responsibility, while distinct from one another, are integrally related in our
proclamation of and obedience to the Gospel. The partnership is, in reality, a marriage. (From the* Grand
Rapids Report, *1982)*

What is the relationship between evangelism and social action?
What priority should be given to each? As the importance of social
action was accepted by evangelicals, so they were increasingly

faced with such questions. For many hard-pressed churches social involvement looked like yet another strain upon their resources. Many have simply made social action a supplement to evangelical thinking and practice. Others, however, have been concerned to rethink the whole evangelical understanding of mission.[1]

In chapter 7 we saw how Arthur Johnston expressed his criticisms of the Lausanne Congress and Covenant in his book *The Battle for World Evangelism* and how Stott replied with an open letter in *Christianity Today*. John Stott then wrote a private letter to Arthur Johnston suggesting that they meet face to face to discuss the issues further. His suggestion was that the LCWE organize a consultation to look specifically at the relationship between evangelism and social responsibility. Johnston agreed and they both served on the organizing committee. The committee invited people from across the evangelical spectrum so that the full range of differing views were represented. The LCWE and the WEF jointly sponsored it although not without a measure of hesitation on the part of the LCWE. Some felt that it would only be divisive and stir up controversy. It also imposed certain limits upon the gathering: the question of the primacy of evangelism, for example, would not be open to discussion.[2]

The Consultation on the Relationship between Evangelism and Social Responsibility (CRESR)[3] met in June 1982, at Grand Rapids in the United States. The conference was potentially a very difficult one. The papers and the responses to them circulated in advance had been sharply critical of one another. 'Before we met', says John Stott, 'I was almost in despair.' He confessed to arriving at it 'with a considerable degree of apprehension'.[4] At times things were pretty tense, especially during the first day or two. In one discussion group one of the participants accused another of advocating that other gospel which was anathema to Paul (a reference to Galatians 1). As the consultation progressed, however, the participants rejoiced at the unity and fellowship God brought to them. The chairmanship of Gottfried Osei-Mensah played a crucial role.[5] In their preface to the conference documents, Bong Rin Ro and Gottfried Osei-Mensah were able to call it 'a model of how Christians should approach a potentially divisive issue'.[6] John Stott comments: 'Adjusting one's position demands a high degree of integrity and humility. Yet this is exactly what I witnessed in brothers

and sisters at CRESR.'[7] In fact when most of the conference participants thought an agreed statement would be impossible Stott went
away and overnight produced the report pretty much as it is in its
final form.

The Grand Rapids Report, *Evangelism and Social Responsibility: An
Evangelical Commitment*, explains the relationship between evangelism and social responsibility in three ways:[8] (i) social activity is
the consequence of evangelism, indeed it is one of its aims; (ii)
social activity can be a bridge to evangelism, although it should not
be a bribe; (iii) social activity is the partner of evangelism, and the
report described this partnership in terms of a marriage.[9] Social
action, then, can precede, accompany and follow evangelism.

Given this relationship, evangelism, according to the report, has
priority only in two senses. First, it has a logical priority since
'Christian social responsibility presupposes socially responsible
Christians'.[10] This, however, need not imply a temporal priority.
Second, evangelism has a priority which stems from the unique
nature of the gospel for it 'relates to people's eternal destiny, and in
bringing them Good News of salvation Christians are doing what
nobody else can do'.[11] The report went on to conclude that in reality
the choice is largely conceptual. In practice the ministry of Jesus, in
which the two were inseparable, is to be our model.[12] And the
report includes a number of short case-studies in which evangelism
and social action have been integrated, each benefiting from the
other. 'It is the churches', the report concludes, 'which visibly
demonstrate the righteousness and peace of the kingdom which
will make the greatest evangelistic and social impact on the
world.'[13]

In fact at points the report seems to go further. It says that
'evangelism and social responsibility, while distinct from one
another, are integrally related in our proclamation of and obedience
to the gospel'.[14] It also speaks of evangelism and service as both
being forms of witness to Christ:[15] 'to give food to the hungry (social
responsibility) has evangelistic implications, since good works of
love, if done in the name of Christ, are a demonstration and commendation of the gospel'.[16] Or again, the report says: 'Evangelism,
even when it does not have a primary social intention, nevertheless
has a social dimension, while social responsibility, even when it does
not have a primarily evangelistic intention, nevertheless has an

evangelistic dimension.'[17] Nevertheless the report continues to maintain that evangelism and social responsibility are distinct activities and as such continues to talk in terms of priorities.[18]

As with the Lausanne Covenant, the Grand Rapids Report gave legitimacy to those whose advocacy of social action was regarded as suspect. Some who went to the consultation regarding evangelical social action with an almost McCarthyite suspicion had their fears dispelled. What the Grand Rapids Report achieved was a statement on evangelism and social responsibility acceptable to the full spectrum of evangelicals. Yet for many it was only 'a milestone', albeit a very significant one, on the way towards a full evangelical theology of mission. 'The Report', writes René Padilla, 'represents a further step in the process of renewal of evangelical missiology.'[19]

Many, especially from the Third World, are unhappy with any talk of priority or primacy. It creates, they would argue, a false distinction. All social action, if it is genuinely Christian, gives witness to the gospel, and all evangelism, if it is true to the biblical gospel, has social implications. The language of priority, it is maintained, is often used to legitimize evangelism conducted in isolation from the social context of the hearers. We do not need to use the language of priority, Steuernagel argues, to affirm that evangelism is essential.[20] The need, they would argue, is for a holistic or integrated[21] approach. In holistic mission our relief and development give witness to the kingdom of God and the gospel is proclaimed in both word and deed. In fact, in Third World contexts the demonstration and proclamation of the gospel are often not clearly distinguishable. This is why social action and holistic mission are not the issues in the Third World which they are still in parts of the West. In some ways the story in the Third World over this period has not been the rediscovery of social action so much as learning to work out the gospel in particular contexts rather than imposing inappropriate Western models upon them.

The Consultation on the Church in Response to Human Need at Wheaton in June 1983, a year after the Grand Rapids consultation, sought to move beyond the Grand Rapids position by emphasizing what it called 'transformation'. Transformation, it was argued, was an all-embracing term which could be used of both personal and social change, both spiritual and physical change, both change in the Third World and change in the First World.[22] Personal, social, spiritual and physical change all belonged together as the church sought to proclaim and live out the gospel. Vinay Samuel and Chris Sugden told the consultation: 'God redeems man as a unity in all his relationships . . . Therefore conceptually there can be no priority between the task of addressing personal and social change.'[23]

In March 1984 at the Leadership '84 conference at Brean Sands, England, the emphasis was upon wholeness. Leadership '84, sponsored by the Evangelical Alliance, was a national conference for British church leaders. The social concern group of the conference produced a findings paper entitled 'Converted to Wholeness'.[24] The gospel, it said, is about the love of God bringing salvation and wholeness to people. Ministry which expresses this wholeness will involve not only compassionate ministries but the challenging of social evils and injustice. The report pointed out that while many in Britain live comfortably there is 'the other Britain' of the unemployed, the lonely, those who lack meaning in life. And they recognize too that as a nation our actions cause damage to poorer countries. The report, it must be said, went largely unnoticed. Nevertheless it was a significant indication of where many British evangelicals were in their thinking. The need now, believes John Stott, 'is to demonstrate in practice that what we're saying about the marriage of evangelism and social action is true'.[25]

With a higher profile, Tear Fund has in recent years sought to place a holistic or integrated understanding of mission at the heart of its thinking. Its concern now is not so much to persuade people that its social action is a valid expression of Christian love. Instead it is concerned to ensure that people do not simply regard it as a kind of in-house relief agency for evangelicals but instead realize that Tear Fund's approach is different from that of other humanitarian agencies. Development is to be approached in a specifically Christian way so that the gospel is proclaimed in both word and deed. As such Tear Fund now sees itself less as a relief agency than as a mission organization with a particular focus on relief and development[26] – a recognition of the fact that evangelism and action against poverty and injustice belong together in the mission of the church. And it is a recognition too that their Third World partners are usually churches within whose work it is often hard to distinguish between evangelism, relief and social action. In its mission statement Tear Fund now describes its main purpose as 'to serve Jesus

Christ by enabling those who share evangelical Christian beliefs to bring good news to the poor, proclaiming and demonstrating the gospel for the whole person through support of Christian relief and development'.

In 1987 a group of about forty evangelicals, generally from a politically conservative and free-market economics background, met in Villars, Switzerland to discuss relief and development. In the Villars Statement on Relief and Development[27] they expressed concern over an emphasis on the redistribution of wealth without a recognition of the importance of initiative, freedom and opportunity. They were concerned too at attempts to synthesize Marxism and Christianity and also at placing a disproportionate emphasis on changing structures when equally oppressive structures often emerge from such changes. At the same time they recognized the need to apply the teaching of the Bible to all areas of life and called for distinctly biblical perspectives on development. Conversion and discipleship, they said, should be essential components of Christian development and development should also be concerned with spiritual transformation.

Increasingly the language of integration seems to be taking over from the language of priority. More and more Christian relief agencies and traditional mission societies are moving towards an holistic approach to mission and as they do so they move closely together. And Jun Vencer, the current International Director of WEF, describes one of its main objectives as being to provide 'a network of information and resources for holistic ministries'.[28] The traditional mission societies are also increasingly recognizing that the gospel needs to be communicated both in word and in deed and that conversion has social implications for both individuals and communities. The Church Missionary Society, for example, now has a threefold aim of encouraging evangelism, renewal and the pursuit of justice. It has appointed Andrew Kirk as its missioner-theologian and Michael Nazir-Ali as its first non-Western General Secretary, both of whom have been actively involved in INFEMIT. Indeed, even while social action has been viewed with suspicion at home, work in education, agriculture and medical care has often continued to be an important if neglected part of mission work. It is sometimes said that in terms of socio-political action mission societies were allowed to do on the mission field what would not have been allowed at home.

Christian relief and development agencies on the other hand are more consciously seeking to carry out development in a specifically Christian way, one that witnesses to the power and love of the kingdom of God. As they do so they face hard questions about the way they engage in development. Is it truly holistic, for example, for the development workers to have new Land Rovers to travel round in while the local pastor must walk? Or does this in fact reflect a Western materialistic view of the world? If God is left out of development projects and the focus is instead upon Western technology and know-how, what message is being communicated?

Increasingly there is a recognition that being holistic cuts both ways. It means caring for physical needs as well as spiritual needs, but it also means caring about spiritual needs and not conducting development in a purely secular way. If care is not taken, overseas aid can sometimes do more harm than good. Overseas money, for example, can distance a local church from its community or it can stunt the church's own involvement in the community.[29] It is all too easy for Western agencies to be paternalistic, to assume that the developing countries need Western solutions, to want to dictate the agenda, to be impatient with local people and to fail to understand their culture. The Third World is littered with ambitious Western projects which have come to nothing or done little for the poorest. It is a total misconception to see Western agencies, whether Christian or not, as heroes coming to the aid of the poor. In reality evangelicals of the First and Third Worlds are still learning about development and still working towards true partnership in Christ.

12

Responding to the media

One conclusion from all of this is that the decision to feature the story of the famine and the manner in which it was treated were largely directed by the internal logic of the media institutions. This is not to say that there was no commitment on the part of individual journalists to the story. Indeed the impact of the October report from Buerk was heightened by the personal commitment which he evidently felt. But overall it is clear that the priorities and internal logic of media organisations can differ sharply from those of Relief Agencies and fieldworkers who are seeking to highlight the genesis of problems in the Third World and to find solutions before the catastrophe strikes. (From a report on television coverage of the Ethiopian famine of 1984–5.)[1]

Right from the first few seconds it was clear that this was a tragedy which the world has somehow contrived not to notice until it had reached a scale which constituted an international scandal. (Bob Geldof, 1986)[2]

In December 1982 Save the Children Fund (SCF), which had been working in Ethiopia since 1936, opened a feeding station in Korem, a town of about seven thousand inhabitants on the main road between Addis Ababa and Asmara, Ethiopia's second city. It was set up in response to a growing number of destitute people arriving there from the surrounding countryside as a result of crop failure. Around three to four hundred children were cared for in the first month of operation.

In April 1983 the Tigrean People's Liberation Front attacked Korem, seizing the SCF workers. Although they were later released, the work at Korem had to close for five months. Within a week of reopening, over one thousand children had been registered for care. By December 1983 it was two thousand and by February 1984 it had risen to three thousand. Then the numbers began to spiral upwards and the cases of malnutrition worsened. In March 1984 there were one hundred deaths a month in Korem; six months later there were about one hundred a day. The situation at Korem was not unique – it was clear that starvation on a major scale threatened and was indeed already becoming a reality.

In March 1984 the Ethiopian Government asked for massive aid but it was largely ignored. The previous year Oxfam had started producing monthly bulletins on the situation and in Britain the quality newspapers included some coverage of the impending famine from the beginning of 1984, yet there was little response and little was being done. In frustration Oxfam made the unprecedented decision in August 1984 to ship grain to Ethiopia. This was normally the function of the large official governmental and UN organizations and in part the Oxfam decision was an attempt to shame them into action. So far the general response had been one of indifference. It so happened that the Food Emergencies Research Unit, supported by the British Government, was working in Ethiopia as the famine spread. Peter Culter, one of their number, returned in September 1984 with news of the famine and tried to get something done. 'We were just banging our heads against a brick wall. I'd tried all the donor agencies and the media. People were sick of my going on and on about it. Then along came BBC Television and everything changed overnight.'[3]

'Dawn, and as the sun breaks through the piercing chill of night on the plain outside Korem, it lights up a biblical famine, now, in the twentieth century. This place, say workers here, is the closest thing to hell on earth.'[4] So began Michael Buerk in the seven-minute film shot by Mohamed Amin. It was first shown on the BBC *Six O'Clock News* on 23 October and subsequently by 425 of the world's broadcasting organizations.[5] In most famines the majority of the victims suffer throughout the affected area. In Ethiopia people travelled to where they heard there was food and so many hundreds of starving people were to be found congregated together in one place. Their concentrated misery created an 'ideal' television image. Earlier in the year a camera crew from ITN had apologized to aid workers – without dramatic shots of starving people they had had to concentrate on the political situation.[6] Now where everything else had failed, these pictures of acute suffering on an unbelievable scale stunned the world into action. An hour-long documentary, *Seeds of Despair*, shown by ITV in July, had already helped to launch a famine appeal which had raised almost £10m. in three months. Now, just when it seemed the appeal would have to close, the public responded as never before and governments too were finally shamed into action.

The old rivalry between the BBC and ITV also played its part. Back in July Michael Buerk, then in Johannesburg, had done a piece on the famine at short notice so that the BBC could match ITV's coverage in *Seeds of Despair*. And the reports in October, which did so much to change the course of events, were shown two days before another ITV documentary, *Bitter Harvest*. *Bitter Harvest* had been made in response to Oxfam's decision in August of 1984 to ship grain to Ethiopia.

The television news coverage sparked a remarkable worldwide response with many acts of great personal generosity. British charities started receiving over £40,000 a day. The switchboards of Oxfam, for example, were jammed for three days after Michael Buerk's report and by January 1985 it had received over £10m. Governments were at last awakened into action. In November 1984 the British MP Russell Johnston said in the Commons: 'The entire aid world has been screaming from the rooftops for the last eighteen months that what has happened in Ethiopia was about to occur, yet it was only when we saw it in colour on the screens in our living rooms that the Government acted.'[7] And the press started to cover the famine; the *Sun* and the *Mirror* competed with each other with their own famine appeals[8] and television crews vied with each other for the best shots of starving people and the most heroic shots of their countrymen helping the victims. One UNICEF representative in Addis Ababa commented: 'We have been asking for help since 1983. It seems you have to have thousands of corpses before people will sit up and take notice.'[9] In August 1984 Oxfam could not get the European Commission to give them 10,000 tonnes of grain for their shipment. After the television reports and the public response they created, the EC leaders sanctioned the sending of 1,200,000 tonnes of grain.

That the famine remained in the public eye for as long as it did was largely the result of the work of one man: the Irish rock singer, Bob Geldof. Geldof organized a Christmas charity record, 'Do They Know It's Christmas?', which was sung by Band Aid – a specially formed collection of British rock and pop artistes. This was followed by a similar venture in the United States in March 1985 with the song 'We Are The World'. Then in July 1985 Geldof organized the massive Live Aid concert. Sixteen hours of music from simultaneous concerts in London and Philadelphia with further contributions from around the world were seen by an estimated television audience of 1,500 million people in over 150 countries. In all Band Aid and Live Aid raised over $90m. They also created a greater awareness in the long term of the issue of poverty. In May 1986 twenty million people from seventy-six countries took part in numerous sponsored events for Sports Aid. Nevertheless, Third World relief and development have failed to become a political issue in any appreciably new way, nor would it seem that they have become a significant vote winner.

The Ethiopian famine proved just how important the television could be in the response to poverty. Michael Buerk's news reports were dramatic not only in their impact upon the public's giving but, by affecting public opinion, upon governments and the UN as well. 'Governments were shamed into responding and so began a huge international airlift which, for a time, gave Addis Ababa's Bole airport something of the atmosphere of Heathrow. All the aircraft involved, including RAF Hercules, were flown in as the direct result of a television report.'[10] Band Aid was also a media event and Live Aid depended almost entirely for its success upon television coverage. Although the concerts played to 72,000 in London and 90,000 in Philadelphia, these numbers were marginal compared to the estimated television audience of 1,500 million.[11]

But what effect did the television coverage have upon the evangelical response to the famine? Any full answer would be impossible to document without detailed research. What can be assessed is the dramatic increase in giving to Tear Fund. November 1984, the month after Michael Buerk's report, was the first time that Tear Fund received over £2m. in one month. And Tear Fund staff are able to point to a very close correlation between news coverage and interest in the Tear Fund's work. If an item is carried in the news they know they can expect to receive enquiring phone calls the next day.

The role of the media in shaping perceptions of Third World poverty is a concern for many working to develop partnership between the First and Third World churches. They would acknowledge that it is right and proper that Christians, as they see human suffering, respond to it with compassion. As such the fact that evangelicals seem to respond to the presentation of suffering on the television is commendable. Nevertheless, those who wish to develop genuine partnership believe there is a danger that the response becomes too tied to television coverage. It sometimes appears that for us in the West an event is not real until it has been caught on the screen – famine is not happening until we have seen starving children on the news.

Yet television coverage of Third World poverty is at best patchy.[12] It covers very little of the on-going day to day grind of poverty. 'In 1984', comments Mike Webb, editor of *Tear Times*, 'journalists discovered 30 million starving people in Africa – ensuring that famine, at least for a time, was headline news. But they ignored the more disturbing fact that 100 million Africans . . . are malnourished as part of "normal" everyday life.'[13] Neither does the media present many positive images of life in the Third World. People in the Third World are typically portrayed as victims. And the media's coverage of crises is affected by many factors. It is assumed, no doubt rightly, that people are more interested in national and regional events than those which take place further away. There can also be a form of concealed racism at work when skin colour and cultural proximity decide newsworthiness. There are also limitations created by cost: satellite link-ups with remote underdeveloped areas are expensive and hard to organize. And not all countries welcome coverage of internal problems. During the early stages of the Ethiopian famine the Marxist regime was sensitive to Western media coverage which might portray the disaster as being of their making.

The combination of factors such of these can have a highly significant effect.[14] In 1991 China suffered its worst flooding this century, thousands were killed and millions were left homeless.[15] Yet while this received negligible attention in the media the San Francisco earthquake received intense coverage. Yet as Christians we are to value people equally wherever they are from. Some evangelicals are beginning to ask whether their compassion is too readily shaped and limited by the nature and extent of television coverage.

There is perhaps an even more important issue involved. Those engaged in social action in the Third World seek not charity but partnership. When involvement is conditioned entirely by images of Third World problems and deprivation it all too easily becomes a form of charitable imperialism rather than an expression of Christian fellowship. The 'First' World sees itself as giving to the 'Third' World because it cannot look after itself. 'News coverage of disasters', writes Mike Webb, 'can perpetuate the myth that Third World people are helpless victims unable to cope without the generous support of outside helpers.'[16] The underlying causes of poverty are forgotten or simplified and positive images of the Third World are ignored. During the Ethopian famine it was convenient for most of the Western media to portray it as a natural disaster. In reality the failure of crops was simply the trigger for a famine the causes of which were much more complex. 'It is easy', comments the journalist Cameron Duodu, 'to create immediate impact with pictures of the dead and dying. It is more difficult to interest people in the trading pattern that decrees that Ethiopia's earnings from coffee should fluctuate from year to year, while the price of wheat or maize or rice climbs steadily upwards.'[17]

Christians in the Third World are looking for justice and partnership. They have a lot to contribute from their experience to the Western church. The temptation for aid organizations is to play upon the image of the starving child in order to raise more money – to market poverty. But, as Mike Webb says,

> Such images, whether used in television news or in the advertisements of aid agencies, enforce the myth that people in developing countries are victims totally dependent on aid. They do not show the causes of poverty, such as the political and economic relationships between rich and poor countries, neither do they show Third World people or their governments doing anything to help themselves.[18]

C. B. Samuel, the director of EFICOR, identifies three levels of partnership: (1) purely funding, (2) funding and other resources (training, personnel, *etc.*), and (3) partnership beyond funding.[19] At levels one and two money and the project are the central factor. Without them there is no partnership. It is, as it were, a marriage of convenience. Most partnerships between evangelical relief and development agencies, Samuel believes, are like this. 'To move to the third level of partnership can be painful; here we relate not by our ability to give or receive but as partners in suffering and pain, in joy and celebration.' 'We need', Samuel believes, 'to constantly affirm the true basis of our relationship in non-monetary terms – not as those who have or have not the funds.' In too many cases so-called partnership involves application forms and investigation. Those with money exercise power over those without it: mammon determines partnership rather than kingdom relationships. 'We must somehow develop an environment', Samuel argues, 'where we share not "projects" but ourselves. Bureaucracies cannot love [one] another; people can. Our professionalism must be clothed with the compassion of God.'

When it comes to social concern the church has often responded to questions raised by the world: questions raised by nuclear proliferation, by environmental crisis, by poverty and injustice. Each succeeding generation of Christians faces the task of articulating the gospel with relevance to its culture and time. With social concern this need is particularly acute if the church is to speak prophetically and relevantly to the social issues of its day. It is inevitable, then, that the church's agenda will to some extent be set for it by the world. Sadly, however, the church sometimes misses the opportunity to speak and to act prophetically, and other voices, who do not speak from a Christian worldview, take up the task. This to a large extent has been the case with the issue of the environment.

The green movement grew during the seventies, though largely at a local level. The eighties, however, saw it gaining national and international prominence. In 1979 the first Green MP was elected in Switzerland followed by more in West Germany four years later. In Britain the movement reached a peak in 1989 when the Green Party took 15% of the vote at elections for the European Parliament.

Christians have been involved in the green movement from the early days. In 1981 a small number of people met informally for prayer at a Green Party conference. As a result Tim Cooper convened a meeting during the following year at which the Christian Ecology Group, now the Christian Ecology Link, was formed. Nevertheless Christian involvement has generally not been great and the church as a whole has been slow to respond. For some this has been because of the association of the New Age movement with environmentalism,[20] although arguably the green movement might not have been so affected by New Age thinking if more Christians had been involved. In fact Christianity is sometimes blamed for having contributed to the environmental crisis by emphasizing humanity's dominion over nature. More recently, however, evangelicals have become more involved in green issues, with a balancing emphasis upon the responsibility we have as stewards of God's creation and God's redemptive purposes to restore and reconcile creation.

An important catalyst in British evangelical interest in green issues has been Spring Harvest, the series of Easter holiday conferences, and the annual Christian arts festival Greenbelt. Important too have been Christian young people. Young people 'rarely have much investment in the economic status quo, but can be simply taught of their investment in the environmental future'.[21] In many cases it is through the enthusiasm of young people that the wider evangelical church has been challenged. In many churches green projects have begun with the youth group.

Part of the Spring Harvest youth programme (catering for twelve- to nineteen-year-olds) has been the taking of an offering. In planning for 1991 it was suggested that a new approach be tried. The offering would focus on a project with which young people could more readily identify. A Youth for Christ project in Burkina Faso was chosen which was following a threefold strategy: evangelism, education and environmental action against deforestation. A video was made introducing the 'Greener Burkina' project, Tear Fund produced a resource pack and a target figure of £25,000 was set – the previous highest collection had been £8,000. In the event £60,000 was raised.

Encouraged by this success it was decided to continue with the environmental theme for the following year, 1992, the year of the United Nations Earth Summit in Rio. The 'Whose Earth?' project as it was called was more ambitious still. It 'sought to be both a prophetic statement to the church to consider our role in the created world, and an evangelistic pronouncement to all people to live in

God's world in his way'.[22] It was a deliberate attempt 'to challenge the rest of the church' through young people.[23]

Tear Fund had been giving more thought to environmental issues and their relationship to poverty over some years. In 1990 they had run a promotion outlining the biblical case for the stewardship of creation under the title 'The Earth is the Lord's'. This had particularly focused on the campaign to save the rainforest in Honduras. A parallel theme had been pursued in their teenage magazine under the title 'Take Care'. As Tear Fund began to plan a development of this, it became clear that Tear Fund and Spring Harvest shared common aims and ideas and so it was agreed to work together on a joint project.

'Whose Earth?' unfolded in three stages. At Spring Harvest, teaching on the environment was given and signatures collected to support a message of Christian concern which was given to the Prime Minister before he left for the Rio summit. This was then followed by a summer of local activities. Finally the project climaxed with a celebration of God's creation and prophetic witness to the nation in Hyde Park in September.

One example of local action was the youth group at a 'Revelation' church in Chichester which organized a can collection and a river clean-up, raising funds in the process for 'Whose Earth?'. Wanting to continue the initiative, the church as a whole, through its 'Green Task Group', prepared teaching material for use in its six congregations and organized an evangelistic 'Creation Celebration' for the summer of 1993. They were also able to use the 'Whose Earth?' resource material in a local school. Yet despite being commended by a recent international forum of evangelicals on the environment,[24] the successes at local level were not entirely matched at a national level, with numbers at the Hyde Park rally disappointing.[25] It would seem that evangelical commitment to environmental issues still has a long way to go. A recent issue of *Tear Times* on the environment led to the criticism that this represented a diversion from the primary task of evangelism, this despite the fact that Tear Fund could point to examples where the integration of an environmental project with witness to the gospel had led to conversions among a people upon whom the gospel had previously made little impact. Nevertheless there are signs that the issue of the environment is coming up the evangelical agenda. The past few years have witnessed a significant number of books looking at the subject from a biblical perspective.[26] And a recent WEF forum[27] initiated an International Evangelical Environment Network (IEEN) for all evangelicals concerned for the environment.

13

Renewal, restoration and social concern

The power we've got is the power to love in a selfish world. It's the power to serve in a gaining, getting, grabbing world. It's the power to lay down our lives rather than preserve them. That's the power we've been given which is the complete antithesis of everything which exists in the world in which we live . . .

I would say that in certain sections (some would say quite a sizable section) of the new churches, house churches – networked and independent – and in a lot of denominational renewal, there is a lot of post-charismatic depression. And the reason is, they've never broken out of realizing that we are here to do more than sing a lot, talk a lot, have truth shot at us from pulpit or platform, pray a lot. And we need to see ourselves – individually and corporately – as bodies . . . just as Jesus is God's gift for the cosmos (John 3:16), we become his gift for the cosmos, to give ourselves away. (Gerald Coates)[1]

During the sixties and seventies the charismatic movement largely changed the face of British evangelicalism. With its emphases on a post-conversion experience of the Holy Spirit, upon the gifts of tongues and prophecy, upon freedom in worship and a spontaneous and loving fellowship, it brought with it not only renewed life for many but also a good deal of controversy. Nor has it been in any way monolithic. Not all charismatics would share the classic Pentecostal understanding of the baptism of the Spirit as a second experience subsequent to conversion. Some have emphasized the importance of miraculous signs and wonders; for others the primary change has been in the style of worship they adopt.

Remaining as they have within mainstream evangelicalism, it is true to say that most charismatics have shared the same influences upon their social concern as other evangelicals. For the most part, the charismatic movement has centred predominantly on church renewal, upon worship and spiritual gifts, and has not been concerned with social involvement as such. This is not to suggest that charismatics have not been socially concerned; rather, if they have been socially concerned, it is not for the most part because they were charismatics *per se*.

Yet this is not the whole picture. The charismatic movement has usually brought with it a greater emphasis on the church as a body and on the mutual love and fellowship of its members. Where this is the case, those involved have often provided a powerful example of caring interrelationships and have lived out at a social level the alternative lifestyle of God's kingdom. Against this background some I have talked to believe the charismatic movement could yet prove a fruitful ground in which simple lifestyle could really take root and be modelled. Furthermore among those who have been socially involved this love and care have spilt over into the world.

Although independent of any denomination, Ichthus Christian Fellowship[2] is very much part of mainstream evangelicalism in Britain and indeed has been very influential. From its beginnings in the seventies the Ichthus Fellowship has always laid a strong emphasis upon local social action. Its founder, Roger Forster, is a Vice-President of Tear Fund. Members have opened their homes to alcoholics, drug addicts, delinquents and disturbed people. They have initiated a life skills course and a job club for the long-term unemployed. In one area of 'concrete jungle' they have set up a laundrette and coffee shop to provide some focus for community life. They have projects providing pre-school care, pregnancy advice from a pro-life standpoint and a credit bank for those with low incomes. They work among the homeless and operate 'discipleship houses' where young people can be housed and cared for. They have bought a pub, the Brown Bear, to use in reaching unchurched young people. They also have a 'Jesus Action' programme in which practical help is offered to neighbourhoods: simple acts of kindness like meals for the elderly, reading to the blind, odd jobs and so on.

The Fellowship is organized in house groups and congregations, and each congregation will have differing emphases depending on the needs of its locality. This kind of work arises from the Fellowship's desire to share the love which they have found in Christ and which they share together. And as a result many have been brought to Christ. Roger Forster cities one occasion, for example, when an elderly lady's home was flooded and the Fellowship arranged for it to be dried out and cleaned up. Later her granddaughter knocked on his door asking: 'Are you the folk who helped my grandmother? I want to know more about this kind of Christianity.'[3]

The Ichthus Fellowship seeks to evangelize with 'words, works and wonders', incorporating in this way 'proclamation, presence and power evangelism'.[4] Roger Forster believes these three elements are all important if evangelism is to be truly holistic. 'It is unfortunate', he says, 'that in our present-day discussion these three have been separated and set against one another theologically, thus denying their essential unity. In the Ichthus Fellowship evangelism is understood as an holistic unity or tri-unity.'[5]

Brian Hathaway, too, speaks of the importance of holding together words, deeds and signs.[6] Hathaway is part of the pastoral team of Te Atatu Bible Chapel, a Brethren assembly in New Zealand which experienced renewal in the late seventies. The new life which the experience of renewal brought led to a greater involvement by the church in its local community. As the church grew the members were in a position to support a full-time pastor but chose instead to appoint a married couple as community workers. 'It is important to note', writes Hathaway, 'that for us, this concern for the needs of people in our community came out of renewal.'[7] Coming out of renewal, then, was a growing involvement in the community as the church recognized God's concern for the whole person and began to seek the kingdom of God through words, deeds and miraculous signs. During this time the church grew from 90 to 650 members.[8]

Another significant factor in the development of social concern which has particularly affected charismatic churches is Spring Harvest, the annual Easter evangelical conference. Spring Harvest began in the late seventies when Peter Meadows went to a conference in Prestatyn to get subscriptions for *Buzz* magazine. Despite having his money stolen he was struck by the potential of the facilities on offer. He shared his thoughts with Clive Calver as they drove together along the M4 motorway. Meadows wanted to run a holiday for Christian young people but Calver persuaded him that it should be a training week in evangelism. To launch it Clive Calver and Graham Kendrick made a tour of fifty towns in sixty-four nights and managed to persuade 2,700 people to come to Prestatyn one rainy morning in 1979. Spring Harvest was originally held under the auspices of *Buzz* magazine and British Youth for Christ, although it now has its own organizational structure, having grown to become the largest regular Christian gathering in Europe.

From the beginning there was a concern that Christians should share their faith, not in some evangelical ghetto, but in the real world. As Spring Harvest developed, this emphasis deepened and it began to encourage Christians seriously and theologically to evaluate the world in which they lived, to relate their faith to it and to question how they lived out their faith in that world. By the mid-eighties, despite tensions within the organization, a radical social dimension was part of the Spring Harvest agenda. The focus is still upon mission but there is a commitment now to understand the context in which that mission takes place and to integrating evangelism and social action.

Although Spring Harvest seeks to draw support from across the charismatic and non-charismatic spectrum, most supporters, particularly in the early years, were at least sympathetic to the renewal wing of the charismatic movement attracted as they are by the lively worship of its evening 'celebrations'. Spring Harvest's sheer size, and the fact that year after year many who attend do so for the first time, make it one of the most significant forces in contemporary British evangelicalism. Its aim from the beginning was to provide worship, teaching and training 'to help equip God's people to be salt and light in their home localities'. And it consciously works within the framework of the Lausanne Covenant. This commitment to working out the Lausanne Covenant is reflected in the range of seminars on offer, including seminars on key political and social issues. This means that many coming to enjoy the celebrations have found themselves challenged about their involvement in the world by well-known evangelical leaders.

It would be hard to measure the significance of this annual event but it has undoubtedly led many to see social involvement as a normal part of Christian discipleship and to enthuse them for it.

Not many evangelicals (including church leaders) in Britain are great readers, and even fewer will have read much on the theology of social action and holistic mission. Spring Harvest, however, has been one of the ways in which an understanding of the social dimension of discipleship has developed among evangelicals in Britain. Important in this is the fact that the majority coming to Spring Harvest come in church groups. As a result the worship at Spring Harvest has had an effect upon whole churches and in the same way, albeit to a lesser extent, so has the emphasis on social issues. Spring Harvest seeks to present a holistic view of the gospel, seen as impinging upon all areas of personal and social life. Nevertheless it is also probably true to say that the best-attended seminars are those on 'spiritual' and personal subjects (prayer, spiritual gifts, marriage, *etc.*).

The experience of the so-called new churches or house churches[9] is somewhat different. Unlike those who remained within their denominations, or at least within mainline evangelicalism, and saw the charismatic movement as a movement for the *renewal* of the church, members of the house churches believed they were part of a *restoration* of the church prior to the return of Christ. Not only were spiritual gifts being restored but so also was the ministry of 'apostles'. During the early seventies, when many such churches left or were forced out of their denominations, they began to take on their own identity.

Initially the Restorationists tended to be somewhat insular, marked as they were by a sense of living in the last times. On the one hand, they were ostracized by the majority of churches and, on the other, they had a sense of God working out his purposes primarily in them. The tremendous importance they placed upon their life together tended to make for a life apart from the world. As such, 'political and social action do not figure highly on a Restorationist list of moral imperatives'.[10] They did, however, participate in the Festival of Light and have remained involved in CARE.[11] And more recently social action has received a higher profile within the new churches. In 1987 Roger Forster contributed an article to *Restoration* magazine which emphasized the fact that the kingdom has implications for social action. Since then articles on politics and society have been regular features of *Restoration*. Tony Morton, who ministers in Southampton, has called for the church to be a prophetic influence in political affairs. Barney Coombes has encouraged Christians to be involved in politics.[12]

Initially, therefore, new church involvement in social action was low: they had other priorities. There was, too, a natural wariness of those non-charismatic evangelicals who had been hostile to them. Organizations such as Tear Fund which arose from the more conservative wing of evangelicalism, although never anti-charismatic, made little attempt to court the new churches. Many members of the new churches carried over from their old churches their support of Tear Fund, but as a whole their insecurity made them reluctant to form links outside their own network.[13] At the same time the new churches have formed their own links with the Third World. And their strong emphasis on relationships also made them wary of institutionalism and bureaucracy. Only more recently have positive attempts been made on both sides to build relationships and work together.

The network formed around Bryn Jones, New Covenant Ministries, has remained largely insular and isolated from the wider church. Members of the network have, however, sent large sums of money overseas to those Third World churches with whom they have contacts, most of it used in a holistic way. Even where they have no formal links they have sent money, to the victims of the Italian earthquake for example. John Houghton, the leader of Hailsham Christian Fellowship, has recently produced a workbook on social issues for the Harvestime 'School of the Word' series – the main teaching programme of the New Covenant churches.[14] This recognizes the changes taking place in evangelical attitudes to social issues and encourages social and political action for the sake of the poor and unborn. Bryn Jones himself recognizes and welcomes the new political and social consciousness emerging in the church.[15]

Those centred around Gerald Coates, John Noble and others on the Pioneer network are much more open both to involvement in the world and towards the rest of the church. Leaders from this wing of the charismatic movement are regular speakers now at Spring Harvest. Gerald Coates has long had contact with the Evangelical Alliance and in many ways the new churches and mainline evangelicalism appear to be moving closer together. Through this wider contact they have become far more involved in social issues to which they bring their own unique contribution, which Gerald Coates sees as being primarily in terms of an emphasis upon relationships and team ministry.[16] One of those involved in the 'Whose Earth?' project was Chris Seaton who is a leader in Revelation, a group of churches which are part of the Pioneer network. More and more the new churches are getting involved in local practical care along similar lines to the Ichthus Fellowship and Te Atatu Bible Chapel.

The Aids Care and Education Trust (ACET), now the largest provider of home care to Aids sufferers in the UK, began when Dr Patrick Dixon came to Gerald Coates and asked him what he and the network were going to do about Aids. Coates suggested that Dixon write a book, which he did. When *The Truth About AIDS* was published it was decided to put the Pioneer address at the back for those wanting further information. As responses came in, an administrator was taken on and Dixon began to speak more widely. The development of ACET was given a major boost when they were put in touch with a trust fund which wanted to give half a million pounds to an Aids initiative offering unconditional care to Aids patients and at the same time providing Aids education along traditional moral lines. ACET was officially launched in June 1988 and is now independent of the original trust and wholly evangelical. Also its work now extends overseas. Tear Fund, for example, supports ACET's care and education programme in Uganda.

In the early days of the charismatic movement the energy and time of those involved were largely directed inwards. The primary concern of those within mainline churches was the renewal of their churches, while those outside were giving themselves to the establishment of new churches. Fellowship among believers and good personal relationships were a priority. The spiritual life which the charismatic movement brought tended to be individualistic and even pietistic in form. The emphasis was upon worship, prayer and a personal experience of God.[17] Many felt that before venturing into the world there needed to be 'a period of strategic introversion'.[18] The energies of those with talent and those concerned to see change were directed towards the process of charismatic renewal.

Since the seventies, however, there has been a growing sense of mission and social action among charismatic churches and the new churches. Indeed, having experienced change, often quite traumatic change, within their churches, there has perhaps been a greater openness to the questioning of traditional ideas on other issues like social involvement. Thus, although initially introverted, many charismatic churches have begun to try and share their community life with the wider community. 'The primary orientation [of social action] in the charismatic movement', says Larry Christenson, 'is not toward a cause, but toward community.'[19] 'If you claim to be filled with the Spirit', says Gerald Coates, 'and you don't have a concern for the needs around you, I think your statement is open to be challenged.'[20]

In the early seventies Murray and Marj Robertson began work in Spreydon Baptist Church, a small church in a working class area of Christchurch, New Zealand.[21] Initially the focus of the work was upon evangelism and the systematic exposition of the Scriptures. These emphases have remained but, encouraged by a visit to New Zealand from David Watson, the church began to look for, and experience, charismatic renewal. It sought to encourage the development of gifts throughout the church and to build up relationships through small fellowship groups. During the early eighties they felt the Lord calling them towards ministry among the poor. They began to integrate the dimensions of evangelism, renewal and justice in their ministry.

Like others, they felt that their small groups had become too insular and so each group was encouraged to specialize in some form of kingdom service appropriate to their gifts and vision. As a result, the ministry of the church now includes day-care provision, a community help centre, work schemes for the unemployed, a medical and counselling centre, homes for people in need, the provision of low-cost retirement housing, prison work, and a 'kingdom bank' which offers interest-free loans on the condition that a budget advisor works with you on your finances. 'We were', says Murray Robertson, 'spending a great deal of time loving each other . . . but the Lord loved the whole world.'[22]

14

Words, works and wonders

We believe that an understanding of the Kingdom of God will bring men and women to a deeper appreciation of the Peace and Justice of God ... We believe that reconciliation is at the heart of the message of the Gospel of the Kingdom and is firstly between God and people, then between people themselves ... We believe the Kingdom of God encourages caring and sharing lifestyles as opposed to materialism and individualism ... We believe that God instituted marriage and family life as the fundamental unit for expressing the life of the Kingdom in society. The rule of Christ brings dignity and sanctity to both the single and married states ... We believe that the proclamation of the Gospel of the Kingdom requires identification with the needs of those to whom we speak ... We believe that God's intention is the transformation of the whole of society and that this is inseparable from the transformation of the inner, spiritual life of people, families and communities ... We believe that God is the rightful owner of this universe, but He has given the management of this planet to men and women ... We believe that the Kingdom of God affects the whole of a person's being ... We believe that commitment to the cause of the Kingdom of God will mean costly discipleship in terms of time, possessions, money and abilities ... (From the Kingdom Manifesto, New Zealand)

A number of those involved in social action, especially those who have a background in the charismatic movement, have come to see the struggle for social justice as a conflict with demonic forces. They have seen demonic confrontation as an important part of their ministry. This involves casting out demons and, less frequently, confronting demonic structures of injustice. They would see any work of the kingdom of God, whether in evangelism or social action, as involving a confrontation with the kingdom of Satan. The Grand Rapids Report, the report of the LCWE and WEF Consultation on the Relationship between Evangelism and Social Responsibility, 1982, says: 'We believe that signs should validate our evangelism . . . The third sign of the kingdom is exorcism . . . Demon possession is a real and terrible condition. Deliverance is possible only in a power encounter in which the name of Jesus is invoked and prevails.'[1]

The language of 'power encounters' is most commonly associated with John Wimber, the founder of the Vineyard Fellowship in California and international charismatic speaker. Wimber maintains that 'signs and wonders', particularly healing and supernatural insights, are important demonstrations of God's presence and power which play a crucial role in effective evangelism and church growth. His thinking is very influential, both in the United States, where he comes from, and, initially through his contact with the late David Watson, in Britain. He himself would claim to be applying lessons learnt among the growing Third World church to a Western context.

John Wimber and Peter Wagner of Fuller Seminary speak of 'a third wave' of the Spirit in this century. The first wave, they maintain, was the rise of Pentecostalism at the beginning of the century and the second was the charismatic movement of the sixties and seventies. The term has now hardened into a name. The distinguishing elements of those who are part of the Third Wave is an emphasis upon the importance of power encounters, signs and wonders as demonstrations of the power of the kingdom, and, increasingly, the importance of spiritual warfare.[2] The Third Wave movement is also closely aligned to the church growth principles associated with the Fuller Seminary School of Mission.

Others have gone further and spoken of territorial spirits.[3] Evil spirits, it is claimed, control geographical areas. Peter Wagner believes that 'Satan delegates high-ranking members of the hierarchy of evil spirits to control nations, regions, cities, tribes, people groups, neighbourhoods and other significant social networks of human beings throughout the world.' 'The implications', he adds later, 'such insights could have for social justice, peace and national righteousness, including evangelization, are obvious.'[4] These ideas have been popularized through the novels of Frank Peretti: *This Present Darkness* and *Piercing the Darkness*. For some involved, the so-called 'marches for Jesus' are seen as a way of 'reclaiming' streets and neighbourhoods for Christ. According to Gerald Coates, one of the prime movers behind the national marches for Jesus, they are intended to make a statement at two levels: to Satan, that we are claiming something from him, and to the nation, that evangelicals are here and that we have an agenda.[5]

If the tensions between charismatics and non-charismatics are growing less, the issues of signs and wonders and particularly spiritual warfare threaten to create new divisions just as great as the old. John Stott, for example, while acknowledging that miracles can and do occur today, disputes Wimber's claims that church growth in Acts took place as a result of signs and wonders and that miracles are supposed to be normal and everyday in the life of the church. The miracles of the New Testament, Stott believes, had a unique eschatological character and marked a fresh epoch of revelation. He doubts, too, whether most of today's signs and wonders are really of the same magnitude as those which took place in the ministry of Jesus and the apostles.[6] The Manila Manifesto, the report of Lausanne II which was drafted by John Stott, says:

> Although the miracles of Jesus were special, being signs of his Messiahship and anticipations of his perfect kingdom when all nature will be subject to him, we have no liberty to place limits on the power of the living Creator today. We reject both the skepticism which denies miracles and the presumption which demands them, both the timidity which shrinks from the fullness of the Spirit and the triumphalism which shrinks from the weakness in which Christ's power is made perfect.[7]

Paul Hiebert, Professor of Mission and Anthropology at Trinity Evangelical Divinity School, Deerfield, Illinois, believes that lying behind the current preoccupation with spiritual warfare is the Indo-European myth of a dualistic battle between good and evil, a struggle for power and control, which continues to pervade Western culture.[8] In contrast, in the Bible, he argues, God is always in control and his victory is secure. Israel was never defeated as a result of a battle in cosmic realms, but rather because God allowed them to be defeated as an act of judgment upon their sin. The issue in spiritual warfare is not to do with power but with holiness and peace. Satan and his forces seek to deceive and tempt people so that they turn from God and in consequence social peace and justice break down. Spiritual warfare is then not a battle for power but a battle for truth and reconciliation. It is not fought in some super-spiritual sense but with the truth of the gospel and with reconciling love. Humans are not the passive victims of some battle fought on a cosmic plane. Instead it is a battle for human hearts which individually and corporately have turned from the truth and from God. If the central issue is power, then, claims Hiebert, it is hard to make sense of the victory of the cross. In fact, however, the cross reveals the truth of Satan's deception and reconciles us with God. People can be demon-possessed but they should be pitied rather than feared. The people we should really fear are those who, possessed by self and deceived by Satan, reject the truth and build oppressive social structures. The ideas of a battle for power and of competition, argues Hiebert, are deeply ingrained in our society. In Christian warfare, however, we are concerned with the truth of God's word and the reconciling love of God in Christ – with holiness and peace.

Speaking from a Third World context Vinay Samuel says: 'I accept the miraculous but I want the miraculous to serve the poor and to bring a change in holiness of life.'[9] He suspects that the preoccupation with spiritual warfare arises from despair: the temptation is 'always for the miraculous to rescue us from the hard graft of struggle'.[10]

Both charismatics and advocates of radical discipleship have made the kingdom of God central to their thought though in differing ways. Charismatics have emphasized the *power* of the kingdom in believers' lives and the importance of the signs and wonders of the kingdom. The radical discipleship group have emphasized the *justice* of the kingdom, the rule of the King in all areas of life and the community of the kingdom as an alternative society.

Since the late eighties, however, discussions have been taking place between charismatics and advocates of radical discipleship. In

January 1988 an international consultation was convened by Michael Harper and Ron Sider in Pasadena, USA, so that charismatics and evangelical social activitists might enter into dialogue.[11] The consultation claimed that both justice for the poor and power and wonders were part of the biblical teaching on the kingdom of God. Also an emphasis on spiritual gifts and ministry was seen as a way of empowering and valuing the poor and disadvantaged who are usually not given the opportunity to make a contribution in the world nor, all too often, in the church.

A second follow-up conference was organized two years later, this time in Britain, by Graham Cray, Roger Forster and Chris Sugden.[12] Many differences remained but the conference also found a good deal of common ground. Brian Hathaway, who was one of the participants, commended to the conference the Kingdom Manifesto which had arisen from similar discussions in New Zealand. The conference not only welcomed the Manifesto but decided to set up a convening committee to facilitate an international process of study with the Manifesto as its focus. This process is due to culminate in a consultation in January 1994 which it is hoped will bring together the three streams of world evangelization, Christian social concern and renewal in the Holy Spirit.[13]

The Kingdom Manifesto[14] calls upon Christians 'to live in the triumph of the kingdom of God over the powers of darkness'. Yet it also recognizes that 'the battle still continues today' and that in the tension between the 'already' and 'not yet' of the kingdom, suffering for the sake of righteousness is a sign of the kingdom's presence. It is a commitment not only to declare the kingdom but to seek the justice, peace and reconciliation of the kingdom in every situation. It is avowedly holistic in approach: 'we are concerned', it says, 'about physical, cultural, social, spiritual, intellectual and emotional wholeness in human lives'. It recognizes the costly discipleship involved in commitment to the kingdom. In particular it contains a commitment 'to living a sacrificial and simpler lifestyle' and the sharing of 'our material abundance to assist the economic and spiritual transformation of the lives of people in poverty in other parts of the world'.

It is probably fair to say that at present the charismatic issue is less divisive than it was. Many organizations and indeed many churches have learnt to live with the tensions that can arise. There is commonly now a respect for one another and a commitment to work together despite the continued differences. Movement has taken place on both sides.

Many involved in the early charismatic movement had a deep commitment to a sacrifical service of their local communities, and especially those who were the poor and under-privileged. One thinks for example of the Church of the Redeemer in down-town Houston, Texas. When Michael Harper wrote about their experience,[15] he did so in order to provide a model for other churches. House groups, now a common feature of evangelical church life, though providing teaching and pastoral care in a new way, have perhaps failed to fulfil the desire from which they originally arose, to 'live together' in the world.[16] John Wimber himself describes as an early achievement of the charismatic movement 'new social experiences, especially in small groups, innovative discipleship, and Christian community'.[17] He points here to the influence of others outside the movement like, for example, Ron Sider. Yet as it has developed, the charismatic movement in England, in contrast to the Pentecostal movement, has remained a largely middle-class and suburban movement.[18] 'If we forget that Luke speaks of being anointed with the Spirit in order to preach good news *to the poor*,' writes Stuart Murray in *Prophecy Today*, 'the anointing of the Spirit is domesticated and frittered away on the excitements demanded by comfortable suburban churches.'[19]

We have already noted how the charismatic movement, if it remains true to its radical origins with its emphasis on community and love, could become a fertile ground for a renewed commitment to simple lifestyle. It could, however, tend towards triumphalism. It seems unlikely that anything like the prosperity gospel in America, in which people are promised 'health and wealth' in return for faith, will ever catch on in Britain in a big way. Yet, as Brian Hathaway pointed out at the International Charismatic Conference at Brighton in 1991, one seldom hears of charismatics being delivered from the demonic power of materialism.[20] And less extreme forms of triumphalism are already here. There seems to be a growing preoccupation with the dramatic, the sensational, a belief that big is best. This is despite a recent report showing that most people are converted through personal contact and over a period of time.[21] Much teaching on healing raises unrealistic hopes. Today, in contrast to cross-centred discipleship, many expect now the victory and glory, the freedom from sickness and weakness, which belong to the future consummated kingdom.

In October 1979 Viv Grigg moved into the Tatalon squatter area of Manila in order to live among the slum dwellers of the Philippines. This first step of identification led to a realization of the need for indigenous discipleship and in turn the need for holistic discipleship. With the support of local workers and a home church whose members were committed to simpler lifestyles, Grigg saw a church planted in the slums and employment opportunities provided. He has also gone on to found Servants to Asia's Urban Poor. Grigg's background was in the renewal movement of New Zealand and his ministry included the confrontation of demonic powers, healing and prophetic visions. Yet what most characterizes Viv Grigg is his commitment to the poor and to sharing their lives, and his commitment to cross-centred discipleship: '[Christ's] cross stands in the midst of suffering. It is a cross of compassionate involvement. If we would take up that cross, we too must enter in to the need, we too must dwell in the midst of suffering and poverty.'[22] 'Many Christians want power; few want holiness. Many want the resurrected life; few want the cross.'[23]

15

Salt and light

*In the sermon on the mount, Jesus said to his disciples
'You are the salt of the earth and you are the light of the
world.'*

In response to this we . . .
*1. affirm the authority of the Bible and the necessity and
relevance of obedient Christian discipleship to every
sphere of life, both personal and social.*
*2. welcome the Decade of Evangelism and commit our-
selves to communicating the Christian gospel in such a
way that individuals allow Jesus Christ to transform
every area of their lives.*
*3. believe that Christian mission requires us to engage
with our culture through reflection, persuasion and
action. Exercising faith in God, Christians must act
together to bring justice, hope and love into our communities in a way which honours Biblical truth.*
*4. commit ourselves to serve humbly those in all cul-
tures, and recognize that we must listen and learn from
each other in order that we might act together to make
our world more pleasing to God.*
*5. pledge ourselves to do this in dependence on God,
through involvement in prayer, worship and action, in
order that we might reflect his glory to a hurting world
and do all in his strength.*
*(The Salt and Light Charter, 1988. Sponsored by the
Evangelical Alliance, the Evangelical Missionary
Alliance and Tear Fund.)*

An important development in the past few years in Britain has been
the 'Salt and Light' process. It began with a conversation between

George Hoffman of Tear Fund and Clive Calver of the Evangelical Alliance. Hoffman was concerned that there were still many negative attitudes to social action among evangelicals in Britain. He suggested a large conference be organized for church leaders at which they could be enthused for social action. In particular, Stephen Rand, the Communications Director of Tear Fund and one of those closely involved in the planning of Salt and Light, felt that contact with Christians from the Third World would have a significant impact upon Christians in Britain.

Calver, with his particular concern for evangelical unity, proposed that a pre-conference consultation be held in order to ensure that all the strands of evangelicalism would support the main conference. This was convened by the Evangelical Alliance, the Evangelical Missionary Alliance and Tear Fund and held in Swanwick in the autumn of 1988.[1] The participants came from across the evangelical spectrum in terms of theology and approach to social action. They included theologians, social activists and Christians involved in secular politics as well as resource people from the Third World. A remarkable degree of consensus was achieved. A central report was agreed upon and about twenty special interest groups produced their own specialist papers. The plan then was, using this foundation, to hold a large conference of around five to six thousand people with the aim of making a significant impact upon attitudes to social action in Britain. This second stage never happened.

What did happen was this. After the conference a number of people who were politically conservative were strongly critical of it. In letters to the EA they accused the process of being a left-wing conspiracy and of going much too far. Instead of uniting evangelicals, the Salt and Light process threatened to create further divisions. It was therefore decided to postpone the main conference and to hold another consultation. This took place in September 1990 in Oxford and this time a deliberate bias to the 'right' was made in terms of participants in order to get them on board. Also, in response to criticisms of the original conference, it sought a wider historical and theological perspective. One or two were still unhappy, but on the whole this consultation dispelled the idea of a conspiracy and was reasonably successful in providing a common basis on which to proceed.

In the meantime, however, something else had changed. There was a growing awareness that evangelicals no longer wanted to come to large conferences. It was felt that another big conference would be difficult to justify in such a climate and that it might only cater for those already convinced of the need for social action. It was decided instead to be involved in other large gatherings, particularly Spring Harvest, and to lobby conference organizers to put Salt and Light on the agenda. A Salt and Light Charter was drawn up and conferences accepting this would be able to badge relevant parts of their event with a Salt and Light logo. Because the large consciousness-raising conference never took place some have felt that the Salt and Light process was scuppered by its politically conservative critics. In reality they delayed it and during that delay there was a realization that a change of tack was needed.

The Salt and Light steering group is also concerned to strengthen the evangelical identity of social activists and is running a project looking at how they use the Bible in dealing with problems they face in their work. It also encourages evangelists to adopt a more integrated approach – something which is increasingly the case. Lowell Sheppard and Eddie Lyle of Youth for Christ, George Verwer of Operation Mobilisation, Jim Smith of the Church Pastoral Aid Society[2] and Steve Chalke of the Oasis Trust are some of the better-known examples. Steve Chalke was particularly affected by a visit he made in 1988 to Bombay. The terrible reality of poverty there convinced him of the importance of social action. As a result he set up Christmas Cracker, a project in which young people run community radio stations and cafés over the Christmas period and which has so far raised over £1.5 million.[3] But in many ways the most significant evangelist to endorse social action was the widely respected late David Watson. Watson played an important role in giving credibility to the charismatic movement but equally his endorsement of social action and simple lifestyle was highly significant in the acceptance of social action among British evangelicals. His preface to *Rich Christians in an Age of Hunger* was crucial in the impact the book made in Britain.

In addition to its participation in the Salt and Light process, the Evangelical Alliance co-ordinates various coalitions which bring together member organizations for mutual fellowship and co-operation. There are, for example, coalitions on sexuality, drugs, education, and community care. The EA seeks to help these organizations retain their evangelical distinctives, to raise awareness among the churches and to challenge them to be more informed, more active and more supportive and to represent these organizations to government and media. There is a feeling in the EA that evangelicals are increasingly in the forefront of social action and that it is high time that politicians knew it.

The EA has also recently appointed a new consultant, Mike Wilson, to advise churches on how to launch community care initiatives. Following the report of Sir Roy Griffiths, *Community Care – An Agenda for Action* (1988), there has been a major shift in government policy towards what is called community care. The aim is to switch provision from institutions to care in the community (through half-way houses, day-care centres, support workers and so on) and to enable people to live in their own homes wherever possible. The problem is that all too often there is no longer a real community in which care can take place. Many people, particularly the mentally ill, find little support in the community and end up on the streets.[4] Funding too is being revised, with encouragement given to voluntary organizations, including churches. Provision will be on the basis of an assessment of the particular needs of an individual and will be found from the best source available, whatever that is, while still being paid for by the local authority. It is hoped that this will lead to a more flexible cost-effective service, a service more adaptable to an individual's particular needs. Some, however, fear that financial constraints will affect the level of care offered.

David Potter, the founder of A Cause for Concern, a Christian charity providing care for those with a mental handicap, believes this represents a great opportunity for church involvement. Churches, he says, can 'be involved in meeting needs and demonstrating practical concern for those around them'. And he gives some examples:

> Running a luncheon club is one option. A support service for a family with a disturbed adult is another; shopping for people who are housebound; a hospital transport service for someone requiring regular treatment or physiotherapy; a sitting service to allow carers

to go out for an evening – the possibilities are as diverse
as are the needs! They will vary from one district to
another, and the ability to respond will vary according
to the skills found among church members.[5]

There are a number of spin-offs, Potter believes, to this sort of
service to the community. It can involve people within the church
whose gifts are often passed over by the normal range of church
activities. It can also maximize the use of church buildings in a way
that makes them part of community life. And churches can meet
people they would not otherwise expect to reach with the gospel.[6]

A Cause for Concern is itself an example of Christian social care
which is funded in part through local authorities. In 1963 David and
Madeleine Potter's new child, Rachel, was found to have Down's
syndrome. As they cared for Rachel the Potters began to face the
question common to most parents of mentally handicapped
children: who will care for our child when we are no longer able to
do so? They found that not only did provision not meet demand but
that there was very little specifically Christian provision. In
November 1973 David wrote an article in the *Evangelical Times*
entitled 'A Cause for Concern'. The article suggested that local
churches, with the assistance of a national charity, might open
homes for the long-term care of the mentally handicapped. The
article led to the foundation of A Cause for Concern, or Christian
Concern for the Mentally Handicapped as it is officially called, and
in 1975 the first home, Plas Lluest, was opened in conjunction with
Alfred Place Baptist Church in Aberystwyth. There are now six
homes, with plans for more, and a concern too to help churches
integrate mentally handicapped people and meet their spiritual
needs.

In Britain the provision of the welfare state has been an important
factor in shaping evangelical social involvement. Evangelicals in
Britain often rediscovered the importance of social involvement as
they learnt how Third World evangelicals were responding to
poverty and injustice. Yet, unless they lived in the inner cities,
British evangelicals have not usually been particularly aware of
social needs. At least since the middle of this century we in Britain
have assumed that the state will meet the needs of the poor.
Things, however, are changing. For whatever reasons gaps are

emerging in the provision of state care. The reasons why evangelicals lost their commitment to social action are complex and in fact I have found little agreement as to which are the most significant factors. Certainly the decline in evangelical social involvement pre-dates the universal provision of the welfare state, and its rediscovery pre-dates the present situation where the gap in provision is growing. Nevertheless the welfare state has in the past somewhat pre-empted evangelical social care. At the same time some evangelicals ceased providing care because of the hostility and difficulties they faced from secular social services. Instead, evangelical social action has largely been directed in the last few decades either overseas or in the UK towards campaigning over moral issues.

Elsewhere in the world government provision, or the lack of it, has also shaped evangelical social action. In Kenya, for example, the state took over the church-run schools and hospitals at the time of independence. It was not until Christian aid agencies provided external finance that the Kenyan church was able to move again into social care. In Germany at the time of unification there was some debate as to whether the church tax, paid by most citizens to the churches, should be abolished or extended to the East. In the end it was decided to extend it to the East not least because the state welfare system depended upon the church provision funded through the church tax. The church's social care had become locked into the state welfare system and, some would say, often secularized in the process. In the Soviet Union prior to the fall of Communism the deregulation of churches was prompted as much by the need for voluntary social provision as by anything else. As the economy failed so state provision could not cope with the needs. This means that most of the indigenous missionary movement in the Soviet Union had a social orientation, albeit with a strong evangelistic thrust.

Even countries with a high level of state provision are finding it increasingly difficult to support this economically. However unwelcome this may be in itself, it does create the opportunity for evangelicals throughout the world to provide care and to provide it in a distinctly Christian , i.e. gospel-orientated, way. Even where state care is good it usually only meets material needs. The challenge is to work out the wholeness of the gospel by bringing holistic care to people. At the same time, believes Tom Houston, the church needs 'to start articulating different reasons and different analyses of the problems of society and providing different solutions that actually say that our secularist views are the problem'.[7] Increasingly it seems that Christians on the left and the right are moving away from any simplistic polarization to a common acknowledgment that social needs cannot be dealt with either through the market or through the secular/humanistic provision of the state.

In Britain the state has for a long time failed to come to grips with the problems of the inner cities. If most evangelicals have not had much contact with social need, those working and living in the inner cities have been all too aware of it and this has uniquely shaped their outlook. In 1974 David Sheppard, then the warden of the Mayflower Centre[8] in London's East End and now the Bishop of Liverpool, wrote about the particular problems of the urban world in *Built as a City*.[9] David Sheppard had been a leading figure in 'Bash' camps, the camps run by Eric Nash (nicknamed 'Bash') for public school pupils, and in the Christian Union in Cambridge. His experience of East End life, however, convinced him that traditional evangelistic models were insufficient. While many evangelicals were withdrawing from the inner cities for the comfort of the suburbs, others, such as the Frontier Youth Trust, were pioneering new models of urban mission.

At the same time the black churches were growing. Many of the early immigrants found that at best the British churches, including evangelical churches, made little attempt to integrate them into church life and at worst treated them with open racism.[10] This led to the formation of a separate Afro-Caribbean Evangelical Alliance. Although traditionally a-political, the black churches have, often unnoticed by the wider evangelical constituency, increasingly been involved in local community projects, particularly in the provision of employment.

In 1972 two working parties, one belonging to the Shaftesbury Project and one from Latimer House, the Anglican study centre in Oxford, merged to form the Evangelical Race Relations Group. In 1985 this became Evangelical Christians for Racial Justice which seeks to combat racism in the church and in society. Originally its make-up was predominantly white Anglican males; now the majority of the executive committee are young, black, lay people from the broad spectrum of evangelicalism.

161

Since the first National Evangelical Anglican Congress at Keele in 1967 an influential network has been growing of those evangelicals concerned to work through new approaches to urban mission. Out of Keele came *Christians in Industrial Areas* – a correspondence-based journal for those involved in urban mission. A number of groups met together in Nottingham in 1974 and the second NEAC in 1977, also in Nottingham, again brought inner-city evangelicals together. After NEAC '77 a weekend consultation was organized by the Mayflower Centre and Frontier Youth Trust in April 1978 and this led to the London Consultative Group on Urban Mission. Finally all these groups came together in Birmingham in March 1980 when a decision was made to form the Evangelical Coalition for Urban Mission (ECUM).[11]

The day of ECUM's public launch in April 1981 could not have been more significant, for it was the day on which riots erupted in the inner cities of Britain. The Brixton and Toxteth riots led to the Archbishops' Commission on Urban Priority Areas and its report *Faith in the City* (1985), and also the Anglican Church Urban Fund. Although viewed with suspicion by many evangelicals, inner-city evangelicals had a significant input to the commission. ECUM, for example, functioned as a resource body, and Michael Eastman, secretary of ECUM and Frontier Youth Trust, served as an advisor.

Evangelicals involved in urban mission have in some measure succeeded in making the wider evangelical constituency aware of the problems of life and ministry in the inner cities.[12] Yet, while things may be changing, their radical thinking and approach have had relatively little impact upon evangelicals as a whole – an indication perhaps of the continuing gap between the inner–city and suburban churches.

Continuing tensions

We affirm that we must demonstrate God's love visibly by caring for those who are deprived of justice, dignity, food and shelter. We affirm that the proclamation of God's kingdom of justice and peace demands the denunciation of all injustice and oppression, both personal and structural; we will not shrink from this prophetic witness . . .

The spiritually poor, who, whatever their economic circumstances, humble themselves before God, receive by faith the free gift of salvation. There is no other way for anybody to enter the kingdom of God. The materially poor and powerless find in addition a new dignity as God's children, and the love of brothers and sisters who will struggle with them for their liberation from everything which demeans or oppresses them. (From the Manila Manifesto, 1989)

Lausanne II met in July 1989 in Manila, Philippines.[1] It was a direct descendant of the Berlin Congress in 1966, but the contrast between them is striking. International evangelicalism had undergone a remarkable change. Lausanne II set itself to call 'the whole church to take the whole gospel to the whole world' – a statement encapsulating the new concern for a holistic gospel with the old concerns of mobilizing the church and evangelizing the world, particularly the unreached. The plenary sessions on 'the whole gospel' included a session on 'Good News for the Poor' led by Tom Houston, the International Director of the Lausanne Committee. And there was a plenary session on 'Social Concern and Evangelization' led by Vinay Samuel, which included a paper on reaching the oppressed by Caesar Molebatsi from South Africa.[2]

The specialist tracks included 'The Poor', 'Gospel and Culture' and 'Simple Lifestyle'.

The Congress statement – the Manila Manifesto – once again claimed that evangelism was primary but added: 'Jesus not only proclaimed the kingdom of God, he also demonstrated its arrival by works of mercy and power. We are called today to a similar integration of words and deeds.' And if evangelism was primary because 'our chief concern is with the gospel', the Manifesto also recognized 'that the biblical gospel has inescapable social implications'. Also the section on co-operation in evangelism went significantly beyond Lausanne towards true partnership between the First and Third World churches.

The choice of subject and speakers, let alone their content, and the language of the Manifesto – all would have been unthinkable to Berlin and even at Lausanne. 'It would be true to say', believes Tom Houston, 'that Manila settled once and for all that social concern was part of the gospel – and it has not pleased everybody.'[3] Tensions remained: the most apparent difficulties were over the charismatic issue, particularly the emphasis on signs and wonders,[4] and on relations with ecumenicals and Catholics. There was, however, also concern again about the imposition of a North American-led strategy. Some felt that the style of the Congress and the influence of Fuller Seminary with its emphases on church-growth theory, signs and wonders and multi-media communication were a far cry from 'the little flock' throughout the world, upon which world evangelization truly depended.[5] Once again John Stott was urged by some of the younger Third World leaders, particularly from Latin America, to go further in the Manifesto. And again there were calls for a large international congress on social action.

On the other hand, there were those, principally from North America, who in their concern for a strategy for world evangelization were beginning to lose patience with the Lausanne movement. Thomas Wang, then the International Director of the LCWE and the Director of the Manila Congress, had noticed over a period of time that a number of strategies had been planned working up to the year 2000. He proposed to the Lausanne Committee that the plans for Manila be altered and that AD 2000 plans should be its focus. Although the committee disagreed they allowed the emerging AD 2000 group to have a specialist track and a plenary session at the Manila Congress. Disappointed with this response, those supporting an AD 2000 focus decided to organize what was called 'The Great Commission Congress', held in Singapore a few months before Manila in January 1989.[6] Problems arose, however, at Singapore, particularly over Catholic involvement, and in the end it was decided that there should be no continuation. At the close of the congress Ralph Winter said there could be no harm in keeping in touch and a small number agreed to set up an office in Pasadena to this end. Then in March 1989 the 'AD 2000 and Beyond' movement was launched in California amidst controversy, with many of the Singapore participants claiming that the organization had no authority to do this.

The aim of the AD 2000 movement is 'a church for every people and the gospel for every person by AD 2000'. The intention is to encourage existing churches, movements and structures to work together towards this aim. The movement seeks primarily to 'motivate', to give a vision of evangelization by the year 2000, and to 'network', to co-ordinate the various projects. One of its foci is upon what it calls the '10/40 window'. This is the area between 10 and 40 degrees north which encompasses northern Africa, the Middle East and most of Asia. It is claimed that 97% of unevangelized people, a large proportion of whom are among the poorest people in the world, live within this area. Yet only 6% of the world's missionary force currently works in this area. Running up to the year 2000 is it planned to hold three Global Consultations on World Evangelization.[7] Although the Lausanne movement helped to launch the AD 2000 initiative and it has also adopted the Lausanne Covenant as 'its philosophical statement,'[8] the two movements are independent. Lausanne, according to AD 2000, represents the broad flow while AD 2000 is a hot current within it.

Within the Theological Track of AD 2000 attention is being given to the meaning and implications of evangelization among the poor, with a consultation on this subject in 1993 jointly sponsored by the Theological Track of AD 2000, the Theological Commission of WEF and INFEMIT. The Least Evangelized Cities Track is also going to focus on the urban poor. One of its aims is the development of a 'slum-dwellers' theology' based on the experience of work among the urban poor. Included in this is a consultation at which it is intended that Latin American and Asian workers among the urban poor will tell of their experience 'in the silent presence of Western funding/mission leaders'.[9]

Whatever these specialist tracks may achieve, the commitment of the strategy as a whole to social action remains uncertain – the proof of the pudding will be in the eating. Despite claims simply to encourage, network and inspire local and national initiatives, the 'AD 2000 and Beyond' organization has a decidedly North American flavour and a North American approach to evangelization is to the fore. Also, apart from the title, it seems that little attention is being given to the work of mission after the initial aim of planting churches among every people group has been achieved, in other words to the discipling of those churches.

Few would now deny the need for Christians to be socially active. There remains within some sections of evangelicalism, however, a continuing suspicion that social action may become an alternative to evangelism. One rarely finds openly negative attitudes to social action; more commonly we are warned not to allow social action to deflect us from the one key task, namely that of proclaiming the gospel.

John Woodhouse, for example, points out that the history of evangelicals over the past twenty to thirty years can be read in two different ways: either that evangelicals have regained something of their heritage, namely social action, or that they are beginning to lose something from their heritage, namely gospel preaching. Woodhouse is one of the evangelical Anglicans from the Diocese of Sydney, Australia, who have an increasing influence in Britain through their contact with the Proclamation Trust and their fine expository ministry. He himself believes in the importance of social action but he also fears that behind much of the renewed emphasis on social action is 'a crisis of confidence in the gospel'.[10] He says:

> It is right that we should be called again and again to care, but when that obligation is given the theological undergirding that belongs properly to the task of evangelism, when the evangelistic task is no longer seen as unique in importance, when evangelistic responsibility

is taken for granted, and our neglect of social action causes deeper remorse than our neglect of evangelism, then the cart has got before the horse, and is trying to grow legs.[11]

Or again: 'Our discussions of social responsibility would be far more clear if we spoke simply in terms of our duty to love our neighbour, rather than in terms of the "mission of the church".'[12]

Clearly one of the on-going tensions has to do with the relationship between social action and the gospel, indeed with the heart of the gospel itself. When Tear Fund recently ran some publicity material under the slogan 'Good News to the Poor' they received a good measure of criticism, particularly from some in Reformed circles.[13] The *Evangelical Times* carried a number of letters critical of Tear Fund and an article by John Legg in which he suggested that Tear Fund was moving towards a social gospel: he himself denied that the gospel had a social dimension.[14] He was particularly critical of a biblical study on poverty written by Roger Forster and produced by Tear Fund. References to poverty in the New Testament, Legg argued, should be understood in terms of spiritual rather than material poverty.

This highlights an important area of debate. Poverty is used in the Gospels to speak of spiritual bankruptcy (Matthew 5:3) and, given its background in Isaiah 61, Legg was probably right to say of the particular example which he gives, namely Luke 4:18, that it refers to 'the faithful people of God, who are poor because of their faithfulness'. In fact, however, this is the point that Forster makes, namely that the gospel brings about a radical change of attitudes to material possessions. The poor person in the Gospels, said Legg, 'is the man who realizes his own spiritual bankruptcy and hopes for salvation from the mercy of God alone'. Others, however, would want to add that those who hope for salvation in this way must also forsake all and take up their cross daily.

Although poverty is used to express spiritual bankruptcy in the Gospels, an increasing number of evangelicals maintain that not all references to poverty in the Gospels are references to spiritual poverty. We can no more spiritualize the poor in Matthew 11:5, they would argue, than we can demythologize the blind, the lame and so on. Furthermore the background to 'the year of the

Lord's favour' in Luke 4:19 is the socio-economic liberation of the year of Jubilee (Leviticus 25). There is a growing consensus that throughout the Old Testament and the New there is a close correlation between material and spiritual poverty. The materially poor are more inclined to turn to God – because they have no-one else to turn to – than the rich whose possessions are often an obstacle to faith. George Hoffman recalled being told by a pastor in Haiti: 'In your country you have God and things. Here we just have God.'[15] And, conversely, the spiritually poor disciples who leave all for Christ often suffer persecution and take up the cause of those experiencing injustice in the world.

In 1980 at the Pattaya Congress the mini-consultation on the Urban Poor concluded in its report: 'Throughout the Bible the majority of references to the poor are to the mercilessly oppressed, the powerless, the destitute and the downtrodden.'[16] In preparation for this consultation Jim Punton, the training officer of Frontier Youth Trust and chair of the consultation, prepared a detailed study of the Bible's use of the word 'poor'. The study is included as an appendix to the report. Colin Marchant, the editor of the report's final draft, describes how Punton tossed this study into his lap on the plane on the way over. Reading it, he says, 'I felt as if I was walking through an avalanche . . . swept away by the cumulative force of hundreds of references.'[17]

Among those who continue to spiritualize the references to poverty in the New Testament there is a very proper concern. They fear that talk of a social dimension to the gospel will lead to a social gospel or some form of liberation theology. The fundamental problem with the social gospel and with liberation theology, however, is not that their advocates speak of the social dimension of the gospel. Rather it is that they transfer that which belongs to the return of Christ to some point in our presently unfolding history, so that the kingdom of God is seen as attainable through either progress or revolution. Evangelical critics of this thinking argue that by saying that this fulness of salvation is a reality now we in fact do a great disservice to the poor. Like all people, they have pointed out, the poor need to be called to repentance and faith. They are not only sinned against but they themselves are sinners before God. The good news to the poor and oppressed is that they can be part of an everlasting kingdom of justice and peace. The good news to the hungry is that they will be filled. The good news to the dying is that they can have eternal life. Evangelicals themselves, often reacting against 'hell-fire' preaching, are sometimes guilty of emphasizing only the present benefits of salvation. At the extreme, conversion is portrayed as a means to self-fulfilment instead of the beginning of self-denial. The fundamental problem facing humanity, namely that it faces the eschatological wrath of God, has all too often been neglected or been the cause of embarrassment.

What evangelical advocates of social action have wanted to say in addition is that the kingdom of God is not only coming but has come. In and through the church the rule of God which brings salvation is already being experienced through the word and the Spirit, and with it the demands of discipleship which that rule brings, both individually and corporately.

The challenge facing evangelicals is to live out the life of the kingdom-present while proclaiming the kingdom-future. Increasingly evangelicals involved in social action and development are realizing that holistic mission is not only seeking to alleviate poverty and suffering as well as preaching the good news of eternal life, but also, as it were, preaching the good news of eternal life while seeking to alleviate poverty and suffering. To separate social action and evangelism is to make our relief and development indistinguishable from that of secular, humanistic organizations.

Recently a number of voices have been raised complaining of what they perceive to be a switch in resources from traditional mission societies to the new social ministries. There is indeed a worrying decline of missionary interest in many evangelical churches and a fall-off in giving to missionary societies. Not all, however, are convinced that this is due to the rise in social concern, not least because most missionary societies have traditionally also been involved in social ministries. For many the greater concern is that over 90% of traditional mission work is directed towards areas where there are already established churches. This leaves much to be done among the 40% of the world's population who are as yet unreached by the gospel.

The contrast between, for example, Tear Fund and the traditional missionary societies is not really a matter of evangelism *versus* social action since it is always Tear Fund's aim to integrate the two. Instead Tear Fund, along with other societies such as the International Fellowship of Evangelical Students and the United Bible Societies, seeks to enable national evangelical churches by supporting specialist ministries. The resources of most traditional societies are usually bound up in sending personnel overseas. This often leaves little money for the support of projects or personnel of local indigenous churches. Tear Fund typically provides resources to enable those already involved in evangelism to run social projects alongside their evangelism. The recognition of this new approach to supporting mission in areas where churches already exist led some within the Evangelical Alliance to propose a body parallel to Tear Fund called EPOCH, Evangelical Partnership with the Overseas Church. This would have provided money for overseas churches to fund evangelism and training. Plans were well under way when it was decided that it would make more sense to set it up as a department within Tear Fund and so in 1979 the Overseas Evangelism and Christian Education department was born. This was never intended to replace traditional missionary societies; rather it was hoped that it would allow them to focus on pioneer work among the unevangelized or, where appropriate, to provide training and teaching for indigenous churches.

17

Getting into politics

*It is a most damning indictment of the evangelical voice
in politics that it has focused on abortion and neglected
employment; denounced trade unions and remained
silent on managerial indolence and corruption; condemned strikes but not closures; said much on scroun-
gers but nothing on overseas aid; called for capital
punishment but not for prison reform; deplored bingo but
not grouse shooting. It is little wonder that the vast
majority of manual workers, unemployed youngsters
and ethnic immigrants have decided that evangelicalism
has nothing for them. We have not balanced judg-
mentalism with compassion. (Donald Macleod, 1992)[1]*

The tensions described in the previous chapter are not the only
ones which operate within the evangelical community. Some evangelicals, while warmly accepting the need for social care, are wary
of support for social reform or political involvement. Others believe
that political involvement is not only important but also the logical
consequence of social care. We have already seen how for many
evangelicals evangelism among the poor has led to social care and
that this in turn has issued in a concern for justice and social
reform. The logic of the Good Samaritan, it is argued, is that love
will eventually ask what can be done to prevent wayside attacks on
the Jericho road.[2] 'What has been happening in the last few years',
says Martyn Eden, 'is that we have begun to recognize that social
activism itself is necessary but it's not sufficient. In some ways it's
like running an ambulance service if you can actually try to prevent
the accident in the first place.'[3]

In Peru , for example, 1980 and 1985 saw organized attempts by
evangelicals to participate in the national elections by nominating

and supporting evangelical candidates.[4] Then in 1990 several evangelicals were elected to Parliament and evangelical support of President Fujimori was decisive in his election. Carlos García, a prominent evangelical, became vice-president. When Fujimori reneged on his election promises evangelicals began publicly to criticize him. And the National Evangelical Council of Peru (CONEP) has been in the forefront of opposition to human rights abuses, despite the personal danger to those involved.

In the wake of the 1972 earthquake which hit Nicaragua, a group of evangelicals formed the Evangelical Committee for Development Aid (CEPAD).[5] In defiance of Somoza, Nicaragua's dictator, they refused to participate in the country's 'common fund', established for the distribution of international aid but corruptly run. In the nineteenth century, conservative governments were pro-Catholic and therefore tended to persecute evangelicals. Liberalism brought evangelicals freedom of religion and so evangelicals were traditionally pro-Liberal. Since the Somoza dynasty was Liberal, technically at least, evangelicals were generally supportive. Somoza was also fiercely anti-Communist, a fact which resonated with many evangelicals who were strongly influenced by the anti-Communist stance of North American missionaries.

The 1972 earthquake was crucial in changing evangelical perceptions of the Somoza regime and in speeding up the awakening evangelical social conscience. As the corruption and cruelty of the regime increased so opposition among evangelicals grew. A minority began to be involved in the Sandinista Front despite the avowed Communism of the Sandinistas. Prior to the Sandinista revolution in 1979 evangelicals were divided; some were accused of being Communists, others of complicity in the crimes of the Somoza regime.

After the revolution evangelicals generally became less suspicious of the Sandinistas and in the 1984 elections two evangelicals were proposed by the Sandinistas and elected to the National Assembly, José Maria Ruíz, a widely respected Baptist pastor, and Sixto Ulloa, the Director of Public Relations of CEPAD. In 1982 CEPAD sent an open letter to American Christians urging them to intercede against the 'intolerant and arrogant attitudes of the Government of the US against Nicaragua'.[6] CEPAD had meanwhile become such a significant part of the life of the evangelical churches in Nicaragua that it was now a *de facto* national body for the evangelical churches. As such it changed its name to the Council of Evangelical Churches Pro-Denominational Alliance (thus retaining its initials). CEPAD was able to play an increasing role in the political life of the nation – even after the Sandinistas were defeated in the 1990 presidential elections – while remaining non-partisan. Perhaps unsurprisingly, CEPAD's co-operation with the (Communist) Sandinista Front led to opposition from both within and without the country. Pat Robertson, for example, the American tele-evangelist and one-time presidential candidate, tried unsuc-cessfully to organize a parallel organization to CEPAD. Yet CEPAD itself has succeeded in gaining freedoms for the evan-gelical churches and in 'contributing the values of the gospel to the construction of a civil society'.[7]

Throughout the world evangelicals have been increasingly involved in politics at local and national levels. In the Philippines, for example, evangelicals were involved in the overthrow of the Marcos regime. In South Africa some evangelicals have been involved in opposition to apartheid and in political reconciliation. In 1986 a multi-racial group of 'Concerned Evangelicals' issued a statement entitled 'Evangelical Witness in South Africa', condemn-ing apartheid and repenting of past evangelical attitudes.[8] They have received support from ESSA, the Evangelical Support for South Africa, which was formed after a request from Concerned Evangelicals in 1987 as a coalition of the EA. In Kenya Bishop David Gitari, Vice-Chairman of INFEMIT, received considerable criticism and even had his life threatened for involving himself in the affairs of coffee farmers, defending the right of the church to speak out on political issues and for attacking vote-rigging.[9] 'We celebrate', said Latin American evangelicals at CLADE III in the Quito Document, 'the growing awareness of the evangelical church with respect to its social and political responsibility and its increasing participation in society.'

In Britain, too, individual evangelicals involved in politics are no longer treated with the suspicion they once received; instead they are actively encouraged. And from the time of the Festival of Light onwards, evangelicals as a whole have again started to be more politically active. An increasing number of books are being written which deal not with the question of 'whether' but with the 'how' of political involvement.[10] The organization Life, which campaigns against abortion and provides pregnancy counselling and care, has an evangelical section, Evangelicals for Life. Through CARE evangelicals have lobbied government over a wide range of issues. And in 1992, Christian Election Forum brought together a number of organizations, the majority of them evangelical, to ensure that Christian concerns were on the General Election agenda.[11] But perhaps the most notable success evangelicals in Britain have had in the political realm was on the issue of Sunday trading.

On 14 April 1986 the Conservative government was defeated at the crucial second reading of a Bill – a unique event during the whole of Margaret Thatcher's premiership. The Shops Bill was intended to deregulate Sunday trading and a government victory had been widely assumed. Opposition to the Bill had largely been co-ordinated by the Keep Sunday Special Campaign – a coalition of churches, the shopworkers' union (USDAW) and many retailers, initiated and organized by the Jubilee Centre. The campaign combined effective parliamentary lobbying with the widescale mobilization of public opinion. Although it had a strongly Christian base, the arguments of the campaign were not couched in theological language: the emphasis was upon deregulation's likely impact on family life, workers' conditions and small shopkeepers' livelihoods. Research also played an important part in the campaign, as did the fact that the campaign was able to put forward a positive alternative proposal. Nearly 750,000 signatures were raised by the Jubilee Centre plus more by USDAW, giving a total of over one million. At one point David Waddington – then a Home Office minister – conceded in a Commons written reply that he had received 16,292 letters against the Bill and only 27 in favour. Against all predictions the government was defeated.

The campaign was a remarkable achievement. It was also an indication of the willingness of evangelical Christians to be politically active. Looking back on the campaign, Michael Schluter of the Jubilee Centre says: 'I didn't realise at the time just how many churches, of all denominations and in every part of the country, had taken the Sunday issue to heart . . . It had been a long time since a Government Bill had touched the churches so extensively and so profoundly.'[12] The support and sacrifice of hundreds of thousands of Christians, he says, was crucial in the campaign's success.

From the widespread support of the Keep Sunday Special Campaign it is clear that the real issue is not whether evangelicals should be involved in politics, but the nature of that involvement, or rather the issues over which evangelicals are prepared to take a stand. Issues which broadly concern social or personal morality seem to command widespread support while issues to do with social justice receive far less attention, perhaps because they are more complex, perhaps because they are perceived to be more 'political'. In a recent book, *Completely Pro-Life*, Ron Sider asks why evangelicals cannot be as radical about poverty as they have been about abortion.[13] Certainly a growing minority of evangelicals, particularly those coming from an inner-city perspective, have been involved with issues across the spectrum. Nevertheless the majority have in the past focused on a fairly narrow political agenda.

The growth of Tear Fund and similar organizations shows that many evangelicals are concerned about poverty. Fewer, however, seem willing to explore the underlying causes of Third World poverty and to question the part the West plays in perpetuating it. Tear Fund itself has been criticized for being too politically cautious although it has had to take care not to fall foul of the Charities Commission. It had its knuckles rapped by the Commission, for example, when it promoted *Rich Christians in an Age of Hunger*. Nevertheless Tear Fund is increasingly committed to educating its supporters about the causes of poverty and suggesting to them lines of action which they might take. 'Tear Fund', says Stephen Rand, 'has tried to steer a steady course between being faithful to its own calling as an evangelical inter-church relief and development charity, and encouraging our supporters to recognize the responsibilities and opportunities of making their voice heard on behalf of the poor.'[14] Recently Tear Fund encouraged its supporters to join a worldwide campaign on behalf of the Miskito Rainforest Indians. The campaign succeeded in persuading the Honduran government to scrap a timber agreement with a US multinational company. Charles Elliot believes that Christians must move beyond what he calls 'comfortable compassion' to ask some uncomfortable questions about the causes of poverty and the relationships between the powerful and the powerless in the world.[15]

The most extreme expression of an exclusively moral agenda is the American fundamentalist New Christian Right and Moral Majority.[16] The entrance of the fundamentalists (such as Jerry Falwell) and Pentecostals (such as Pat Robertson) into American politics came after years of strict separatism. The issues of abortion, pornography and school prayers were the causes of this new involvement. The Roe v. Wade Supreme Court case in 1973 which paved the way for the legalization of abortion was particularly significant[17] – the decline in moral standards was forcing them, the fundamentalists argued, into political involvement. During the seventies Jerry Falwell, the tele-evangelist and minister of Liberty Baptist Church, Lynchburg, Virginia, began to hold 'I Love America' rallies and launched a 'Clean Up America' campaign. In 1979 Falwell, Pat Robertson and other Christian leaders met together with a group of professional right-wing political organizers and formed Moral Majority.[18] During the 1980 election campaign Moral Majority sought to highlight moral issues, particularly abortion, and to endorse candidates with a moral stance of which they approved. They also managed to register thousands of voters – fundamentalists who had never voted before. The New Christian Right targeted 27 congressional liberals – 23 were defeated – and late in the day Falwell gave his endorsement to Ronald Reagan. Then, 'in 1984', Charles Colson writes, 'the fault line broke wide open with a presidential campaign that resembled a holy crusade more than an election'.[19] It was perhaps their finest hour.

Once involved in politics the agenda of the New Right widened: they were fiercely patriotic, vehemently opposed to liberalism, Communism and humanism, against spending on welfare provision and in favour of high military spending. In the run-up to the 1988 election Pat Robertson ran for the Republican nomination for president. Two years before, in January 1986, Falwell had created the Liberty Foundation in order to be able to 'address economic, social and political issues'. Falwell has also involved himself in foreign issues: he has been consistently pro-Israel, expressed support for the Marcos regime before its fall, supported the white regime in South Africa – calling Desmond Tutu a 'phoney' – and argued for aid to the Contra rebels in Nicaragua.[20] Yet despite raising and spending millions of dollars Pat Robertson's attempt to run for president failed. And in the late eighties money for Moral Majority started to dry up, with the result that in 1989 the organization was wound up. The Liberty Foundation continues but Falwell has announced an end to his political career. The election of the Democrat Bill Clinton in 1992 was a further bitter blow to the Christian Right in America although in fact the evangelical vote as a whole was split approximately fifty-fifty.

Very little of this kind of campaigning exists in Britain. Politically and theologically we have very different roots. In an article in *The Independent* newspaper just before the 1992 American presidential elections, Clive Calver was at pains to disassociate British evangelicals and the Evangelical Alliance from the political involvement of American evangelicals and fundamentalists. Claims, said Calver, that 'To vote for Clinton is a sin against God' and that 'We are here to re-elect the living God' are not only totally alien to British evangelicals but also serve as a setback in their efforts to shake off the American fundamentalist caricature. 'Middle-class church-goers in Britain', says Calver, 'are now less prone than Americans to identify biblical values with their own well-being and thereby fail to challenge social injustices.'[21]

Yet not all would agree with this judgment. Donald Macleod, Professor of Systematic Thelogy at the Free Church College in Edinburgh, writing in *Evangelicals Now* after the 1992 British General Election, could not hide his frustration with the political attitudes of English evangelicals.'[22] Evangelicals, he believes, are guilty of 'simplistic judgments' and of 'voting with their pockets'. He says:

> The problem can be summed up in one sentence: we are interested in morality, not injustice. The symptoms are clear enough. We major on such issues as abortion, euthanasia, capital punishment and homosexuality and forget that, even if we had satisfactory legislation on all of these, we would still be an unjust society in which equal opportunity is a myth, the gap between rich and poor is constantly widening and even the most talented young people face a bleak future. . . . We simply cannot afford to spend most of our lives in political hibernation.

Things, however, are changing. 'There has been', acknowledges Martyn Eden, 'a political tension [between social justice and social morality] because social morality tended to be a right-wing agenda and social justice a left-wing agenda, but increasingly . . . there are a growing number of evangelicals who are coming to see that the old left–right divide is simply an anachronism that we have got to dump.'[23] The old either/or of social morality and social justice is being replaced by a both/and. This is reflected, for example, in the range of issues which Christian Election Forum 1992 sought to highlight, namely overseas development, Sunday trading, abortion, homelessness, poverty, pornography, and debt.

For the most part evangelicals in Britain have said that involvement by the church in politics need not, or should not, mean involvement in party politics or telling people how they should vote. They have sought to reach agreement on the values which should shape society and the priorities and goals which government should seek to achieve. But how these objectives can best be realized – the political rather than theological question – they have left as a matter of individual conscience. The church as a whole, it is commonly argued, should seek to speak with a united voice on the needs and priorities facing a nation even though individual Christians disagree over how those goals can best be achieved. This approach has enabled many churches to steer clear of party politics while at the same time encouraging their members to be involved in the different parties. And the EA would never, according to Clive Calver, dream of endorsing a particular candidate, as its US equivalent, the National Association of Evangelicals, has done.[24] Much good cross-party work is done in Britain although it usually gets eclipsed by the dramatic confrontations and debates of adversarial politics. At this cross-party level evangelicals are increasingly making a contribution which, though it often goes unnoticed by the media, is not without influence.

Although most evangelicals in Britain are not overtly partisan,[25] a minority, people such as Richard Russell and Alan Storkey, have suggested that evangelicals should consider forming a Christian political party. Among this group the Dutch Reformed tradition is a strong influence. In emphasizing the lordship of Christ over all of life, this tradition has a long history of involvement in the political life of the nation, most notably when Abraham Kuyper (1837–1920) was Prime Minister of Holland (1900–05).[26]

Even among those who do not favour a Christian party there are differing views concerning the relationship between the church and the state. Some feel that Britain is, or at least was, a Christian country and that this specifically Christian character should be preserved. The Movement for Christian Democracy receives evangelical support in its aim of developing consensus politics upon a Christian basis. Anglicans in particular often see the church as part of the fabric of society, a view related to their position as an established church.

The Mennonite witness has been a small but highly significant alternative influence upon evangelical political involvement in both Britain and North America.[27] The Anabaptist tradition to which the Mennonites belong makes a sharp distinction between church and state and so would not want to call any society Christian. Yet they are far from being non-political; instead they seek to be a radical and subversive element within society for its good. They are, for example, generally pacifists and have often participated in anti-nuclear campaigns. While they are criticized for being politically unrealistic, their adherence to the radical values of the kingdom of God is a healthy corrective to the complacency of the wider church.

Different understandings of the implications of Romans 13 and 1 Peter 2 play their part in determining views of the relationship between church and state but such views often have more to do with one's perspective. For the rural and suburban middle class it is easy to see the state as fundamentally good, maintaining law and order and providing opportunities for its citizens. To those who live in poverty or minister in the inner cities, however, the state can appear in contrast to be working against people and denying opportunities. Perhaps the most common model for relating to society at large, however, is that of salt and light (from Matthew 5:13–16). The church, by its presence in society and as it speaks out, seeks to act like salt, preserving that which is good in society. At the same time it gives witness to the transforming light of the gospel.

Underlying a number of these tensions is a deeper theological issue. In emphasizing the importance of social action some have chosen to work primarily from the pattern of creation, and others from their understanding of the kingdom of God. Should social action centre on 'creation ethics' or on 'kingdom ethics'?[28]

Those who advocate kingdom ethics believe that our approach to social action should primarily be governed by the ideals of the kingdom and by God's kingdom activity in the world. The question we must ask, according to Vinay Samuel and Chris Sugden, is: 'How can I take part in, express, and produce the quality of personal and corporate life that will be fulfilled in God's kingdom?'[29] This approach to social action, its advocates argue, means that our social action is related to the gospel of the kingdom. They fear that the creation-centred approach leaves Christ and the gospel out of our social action. Another common feature of kingdom ethics is the denial of any separation of God's activity in the church and outside the church: God's activity has but one goal, the kingdom of God. This means that the good done by non-Christians must also be seen in terms of God's kingdom activity.[30] Also controversial is the insistence by some advocates of kingdom ethics that sin can be structural or institutional. Sin, they argue, can permeate social structures such as apartheid. Others prefer to speak of structural evil. Sin does affect all areas of life but sin is committed by people, not by structures. They fear that if we speak of structural sin then we must also speak of the possibility of structural redemption.

Advocates of creation ethics believe that the use of salvation and kingdom language for the activity of God outside the church is unbiblical and inappropriate. They begin from the perspective of creation. Certain ethical principles can be derived from the order of created reality. Although the fall leads to additional ordinances (for example, the state), the basic structure of creation principles holds true. These principles were expressed in the law of Moses and, in particular, in the Ten Commandments. Advocates of this approach to social action believe that a creation-based ethic provides a better way forward because its principles are applicable to all people – all are part of creation but not all are part of the kingdom. As such they can be commended to all people as being for the common good. Advocates of creation ethics would prefer to see the activity of God outside the church in terms of common grace.

Others, however, view these approaches as an unnecessary polarization. Both Chris Wright and the Jubilee Centre, for example, have sought to steer a middle line between creation and kingdom ethics in their respective approaches to the use of the Old Testament.[31] But perhaps the one of the most important contributors to this debate, in Britain at least, has been Oliver O'Donovan, Regius Professor of Moral and Pastoral Theology at Oxford University. At the National Evangelical Conference on Social Ethics at High Leigh in 1978 O'Donovan argued that in fact we need not be forced to choose between a creation approach and a kingdom approach.[32] Creation and kingdom are not independent of one another, for creation is fulfilled and restored in the kingdom.

It is the problems which we face, O'Donovan pointed out, which determine to a large extent whether our primary concern is to preserve the *status quo* – keeping it in line with the creation order – or to transform it – making it more in line with the kingdom. In his important book, *Resurrection and Moral Order*, O'Donovan writes: 'In the resurrection of Christ creation is restored and the kingdom of God dawns. Ethics which starts from this point may sometimes emphasize the newness, sometimes the primitiveness of the order that is there affirmed. But it will not be tempted to overthrow or deny either in the name of the other.'[33] In a recent article Ron Sider reflected on the divide in the United States between the conservatism of Jerry Falwell and Pat Robertson and the radicalism of the Sojourners and Evangelicals for Social Action – a divide much greater than anything we experience in Britain. He says: 'I want to plead for conserving radicals who gladly affirm the conservatives' desire to preserve what is good in the past . . . At the same time, I want to plead for radical conservatives who are ready to critique and abandon what is not good in the past.'[34]

Increasingly there is a feeling among those involved in evangelical social action that the most fruitful way forward in evangelical ethics will prove to be through a creative synthesis of creation and kingdom ethics. Such a synthesis may well not only appeal to both conservative and radical evangelicals but serve to hold both groups together, thus preventing unnecessary and wasteful polarization.

Conclusion: a personal reflection on faith, hope and love

Evangelism in our day has largely become a packaged production, a mass-marketed experience in which evangelists strain to answer that question which nobody is asking. Modern evangelists must go through endless contortions to convince people that they are missing something that Christians have. Without the visible witness of a distinct style of life, evangelists must become aggressive and gimmicky, their methods reduced to salesmanship and showmanship. Evangelism often becomes a special activity awkwardly conducted ... instead of being a simple testimony rising out of a community whose life together invites questions from the surrounding society. When the life of the church no longer raises any questions, evangelism degenerates ...

I no longer believe that either self-interest or hypocrisy is the root cause of the great contradictions in the church's life. They have more to do with lack of faith. Our communion with God and with one another is so small that we just do not have the strength or the resources to live the way Jesus taught ... At bottom, our conformity to the world about us is due to a lack of faith. (Jim Wallis commenting on 1 Peter 3:15)[1]

Since, then, you have been raised with Christ, set your hearts on things above, where Christ is seated at the right hand of God. Set your minds on things above, not on earthly things. For you died, and your life is now hidden with Christ in God. When Christ, who is your life, appears, then you also will appear with him in glory. (Colossians 3:1–4)

The church faces tremendous challenges today. There is the dramatic spread of Aids. Estimates of the number of people who will be HIV positive by the turn of the century range from 35 to 100 million. Still today over one billion people live in poverty, yet the Third World pays £3 in debt repayments for every £1 received from the West. A country like Uganda has to set aside 90% of its foreign exchange earnings simply to service its foreign debt. In Britain there are signs of a growing underclass of people, particularly among the young, who lack access to the economic mainstream and the moral framework which guided a previous generation. And still over two billion people have not heard the gospel of Jesus.

The needs are great and the reality of suffering much greater than statistics can ever reveal. No-one can love figures but we are called to show love to those in need. But how can we love when the needs are so great? What kind of love will overcome the stigma to care for those suffering from Aids? Or what kind of love will speak the truth, telling the world a message about God's standards which it does not want to hear? What kind of love will care for those whom society rejects? What kind of love will go on caring when there are no easy solutions? What kind of love will move beyond charity to partnership, to sharing in the struggles and joys of our brothers and sisters in Christ throughout the world? What kind of love will care enough to give time to research the causes of poverty? Or what kind of love is prepared to question the way we live in a world in need?

Only the kind of love which Jesus called us to when he commanded us to deny ourselves and take up our cross daily: sacrificial love modelled on the cross itself in which we give our whole lives in the service of others. Only faith and hope can sustain such love. Yet that I suspect is the greatest problem facing evangelical social action. What hinders our love most is a lack of faith, and a lack of hope. This has two clear consequences.

1. *Lacking faith, we seek security in the things of this world.* In the Sermon on the Mount Jesus told his disciples not to worry about life, about food, clothes and so on. Our heavenly Father, he said, is able to care for all these things just as he cares for the sparrows and the lilies. It is familiar teaching, and yet so alien to the reality of our lives.

We give to the needs of the poor and to the mission of the church but all too often only after we have paid our mortgage, our pension contributions, our insurance, our health plan. Of course none of these things is intrinsically wrong but money has a powerful effect upon our thinking. Theo Donner from the Bible Seminary of Colombia in Medellín speaks of how our culture has corrupted the idea of stewardship: 'it becomes a wonderful capitalist model, by which we are in fact saying that whatever is a sound investment, whatever is good for money, is also good for God.'[2] True biblical stewardship is to use the earth's resources for the good of all people and for the good of the earth, not for the good of money. We must use money wisely but we must always ask ourselves whether in fact money itself has become the main criterion of our financial decision-making. Are we serving mammon or God?

The purpose of Jesus' teaching on worry was not to comfort us when things are financially tight, though it certainly is a comfort in such circumstances. Rather we are told not to worry about these things so that instead we can give ourselves in the service of God. 'So do not worry, saying, "What shall we eat?" or "What shall we drink?" or "What shall we wear?" For the pagans run after these things, and your heavenly Father knows that you need them. But seek first his kingdom and his righteousness, and all these things will be given to you as well' (Matthew 6:31–33). We are not to worry, not to concern ourselves with the things of this life, so that we can put first God's kingdom and his righteousness. The reality of so much of our lives, however, is that like the pagans we run after the things of this world. Lacking faith in God's ability to care for us, our priorities are askew.

Who will give generously for the sake of the kingdom? Who will serve God overseas or in the inner cities? Who will offer care when it costs? Only those who truly trust God for all their needs. And who has not found that in seeking first the kingdom of God, God has blessed them beyond measure (Mark 10:29–31)? Or that giving up all for the sake of the kingdom they have found a pearl of great value (Matthew 13:45–46)? Lacking faith, we seek security in the things of this world.

2. *Lacking hope, we seek blessing in the things of this world.* For evangelicals in the Third World the story of the last twenty to thirty years is the story of how they have sought to escape from the 'pie in the sky' view of Christianity. They have spoken of the new dignity that the poor find as children of God, the power that is given to

185

those who are powerless, the new community in which the justice and love of the kingdom are already at work. They have emphasized the presence of the kingdom.

But this is not the message we in the prosperous West need to hear. What makes the gospel good news to the poor comes to the rich as a call to repentance. We need to be reminded of the future of the kingdom. We need to be told to lay up treasure in heaven. Indeed we are often so prosperous now that for the most part we have stopped longing for heaven much at all. In the New Testament, believers prayed for the return of Christ in glory. I hear very few evangelicals pray for this today.

While it is seen as separate from social action, evangelism will continue to be perceived as its rival. When much of our evangelism is ineffective this is compounded: people call for the church to turn from 'secondary' things in order to focus on evangelism. The New Testament, however, has little to say on how and when we should evangelize. Instead it has much to say on how Christians should *live* and particularly how they should live in the light of Christ's coming.

One of the most famous passages which does speak of explaining our faith is 1 Peter 3:13–16. Peter tells us we must 'always be prepared to give an answer to everyone who asks you . . .'. But what are we being asked for? 'The reason for the hope that you have.' If we live for present blessings is it surprising that we are not asked to explain our hope? Little wonder, then, that our evangelism is ineffective: we are forced to answer questions which people are not asking.

Peter is speaking to those who are suffering for doing good – those whose lifestyles are so radically different that the world finds them threatening – and, citing Isaiah 8:12, he tells them not to fear. In Isaiah 8 the people are not to fear what others fear (verse 12), but to fear God (verse 13), and, fearing God, to trust him for the future (verse 14). Peter quotes this but focuses it on Christ, identifying Christ with Yahweh. 'In your hearts set apart Christ as Lord,' he tells his readers. Setting apart Christ as Lord, we trust him for the future and so, freed from fear, commit ourselves to the radical lifestyle of the kingdom. Christians cannot commit themselves to such a lifestyle, with its cost and uncertainty, unless they truly trust God and have a confident hope for the future based upon that trust.

Only when such trust and hope enable us to seek first God's kingdom and his justice, to take up our crosses in a daily life of service, submission and suffering, will people ask about our lives and the hope which lies behind what we do. Our aim must be godliness with contentment (1 Timothy 6:6), which, if it is real, means that we gratefully enjoy all that God has given us while not being enslaved by the desire for more.

While we lay up treasure on earth or while we make future security a priority, people are not going to ask about our hope. Having become like everyone else we have nothing to tell them because our lives do not provoke their questions. And when that happens our evangelism ceases to be based upon a lifestyle of trust and hope and becomes a technique. So books abound telling us how to evangelize effectively, how to turn conversations around to Christ, when if Christ is Lord of *all* our lives no conversation will need to be turned around. We are taught how to speak of spiritual things when in fact to be spiritual is to walk in step with the Spirit in all of life. Writing to the Thessalonians Paul says: 'we loved you so much that we were delighted to share with you not only the gospel of God but our lives as well, because you had become so dear to us' (1 Thessalonians 2:8). True evangelism starts with love and does not stop at sharing the gospel with people, as most of our evangelism does, but involves sharing our lives with people. It is love in action.

Too often we reveal ourselves to be primarily interested in present blessing. Yet the New Testament pattern is of suffering followed by glory. This was the pattern that Christ himself experienced (1 Peter 1:11): it is the pattern of cross–resurrection. And it is the pattern for Christian discipleship (Romans 8:17–18). Suffering in this case is defined by the cross: it is to follow the way of the cross (Luke 9:23), the way of submissive service, self-denial, sacrificial love and patient endurance. Of course by the Holy Spirit we know resurrection power now but that power is given precisely that we might follow the way of the cross (Philippians 3:10). It is, if you like, power to be weak (2 Corinthians 13:4). We are freed that we might serve one another in love (Galatians 5:13). What is the sign that we have resurrection life? Is it glory, victory, power? No, for all these things are hidden (Colossians 3:3). Our resurrection life is revealed as we share in the death of Christ (2 Corinthians 4:10–12). That is why in the New Testament suffering is a cause for rejoicing. Seeing the evidence that we are united with Christ in his death we can be confident that we are united with him in his resurrection and will share in his glory when it is revealed (1 Peter 4:13).

Martin Luther used to speak of a theology of glory and a theology of the cross.[3] Those who follow a theology of glory want direct knowledge of God through powerful acts of revelation or human insight. After the fall, however, says Luther, God is hidden from humanity. He is known now only through redemption, that is, through his grace. God reveals himself to us ultimately in the cross. There we see God's power but indirectly; through faith we see it hidden in weakness. And we see his wisdom in foolishness, his victory in defeat and his glory in shame.

What is needed today is an eschatology of the cross.[4] Too often there is a tendency towards an eschatology of glory. People want to know all the blessings of the future kingdom now, whether prosperity or healing or political liberation or self-fulfilment. An eschatology of the cross, on the other hand, will accept the way of the cross – the way of submissive service, self-denial and sacrificial love – in the hope of the glory that is to follow. Just as God's power is hidden in the weakness of the cross, so our resurrection glory is hidden now in our fellowship with Christ in his death (2 Corinthians 4:10–11; Colossians 3:3).

It is not my intention to make us feel guilty. That is easily done when we are the rich in a world where the contrast between rich and poor is so great. But guilt is a poor basis for motivation in the long run. We are indeed guilty, but in Christ we are forgiven and freed from guilt. Our actions are more biblical when they arise in response to redemption rather than in response to guilt. My concern is that, growing in faith and hope, we might 'love not with words or tongue but with actions and in truth' (1 John 3:18).

And how do we know greater faith and hope? Only as we know God more. Our trust in God will only become stronger as by his Spirit we come to know him more through his Word. And knowing him our hope will increase as we consider 'him faithful who had made the promise' (Hebrews 11:11). Abraham is our father in the faith because when he heard the promise of God that all nations would be blessed through his seed he did not look to the natural circumstances, his age and Sarah's barrenness, but instead to him who made the promise (Romans 4:19–21). When we look to the needs of the world it is easy to grow despondent. But hope arises when we look in faith to him who makes the promise, the King eternal, immortal, invisible, the only God. If only we could be grasped by the excitement of serving the God who promises that one day 'the earth will be filled with the knowledge of the glory of the LORD, as the waters cover the sea' (Habakkuk 2:14).

Postscript
by Stephen Rand

I can still remember his infectious enthusiasm. He was crouching down, showing me a tiny sapling a few inches high, and explaining the theory behind the project. We were in an area of southern Ethiopia, surrounded by parched ground that resembled a lunar landscape, sculpted by the damaging processes of deforestation and soil erosion.

But this Ethiopian Christian, a graduate of Addis Ababa University, was not focusing on the size of the problem. He was describing nothing short of transformation, his mind clearly fixed on what could be. The land would be terraced, these tiny saplings planted; the grazing would return, the animals would be fed; the trees would be managed, and would provide fuel, fruit and fodder. The local people would contribute their labour and be paid in food. They could participate in the process and benefit from it. They would see barren land become fruitful before their eyes.

That was the moment, he explained, when he would put the sign up, revealing to all who passed on the main road that this was a church project. They would all know that the church was in the business of transforming the environment, of restoring the land to fruitfulness. That was not all. The people of this area were Muslims; he wanted them to know that not only did God care about the land, but God loved them. They would experience the gospel, the gospel that is good news to the poor.

That was in 1984, the height of the TV famine focus – Michael Buerk, Bob Geldof, Band Aid, Live Aid. Three years later, that same Ethiopian Christian was in the Tear Fund office in Teddington. I asked him how the project was going. He was delighted: the saplings were now an incredible 30ft tall, the grazing had returned. The government was so impressed that they had given a further large area for similar treatment: the Marxist regime giving

191

land to the Christian church. Something else had happened: some of the local Muslim people had come asking why Christians were prepared to help them and their area in this way. The church leaders had explained that the help was a response to a God of love; the result was that a small church had been formed. In an important sense, evangelical Christians in Ethiopia did not have to awaken to a world of need; they were surrounded by it day by day. Despite persecution, despite the scale of the problem, the church was seeking to respond, and Tear Fund was seeking to enable them to do so, sharing resources released by Christians who had themselves been awakened to the world of need in Ethiopia as a result of television.

Tear Fund was founded in 1968, in itself a result of the awakening described by Timothy Chester in these pages. Its growth and influence have been a catalyst to that process as well. So as Tear Fund's 25th Anniversary approached, we felt that it would be an appropriate moment to commission a record and analysis of this world-wide rediscovery of evangelical social concern. Here was an opportunity to look back, and hopefully to learn, for as a historian I have always believed that proper analysis of the past should illuminate the present and help chart the way for the future. As I look back on that visit to Ethiopia in 1984 it seems to represent so many of the crucial issues of the past twenty-five years that have also become the major challenges facing the church, particularly in the wealthy nations, in these last years of the twentieth century.

Much has been achieved over the past twenty-five years. Rates of infant mortality have fallen, food production has increased, education leading to literacy has become more widely available and more people now have access to safe water supplies. These are all positive achievements in a world with a rapidly expanding population. At the same time there is no room for complacency. The gap between rich and poor still grows. The international debt crisis results in a net outflow of wealth from the Third World to the rich nations. Outbreaks of mass famine point up the daily reality of malnutrition for millions. The worldwide Aids epidemic not only reflects a moral crisis for the world community but also reveals a further link in the chain of injustice, as increasing numbers of babies are born HIV positive and the healthcare budgets of Third World countries, already completely inadequate, struggle to provide any semblance of care for those already suffering. Meanwhile the approach of the new millennium encourages many Christians to escape their responsibilities to this world by an unbalanced and unbiblical emphasis on the next.

But in the past twenty-five years academic debates and conference resolutions have rehearsed, repeated and refined the argument about the relationship between evangelism and social concern; this book has charted these waters. Tear Fund itself has reflected the same debate. In the search for holistic balance, Tear Fund began by being seen as one side only, providing in its social concern of relief and development a complementary counterweight to the assumed existing emphasis on evangelism. Then, when the Evangelism and Christian Education Department was added to Tear Fund at the request of the Evangelical Missionary Alliance and the Evangelical Alliance in 1979, it was argued that Tear Fund was now internally holistic and balanced, in that it supported both evangelism and social concern. Only in the last few years has the emphasis begun to shift again, as we seek to maximize the way in which each project and programme can reflect God's concern with wholeness. We want to develop in theory and practice how a Christian well-drilling programme differs from any other. We want to hear the cry of those in one Indian village who said to visiting Christians, 'Once you taught us to pray, now you teach us to fill in project proposals.'

That was the beauty of the explanation I heard on that hot Ethiopian day in 1984. In an African context, less burdened by the Western inheritance of Greek dualism and closer to the everyday realities of land, food and people, it was possible to see an integrated approach to Christian mission that did not isolate evangelism from social action, or even see them as two activities to be held in balance. Concern for the land, for the environment, for the people were all seen as the natural outworking of Christian witness. The gospel was demonstrated and articulated in response to the whole needs of whole people. The result was the beginnings of transformation in the environment, in the community and in individual lives, as the Holy Spirit was released in power. They knew that evangelism without social action is bad evangelism, and social action without evangelism is incomplete social action.

My many visits to different countries have revealed to me that ultimately the full story of evangelical social concern is not found in conference papers and on library shelves. It is found in the home of the Brazilian bank clerk who gave up his job to share his family life with six abandoned street children. It is found in the story of the black teenager, left with an artificial limb as a permanent reminder of the evil and injustice of apartheid, and now the director of an influential and radically holistic youth movement. It is found in a lathe made out of washing-machine parts by a Sri Lankan evangelist who gave up his home and his job to start a handicraft project for unemployed young men. It is found in the rice-paddies of the Philippines, where the pastor stands ankle deep in mud working alongside his congregation. It is found in a house in Calcutta where the urchin children of the station platform find security and love. All round the world the silent minority, the unseen saints, have been at work.

That is why I am so glad that one of the features of this book is the recognition of the leading role taken by theologians and activists from the so-called Third World. Indeed, it could be argued that the story of the evangelical awakening to a world of need is the story of how well the wealthy have listened to those living right in the world of need. The balance of numbers now lies in favour of the poor – the majority of the world's Christians live in the Third World, where the church is growing fastest. Since the sixties, their leaders have spoken, their new missionary force has been mobilized, their biblical understanding has informed and challenged. The pendulum has swung – and one of the challenges that faces the church of the rich in the West is the extent to which the balance of power will be allowed to shift. Wealth brings power and responsibility: charity is a legitimate but insufficient response to the challenge of justice, and of true Christian fellowship, in a divided world.

Mass communication is a symbol and weapon of wealth and power, television perhaps its most powerful medium. It was television that made Ethiopia a household name; it was television that made it synonymous with famine. It was the week after Michael Buerk's news reports which graphically portrayed the helpless victims of famine that I saw for myself the dynamic activity of Ethiopian Christians in that reforestation programme. It was the week after those camps of masses of emaciated and stricken people had made such gripping television that I met and talked to Tiekle; just one individual, but enough to remind me that famine victims are real people, made in the image of God. And it was the week after Britain was shown just one aspect of life in Ethiopia that I discovered Ethiopia was being shown just one aspect of life in Britain – the only item about Britain on Ethiopian television was a report of violence on the picket lines during the miners' strike. It was a salutary reminder of the power of television to create and sustain national stereotypes, to reinforce a one-eyed view of the world. This is a real challenge in our communications as a Third World charity. There are those who emphasize that Tear Fund has much to gain from a consistent portrayal of the poor as helpless victims; but we believe it is part of our calling to help people see beyond the TV stereotype of horror and suffering; not least to see a vibrant, active church, often taking the lead in demonstrating joyful and consistent care for the needy.

Yet it cannot be denied that television has revealed the world of need in all its awful detail. Since the sixties we have become dominated by visual news reports, suffering revealed in glowing colour in the corner of our living rooms. I believe this has been the dominant cause in our society for evangelicals awakening to a world of need. A symbol of our wealth has shown us poverty: the source of anaesthetic entertainment has sometimes broken through to our conscience. There is a sense in which this causes grave disquiet. Are we all victims of mass media manipulation? Are we forced to follow the news editors' agenda, rather than a biblical agenda? Who prompts our actions – the Holy Spirit or the BBC? Every year at Tear Fund we seek to plan ahead, to prepare a strategy of communication and education, to encourage a committed, biblical response to the needs of the poor. At the same time we know that reports on *News at Ten* may generate more immediate financial response than any activity we initiate. One of our basic and most vital strategies is to ensure that our supporters are aware as quickly as possible of a Christian perspective on an area featured on the news. As information overload increases, the church will face a greater and greater challenge: how to maintain and communicate a Christian understanding of what is happening in this world of need.

At the same time, I do not wish in any way to belittle the importance of response to the news. The last thing I would want to suggest is that we should become immune to the needs of others revealed by the television. Christians of all people should not suffer from compassion fatigue. I firmly believe that television has helped to save evangelicalism from being lost in its own world of sanctified irrelevance. Since industrialization the church in Britain has been predominantly middle class. After the Second World War that middle class lapsed into increasing suburban affluence, and the church often reflected that sense of safe, unthreatening parochialism. The difference between the church in Britain and the church in Ethiopia was that the former had almost completely cut itself off from a world of need. I remember visiting an Ethiopian church building in 1984. The Orthodox Church in Ethiopia predates Christianity in Britain; the architectural features of the building reflected much of what I recognized as features of a Jewish synagogue; but perhaps the most thought-provoking biblical resonance was the beggar at the gate. How would my experience of church be affected if every time I attended I had to force my way past a hungry face and an outstretched hand?

The point was driven home by a pastor at an evangelical church that had become a base for a large feeding programme. I had asked him why he was involved in feeding the hungry: was he not more concerned with spiritual tasks? His answer was direct: 'I simply could not stand by and watch people suffer.' It immediately struck me that this was the authentic Christian response. 'How does God's love abide in anyone who has the world's goods and sees a brother or sister in need and yet refuses to help?' (1 Jn. 3:17, New Revised Standard Version). The television, one item of the world's goods, enables us to participate in that Ethiopian pastor's experience. We can see our brother in need; and if God's love is real in our lives we will not be able to close our heart.

Love is the key. The story of the awakening of evangelical social concern is nothing less than the awakening to a full experience of God's love in action. Love does not debate theoretical priorities so much as demand that others are put first; love does not spend time criticizing the failures of fellow-Christians so much as work to overcome the weakness of self; love does not see the church as a religious club for our comfort and benefit so much as make it the base for an impact on the community; love does not draw curtains but opens doors. As the song says, 'What the world needs now is love, sweet love': God's love in action, poured into his people, through his people, reaching out to a world in need.

All of us who were able to comment on this book as the manuscript was prepared were convinced that it needed to end, not by looking back in simple reflection, nor by ensuring that the analysis was neat and satisfying, but by recognizing the challenge that faces us all. That is why the Conclusion was written. I would want to endorse its message and recognize its challenge: to me first, to Tear Fund as an organization, and to the church as a whole. Evangelicals may have reawakened to a world of need, but there is still a lot of sleep in the eyes. Evangelicals who understand the necessity and possibility of individual salvation, and who accept biblical doctrines of wholeness and compassion, have a primary responsibility to demonstrate the reality of their beliefs in the pursuit of Christian development for every society in every location. But with the possibility of making this unique contribution goes the possibility of doing nothing at all. There is always the tendency to opt for religion rather than obedience, to choose comfort rather than truth, to prefer talk to action. Disciples are called to take up their cross and to follow Jesus; the world is dying to see obedient, willing, enthusiastic and, above all, loving disciples – disciples who follow the example, not of their forerunners who fell asleep while Jesus faced the cross, but of Jesus himself. 'This is how we know what love is: Jesus Christ laid down his life for us. And we ought to lay down our lives for our brothers' (1 John. 3:16).

Stephen Rand
Communications Director
Tear Fund

Notes

Preface

[1]See, for example, Robin Thomson (ed.), *The World Christian: A Workbook for those aiming to take the gospel from culture to culture* (Oxford: Lynx, 1991), pp. 15–16.

Chapter 1: Back into the arena

[1]Carl F. H. Henry, *The Uneasy Conscience of Modern Fundamentalism* (Grand Rapids: Eerdmans, 1947), p. 84.

[2]Valdir Steuernagel, 'The Theology of Mission in its Relation to Social Responsibility within the Lausanne Movement', DTh Dissertation, Lutheran School of Theology, Chicago, Illinois, May 1988, p. 71.

[3]Cited in *ibid.*, p. 79.

[4]Interview with Clive Calver, 3 December 1992.

[5]*Ibid.*

[6]The polarization was not perhaps as strong initially as it was to become. One of the contributors to *The Fundamentals* series wrote: 'A true gospel of grace is inseparable from a gospel of good works. Christian doctrines and Christian duties cannot be divorced. The New Testament no more clearly defines the relation of the believer to Christ than to the members of one's family, to his neighbours in society and to his fellow-citizens in the state. These social teachings of the Gospel need a new emphasis today by those who accept the whole Gospel, and should not be left to be interpreted and applied by those alone who deny essential Christianity ... Some are quite comfortable under what they regard as orthodox preaching, even though they know their wealth has come from the watering of stocks and from wrecking railroads, and from grinding the faces of the poor. The supposed orthodoxy of such preaching is palpably defective in its statements of the social teaching of the Gospels. One might be a social bandit and buccaneer and yet believe in the virgin birth and the resurrection of Christ' (C. R. Erdman, 'The Church and Socialism', in *The Fundamentals*, Vol. xii [1911], cited by Samuel Escobar, 'Evangelization and Man's Search for Freedom, Justice and Fulfilment', in J. D. Douglas (ed.), *Let the Earth Hear His Voice* [Minneapolis: World Wide Publications, 1975], p. 311). This also shows that a reaction to the social gospel is at best only a partial

explanation for the loss of evangelical social action during the beginning of this century.

[7]See George M. Marsden, *Reforming Fundamentalism: Fuller Seminary and the New Evangelicalism* (Grand Rapids: Eerdmans, 1987).

[8]See William Martin, *The Billy Graham Story: A Prophet with Honour* (London: Hutchinson, 1991), pp. 211–217.

[9]Carl Henry, *The Uneasy Conscience*, p. 17.

[10]*Ibid.*, p. 20.

[11]*Ibid.*, pp. 26, 30.

[12]Carl F. H. Henry, *Evangelicals in Search of Identity* (Waco, Texas: Word Books, 1976), pp. 30–31. Cited by Ray S. Anderson, 'Evangelical Theology', in David Ford (ed.), *Modern Theologians*, vol. 2 (Oxford: Blackwell, 1989), p. 143.

[13]See, for example, William Martin, *The Billy Graham Story*, p. 343.

[14]Billy Graham's statement was made in a talk to students at Harvard University and cited in *Billy Graham: The Man and his Mission*, the official publicity material for Mission England (1984), p. 45 and in William Martin, *The Story of Billy Graham*, p. 588.

[15]Before the Harringay crusade only 7% of Anglican ordinands described themselves as evangelical. In 1956 23 out of the 33 men ordained in the Anglican dioceses of London were evangelicals. In 1957 it was 22 out of 32. Cited by William Martin, *The Billy Graham Story*, p. 185.

[16]For a discussion of the effect of millennial views upon social concern see Peter Kuzmic, 'History and Eschatology: Evangelical Views', in Bruce Nicholls (ed.), *In Word and Deed* (Exeter: Paternoster, 1985), pp. 135–164. Not all pre-millennialists are opposed to social action – the Earl of Shaftesbury, the noted Victorian reformer known especially for his campaigns against child labour, was a premillennialist. Clive Calver draws a distinction between premillennialism in general and what he calls 'an aberrant strain': 'I don't believe that the premillennialism of the end of the nineteenth century is the same as the premillennialism of the 1830s. I believe there's actually an aberrant strain and that aberrant strain still exists in the USA' (interview with Clive Calver, 3 December 1882).

[17]D. W. Bebbington, *Evangelicalism in Modern Britain: A History from the 1730s to the 1980s* (London: Unwin Hyman, 1989), p. 264.

[18]*Ibid.*

[19]*Ibid.*, p. 249.

[20]How great a factor this was it is not easy to tell at this stage. Despite the changes in British society, a great number of prominent evangelical Anglicans at the time were 'Bash Boys'. Eric Nash, or 'Bash' as he was known, organized Christian Unions and 'Bash' camps exclusively within the public schools. Those converted or influenced in this way included John Stott, David Sheppard, David Watson, Dick Lucas, Michael Green, Fred Catherwood and John Marsh. Yet despite their public school background a number of these have played a significant part in the rediscovery of social action by evangelicals.

[21]Michael Saward, *Evangelicals on the Move* (Oxford: Mowbray, 1987), p. 63.

[22]Anderson's paper, 'Christian Worldliness: the need and limits of Christian

involvement' was published, together with the other Keele papers, in J. I. Packer (ed.), *Guidelines: Anglican Evangelicals Face the Future* (London: Falcon Books, 1967), pp. 211–232.

[23]J. N. D. Anderson, *Into the World: The Need and Limits of Christian Involvement* (London: Falcon Books, 1968).

[24]J. N. D. Anderson, 'Christian Worldliness', *Guidelines*, p. 218.

[25]H. F. R. (Sir Fred) Catherwood, *The Christian In Industrial Society* (London: Tyndale Press, 1964); *The Christian Citizen* (London: Hodder, 1969); *A Better Way* (London: IVP, 1975); *Pro-Europe?* (Leicester: IVP, 1992).

[26]See John Capon, *And There Was Light: The Story of the Nationwide Festival of Light* (London: Lutterworth, 1972).

[27]Gerald Coates was told this by Malcolm Muggeridge himself. Interview with Gerald Coates, 27 November 1992. See also Gerald Coates, *An Intelligent Fire* (Eastbourne: Kingsway, 1991), p. 83.

Chapter 2: The debate begins

[1]The meeting in Montreux, Switzerland, took place 16–19 August 1960. The 33 world evangelical leaders who gathered did so for both prayer and Bible study. It was funded by the BGEA.

[2]The story is told by Carl Henry in his autobiography, *Confessions of a Theologian: An Autobiography* (Waco, Texas: Word Books, 1986), p 252.

[3]Cited by David Bosch, *Witness to the World: The Christian Mission in Theological Perspective* (London: Marshall, Morgan and Scott, 1980), p. 181.

[4]*Ibid.*

[5]The World Congress on Evangelism was held in Berlin 25 October–4 November under the title One Race, One Gospel, One Task. It was sponsored by *Christianity Today* to celebrate their tenth anniversary. The conference papers were published in Carl F. H. Henry and Stanley Mooneyham (eds.), *The Official Reference Volumes: One Race, One Gospel, One Task*, 2 vols. (Minneapolis: World Wide Publications, 1967).

[6]Carl F. H. Henry and Stanley Mooneyham (eds.), *The Official Reference Volumes: One Race, One Gospel, One Task*, Vol. 1, p. 5. The final statement is also printed in Arthur Johnston, *The Battle for World Evangelism* (Wheaton, IL: Tyndale House, 1978), pp. 365–368.

[7]Carl F. H. Henry and Stanley Mooneyham (eds.), *The Official Reference Volumes: One Race, One Gospel, One Task*, Vol. 1, p. 41.

[8]*Ibid.*, Vol. 1, p. 307.

[9]*Ibid.*, Vol. 1, p. 308.

[10]See the closing statement, *ibid.*, Vol. 1, p. 6.

[11]*Ibid.*, Vol. 1, p. 28. At the Congress, the black evangelist William Pannell complained that while this traditional view might be true 'ideally', it 'is now being used as an excuse for almost complete non-involvement at all levels'. Cited by Carl Henry, *Evangelicals at the Brink of Crisis: The Significance of the World Congress on Evangelism* (Waco, Texas: Word Books, 1967), p. 70.

[12]Cited by Carl Henry, *Evangelicals at the Brink of Crisis*, p. 64. Henry himself

criticizes this preoccupation with just one aspect of Christian activity. It should be remembered too that Harak was from Yugoslavia, then a Communist country in which socio-political action was not a very realistic possibility.

[13]The closing statement, Carl F. H. Henry and Stanley Mooneyham (eds.), *The Official Reference Volumes: One Race, One Gospel, One Task*, Vol. 1, p. 5.

[14]*Decision*, May 1966.

[15]Carl F. H. Henry and Stanley Mooneyham (eds.), *The Official Reference Volumes: One Race, One Gospel, One Task*, Vol. 1, p. 2.

[16]*Ibid.*, Vol. 1, p. 120.

[17]Carl F. H. Henry, *Evangelicals at the Brink of Crisis*, p. 2.

[18]The Congress on the Church's Worldwide Mission was held in Wheaton, USA, 9–16 April 1966. It was co-sponsored by the Evangelical Foreign Missions Association and the Interdenominational Foreign Missions Association, who together represented nearly a half of all North American missionaries. Altogether 938 people attended from 71 countries. The conference papers were published in Harold Lindsell (ed.), *The Church's Worldwide Mission* (Waco, Texas: Word Publishing, 1966).

[19]The main address on social action at the Wheaton Congress was 'Mission and Social Concern' given by Horace Fenton, a North American but head of Latin American Mission. He pointed out that Jesus never ignored people's physical needs and that evangelicals throughout history have always been involved in social action, and he stressed the need for discipleship to be seen as part of our mission.

[20]The Asia and South Pacific Congress on Evangelism was sponsored by the BGEA and held in Singapore, 5–13 November 1968 under the title Christ Seeks Asia. There were 1,100 participants from 24 countries. Its aim was to bring the challenge of Berlin '66 to the continent of Asia. The conference papers were published in Stanley Mooneyham (ed.), *Christ Seeks Asia* (Hong Kong: The Rock House, 1969). Benjamin Fernando's address, although short, was described by Valdir Steuernagel as 'pioneering within evangelical ranks' ('Social Responsibility within the Lausanne Movement', DTh Dissertation, Lutheran School of Theology, Chicago, 1988, p. 117).

The first Berlin follow-up conference was actually the West African Congress on Evangelism, where 459 people gathered in Nigeria during July 1968. It included little on social action but focused instead on the definition of the gospel, the relevance of its message to an African context and the need to present that message to all.

[21]The US Congress on Evangelism was sponsored by the BGEA and held in Minneapolis 8–13 September 1969. There were 4,700 delegates from 93 denominations who met under the title Much is Given – Much is Required. The Congress proceedings were published in *Evangelism Now* (Minneapolis: World Wide Publications, 1970).

[22]*Decision*, December 1969.

[23]See Leighton Ford, 'The Church and Evangelism in a Day of Revolution', in *Evangelism Now*, pp. 50–63. Leighton Ford was then with the BGEA and is currently Chairman of the Lausanne Committee for World Evangelization. Also

at the Minneapolis Congress Myron Augsburger called upon the church 'to affirm Christ's lordship in judgment on social evils' (*ibid.*, p. 200).

[24]The Latin American Congress on Evangelism, or CLADE from the Spanish title (*Congreso Latinoamericano de Evangelización*), was held in Bogotá, 21–30 November 1969. There were 920 participants from 25 countries who met under the title Action in Christ for a Continent in Crisis. CLADE II was held in Lima ten years later and CLADE III in Quito in 1992.

[25]Translated and reprinted in Brian Griffiths (ed.), *Is Revolution Change?* (Leicester: IVP, 1972), pp. 84–111. It was described as the most popular address by Arthur Johnston, *The Battle for World Evangelism*, p. 255.

[26]*Decision*, March 1970.

[27]Cited by Arthur Johnston, *The Battle for World Evangelism*, p. 257.

[28]W. Dayton Roberts, 'Latin American Protestants: Which Way Will They Go?', *Christianity Today*, Vol. 14, No. 1, October 1969, p. 14.

[29]The European Congress on Evangelism was sponsored by the European Evangelical Alliance and was held in Amsterdam, 28 August–4 September, 1971. There were 1,064 participants from 36 countries in Europe and the Middle East. A smaller conference for Eastern Europe had been held in Novi Sad, Yugoslavia in 1969. The papers for the European Congress were published in Gilbert W. Kirby (ed.), *Evangelism Alert* (London: World Wide Publications, 1972).

[30]Paavo Kortekangas, 'Social Implications of Evangelism', in G. W. Kirby (ed.), *Evangelism Alert*, p. 131.

[31]*Decision*, November 1971.

[32]Samuel Escobar, 'Evangelism and Man's Search for Freedom, Justice and Fulfilment', in J. D. Douglas (ed.), *Let the Earth Hear His Voice* (Minneapolis: World Wide Publications, 1975), p. 306. He goes on to cite a number of examples, pp. 306–307.

[33]Carl F. H. Henry and Stanley Mooneyham (eds.), *The Official Reference Volumes: One Race, One Gospel, One Task*, Vol. 1, p. 278.

[34]*Ibid.*, Vol. 1, p. 193. In contrast, the report from South Africa itself speaks enthusiastically of the evangelistic opportunities while failing even to mention the problem of apartheid. And when Michael Cassidy described the group ethic, the distinction of groups along racial lines, as 'a basic problem for Christian witness and evangelism in South Africa', one of the Afrikaner delegates demanded that his contribution be withdrawn as damaging to evangelism in South Africa.

[35]*Decision*, December 1969.

[36]Valdir Steuernagel, 'Social Responsibility within the Lausanne Movement', p. 99.

[37]Interview with Vinay Samuel, 7 December 1992.

Chapter 3: Face to face with need

[1]Cited by Mary Endersbee, *They Can't Eat Prayer: The Story of Tear Fund* (London: Hodder, 1973), p. 11.

[2]George Eldon Ladd, *Jesus and the Kingdom* (New York: Harper and Row, 1964),

later revised and published as *The Presence of the Future* (Grand Rapids: Eerdmans, 1974, and London: SPCK, 1980). See also G. E. Ladd, 'The Kingdom of God: Reign or Realm?', *Journal of Biblical Literature*, 81, 1962, pp. 230–238 and G. E. Ladd, *A Theology of the New Testament* (Grand Rapids: Eerdmans, 1974, and Guildford: Lutterworth, 1975).

[3]Interview with Vinay Samuel, 7 December 1992; interview with Chris Sugden, 12 November 1992.

[4]That evangelicals respond to perceived needs with compassion is borne out in part by the opposite case. Don Mason of the Hard of Hearing Christian Fellowship believes that one of the major reasons that the fellowship has not grown or had the influence it might have wished for is that poor hearing is not perceived as a serious need. 'The church generally', he writes, 'doesn't perceive poor hearing as being a handicap, and deaf people are often afforded little sympathy even by otherwise caring Christians. Partial hearing is often observed with mild amusement, and sometimes irritation. These attitudes are a mirror of society's attitudes to the hard of hearing' (Don Mason, personal letter to the author, 24 November 1992).

[5]The All India Congress on Evangelism was a follow-up to the Asia and South Pacific Congress on Evangelism, 1968 (itself a follow-up to Berlin '66). It was organized by the Evangelical Fellowship of India in its 20th anniversary year. Three hundred participants gathered in Deolali, Maharashtra, 4 January 1970.

[6]Dr. I. Ben Wati, 'Evangelism and Social Concern', in *idem, Whither Evangelicals? The Evangelical Movement in India* (New Delhi: Evangelical Fellowship of India, 1975), pp. 71–72.

[7]See Mary Endersbee, *They Can't Eat Prayer*, p. 30, and also, for example, the report on Tear Fund in the *Life of Faith*, 14 November 1968. Peter Meadows is also quoted as saying: 'Evangelicals are now without excuse.'

[8]The members of IRDA are: AEA (Angola), AEAM (Kenya), AGEMPEM (Mali), AHS (Switzerland), CCSD/EFT (Thailand), EFICOR (India), EFZ (Zambia), FEME (Burkina Faso), KOINONIA (Bangladesh), LEADS (Sri Lanka), PAEDAS (Central African Republic), PHILRADS (Philippines), SCC (Swaziland), SEL (France), TEAR Australia, Tear Fund Belgium, Tear Fund Holland, Tear Fund New Zealand, Tear Fund (UK and Ireland), World Relief (Canada), World Relief (USA).

[9]Cited by Philip Schlesinger, *Putting 'Reality' Together: BBC News* (London: Constable, 1978, and Methuen, 1987), p. 34. In 1955 there were 4,504,000 television licences issued; in 1960 it was 10,470,000 and in 1965 it was 13,253,000. Source: B. R. Mitchell and H. G. Jones, *Second Abstract of British Historical Statistics*, University of Cambridge Department of Applied Economics, Monograph No. 18 (Cambridge: Cambridge University Press, 1971). Television licences were introduced in 1947 when 15,000 were obtained. In 1991, 19,546,000 licences were obtained. Source: Central Statistical Office, *Annual Abstract of Statistics 1992*, London: HMSO, 1992).

[10]See Philip Schlesinger, *Putting 'Reality' Together: BBC News*, p. 37.

[11]*Ibid.*, p. 41.

[12]Cited in Jeremy Tunstall, *The Media in Britain* (London: Constable, 1983), p. 39.

[13]See Colin Seymour-Ure, *The British Press and Broadcasting Since 1945* (London: The Institute of Contemporary British History, and Oxford: Blackwell, 1991), p. 140.

[14]Interview with Stephen Rand, 8 October 1992. It is a source of some pride within Tear Fund that while it is the twenty-fifth largest charity in terms of income, it is the fourth largest in terms of covenanted, *i.e.* committed, giving.

Chapter 4: The turbulent sixties

[1]John C. King, *The Evangelicals* (London: Hodder, 1969), p. 157.

[2]Paul Henry, *Christianity Today*, Vol. 14, No. 7, January 1970, p. 28. See also Paul Henry, *Politics for Evangelicals* (Valley Forge, PA: Judson Press, 1974).

[3]John Stott, *Issues Facing Christians Today* (Basingstoke: Marshall, Morgan and Scott, 1984), p. 9.

[4]Vinay Samuel and Chris Sugden, 'Towards a Theology of Social Change', in Ronald Sider (ed.), *Evangelicals and Development* (Exeter: Paternoster, 1981), p. 48.

[5]Cited by Marshall Frady, *Billy Graham: A Parable of American Righteousness* (London: Hodder, 1979), p. 417.

[6]See, for example, the editorials of *Christianity Today*; *e.g.* Harold Lindsell's criticism of the Washington peace protests, Vol. 14, No. 5, December 1969.

[7]I owe this observation to Tom Houston, interview on 28 November 1992.

[8]Brian Griffiths (ed.), *Is Revolution Change?* (London: IVP, 1972), p. 106. The other contributors were Fred Catherwood, Alan Krieder, René Padilla and Samuel Escobar.

[9]Two internal support surveys were conducted by Tear Fund in 1986 and 1991. The two reports are not directly comparable since the first looked at general support while the second focused on church representatives. Nevertheless the first report shows that in 1986 45% of Tear Fund's support came from under-35-year-olds compared to 25% from 35–44-year-olds. In 1991 23% of church representatives were under 35 while 35% were 35–44. In 1991 the average age of church representatives was 45, *i.e.* someone who was 24 at the end of the sixties. Figures of course can be misleading but there is a perception within Tear Fund that its main support comes from the sixties generation and that this support is not being matched by subsequent generations. As a result, as this generation gets older so Tear Fund's support profile shifts.

[10]Interview with Chris Sugden, 12 November 1992.

[11]Interview with Clive Calver, 3 December 1992.

[12]Jim Wallis, *The New Radical* (Tring: Lion, 1983), p. 72.

[13]*Ibid.*, p. 11.

[14]John Perkins, *A Quiet Revolution* (Waco, Texas: Word Books, 1976, and Basingstoke: Marshall Pickering, 1985), p. 62. See also Will Norton, 'An interview with John Perkins, the Prophet', *Christianity Today*, 1 January 1982, pp. 20–22.

[15]John Perkins, *A Quiet Revolution*, pp. 82–92.

[16]*Ibid.*, p. 70.

[17]It also shows something of the Berlin Congress's preoccupation with US

concerns. The only social issue of prominence was the main one North Americans were facing.

[18]Carl F. H. Henry and Stanley Mooneyham (eds.), *The Official Reference Volumes: One Race, One Gospel, One Task* (Minneapolis: World Wide Publications, 1967), Vol. 1, p. 5.

[19]David E. Kucharsky, 'U.S. Congress on Evangelism: A Turning Point?', *Christianity Today*, Vol. 14, No. 1, 10 October 1969, p. 28.

[20]Tom Skinner, 'Evangelism in Our Modern Community', in G. M. Wilson (ed.), *Evangelism Now* (Minneapolis: World Wide Publications, 1970), p. 145.

[21]Ralph Abernathy, 'What this Congress Can Mean to Society', in *ibid.*, pp. 176–185; citations from pp. 181, 184.

[22]US Congress on Evangelism: Statement of Purpose, in *ibid.*, p. v.

[23]*Decision*, December 1969.

[24]One positive outcome of the meeting was that Nixon arranged for the Office of Economic Opportunity and the Department of Housing and Urban Development to be more forthcoming with funds for local housing projects – a particular grievance raised by the church leaders. See William Martin, *The Billy Graham Story: A Prophet with Honour* (London: Hutchinson, 1991), pp. 364–365.

[25]Jim Wallis, *The New Radical*, p. 62.

[26]Mark O. Hatfield, 'Evangelism and Coming World Peace', in G. M. Wilson (ed.), *Evangelism Now*, pp. 104–115, citations from pp. 111 and 106 respectively. An edited version was also printed in *Decision*, November 1969.

[27]Jim Wallis, *The New Radical*, p. 80.

[28]There were about 50 participants at the Thanksgiving Workshop on Evangelical Social Action which was held in Chicago 23–25 November 1973. A partial list of participants was printed in the *International Review of Mission*, Vol. 63, No. 250, April 1974, pp. 274–275. A twentieth anniversary gathering is due to be held during 1993.

[29]The Chicago Declaration of Evangelical Social Concern was published together with the conference papers in Ronald J. Sider (ed.), *The Chicago Declaration* (Chicago: Creation House, 1974). The declaration was also published in the *International Review of Mission*, Vol. 63, No. 250, April 1974, p. 274; in *Christianity Today*, Vol. 17, No. 6, 1973, p. 38; and in C. René Padilla and Chris Sugden (eds.), *Texts on Evangelical Social Ethics 1974–1983* (Bramcote, Nottingham: Grove Books, 1985), pp. 4–5.

[30]René Padilla says the Chicago Declaration 'was enthusiastically received by many people who saw in it clear evidence that evangelicals were transcending the traditional dichotomy between evangelism and social responsibility'. 'How Evangelicals Endorsed Social Responsibility', *Transformation*, Vol. 2, No. 3, p. 28.

[31]John Howard Yoder, *The Politics of Jesus* (Grand Rapids: Eerdmans, 1972).

[32]Vinay Samuel and Chris Sugden, 'Toward a Theology of Social Change', p. 49.

[33]René Padilla, 'The Politics of the Kingdom of God and the Political Mission of the Church', in Vinay Samuel and Albrecht Hauser (eds.), *Proclaiming Christ in Christ's Way: Studies in Integral Evangelism* (Oxford: Regnum, 1989), p. 180.

[34]John Howard Yoder, *The Politics of Jesus*, p. 15.

[35]A. N. Triton, *Whose World?* (London: IVP, 1970). See also A. N. Triton, *Salt to*

the World: The Christian and Social Involvement (Leicester: IVP, 1978).

[36]D. W. Bebbington, *Evangelicalism in Modern Britain* (London: Unwin Hyman, 1989), p. 266.

[37]Urbana '70 was held on the campus of the University of Illinois, Urbana, 27–31 December 1970. There were 10,937 students gathered from across the United States and Canada and 113 missionary agencies were also represented. The convention theme was 'World Evangelism: Why? How? Who?'

[38]Carey Moore, *Decision*, April 1971.

[39]Samuel Escobar, quoted in *ibid*.

[40]Cited by David O. Moberg, *The Great Reversal: Evangelism Versus Social Concern* (London: Scripture Union, 1973), p. 164.

[41]Tom Skinner, *Decision*, April 1971.

[42]Cited by David O. Moberg, *The Great Reversal*, p. 17.

[43]See Raymond Williams, *Television: Technology and Cultural Form* (London: Fontana, 1974), pp. 48–49.

[44]Athol Gill, 'Christian Social Responsibility', in C. René Padilla (ed.), *The New Face of Evangelicalism: An International Symposium on the Lausanne Covenant* (London: Hodder, 1975; Downers Grove, IL: IVP, 1976), p. 96. Gill adds: 'In some areas "culture Christianity" concepts die hard, but the resignation of President Nixon will undoubtedly have a far-reaching effect on American evangelical theology. Perhaps, at last, corporate evil will be taken seriously' (p. 272, n. 26).

[45]Cited by Marshall Frady, *Billy Graham: A Parable of American Righteousness* (London: Hodder, 1979), p. 438.

[46]Reading over William Martin's account of Graham's involvement with the Nixon administration and with Watergate, Graham commented: 'I knew what I had said to the President and I knew what he had said to me. But I was unaware of all those memos circulating in the background. When I read about that, I felt like a sheep led to the slaughter' (William Martin, *The Billy Graham Story*, p. 399). There is no doubt that the Watergate scandal hit Graham hard. When he finally read the transcripts of the Watergate tapes he wept and even vomited (*ibid*., p. 431). He has certainly been far more wary with later Presidents.

[47]This is, for example, John Stott's assessment of his success as a preacher, cited by William Martin, *ibid*., p. 595.

[48]Graham himself was to acknowledge: 'maybe I was naive at that time; maybe I was used'. Cited by William Martin, *ibid*., p. 435.

[49]Billy Graham, 'Why Lausanne?', in J. D. Douglas (ed.), *Let the Earth Hear His Voice* (Minneapolis: World Wide Publications, 1975), p. 30. This statement produced sustained applause from the Congress delegates (see William Martin, *The Billy Graham Story*, p. 432).

[50]Cited by William Martin, *ibid*., p. 472.

[51]Paul Henry, *Christianity Today*, Vol. 14, No. 7, January 1970, p. 28.

Chapter 5: Mission in the melting pot

[1]For a detailed examination of developments in the WCC's understanding of mission from an evangelical perspective see Harvey T. Hoekstra, *Evangelism in Eclipse: World Mission and the World Council of Churches* (Exeter: Paternoster, 1979). See also Orlando Costas, *The Church and Its Mission: A Shattering Critique from the Third World* (Wheaton, IL: Tyndale, 1974), pp. 153–301; David Bosch, *Witness to the World: The Christian Mission in Theological Perspective* (London: Marshall, Morgan & Stott, 1980), pp. 159–195 and Arthur Johnston, *The Battle for World Evangelism* Wheaton, IL: Tyndale House, 1978).

[2]See Harvey T. Hoekstra, *ibid.*, pp. 237–242.

[3]Donald A. McGavran, 'Will Uppsala Betray the Two Billion?', *Church Growth Bulletin*, Vol. 4, No. 5, May 1968.

[4]See Orlando Costas, *The Church and Its Mission*, pp. 182–186.

[5]Peter Beyerhaus, 'The Frankfurt Declaration', in Sinclair B. Ferguson, David F. Wright, J. I. Packer (eds.), *New Dictionary of Theology* (Leicester, and Downers Grove, IL: IVP, 1988), p. 263.

[6]Cited by Orlando Costas, *The Church and Its Mission*, p. 190. Costas, himself critical of the conception of mission in the WCC, gives a critique of the Frankfurt Declaration, pp. 189–217.

[7]Peter Beyerhaus, *Missions: Which Way? Humanization and Redemption* (Grand Rapids: Zondervan, 1971). The Frankfurt Declaration was published in *Christianity Today*, Vol. 14, No. 19, June 1970, pp. 3–6. The Frankfurt Declaration contained 'seven indispensable basic elements of mission . . . 1. the sole authority of the Bible over against situational hermeneutics; 2. the primacy of doxology over against humanization as the goal of mission; 3. biblical christology over against an anonymous Christ-presence in human history; 4. the significance of personal faith in salvation over against universalism; 5. the spiritual nature of the church over against a merely functional understanding of it; 6. the uniqueness of the gospel over against other religions; 7. the reality of Christ's second coming for the eschatological orientation of mission over against an ideology of progress or revolution' (cited in Peter Beyerhaus, 'The Frankfurt Declaration', *loc. cit.*, p. 263).

[8]John Stott, 'The Biblical Basis of Evangelism', in J. D. Douglas (ed.), *Let the Earth Hear His Voice* (Minneapolis: World Wide Publications, 1975), p. 65.

[9]*Ibid.*, p. 74.

[10]Cited by Carl Henry, *Evangelicals at the Brink of Crisis* (Waco, Texas: Word Books, 1967), p. 67.

[11]Francis Schaeffer, *A Christian Manifesto* (Basingstoke: Pickering and Inglis, 1981, 1982), p. 19.

[12]See, for example, Francis Schaeffer, *Art and the Bible* (London: Hodder, 1973).

[13]See, for example, Francis Schaeffer, *True Spirituality* (Wheaton: Tyndale House, and London: Coverdale House, 1971).

[14]For the story behind L'Abri see Edith Schaeffer, *L'Abri* (Worthing: Henry Walter, 1969).

[15]See, for example, Francis Schaeffer, *The God Who is There* (London: Hodder,

1968), *Escape from Reason* (London: IVP, 1968), *He is There and He is Not Silent* (London: Hodder, 1972), *Death in the City* (London: IVP, 1969), and the book and film *How Should We Then Live?: The Rise and Decline of Western Thought and Culture* (New Jersey: Fleming H. Revell, 1976).

[16]Francis Schaeffer, *A Christian Manifesto*, p. 13.

[17]Francis Schaeffer, *ibid.*

[18]See Francis Schaeffer, *Pollution and the Death of Man: The Christian View of Ecology* (London: Hodder, 1970).

[19]Francis Schaeffer and C. Everett Koop, *Whatever Happened to the Human Race?* (New Jersey: Fleming H. Revell, 1979, and London: Marshall, Morgan and Scott, 1980).

[20]*Ibid.*, p. 153.

[21]Cited by John Zens, ' "Christian Consensus" or Christian Counter-Culture? *A Christian Manifesto* Examined', *Searching Together*, Vol. 11, No. 4, 1982, p. 41.

[22]Conrad Brunk, cited by John Zens, *ibid.*

[23]I. Hexham, 'Civil Religion', in *New Dictionary of Theology*, p. 148.

[24]See, for example, Andrew Kirk's testimony at the end of Francis Schaeffer's *The God Who is There*, pp. 171–176.

Chapter 6: Lausanne – congress, covenant, movement

[1]D. W. Bebbington, *Evangelicalism in Modern Britain* (London: Unwin Hyman, 1989), p. 266.

[2]Interview with Tom Houston, 1 December 1992.

[3]Peter Beyerhaus, cited by Valdir Steuernagel, 'Social Responsibility within the Lausanne Movement', DTh Dissertation, Lutheran School of Theology, Chicago, 1988, p. 135.

[4]The International Congress on World Evangelization met 16–25 July 1974 at the Palais de Beaulieu in Lausanne, Switzerland. The 2,473 participants from 150 countries met – together with 570 observers and 410 reporters – under the title Let the Earth Hear His Voice. The congress papers were published in J. D. Douglas (ed.), *Let the Earth Hear His Voice* (Minneapolis: World Wide Publications, 1975). Concrete planning for the Congress began on 2 December 1971, when Billy Graham met with 16 international leaders at White Sulphur Springs, West Virginia.

[5]Cited by William Martin, *The Billy Graham Story* (London: Hutchinson, 1991), p. 439 and by René Padilla, 'How Evangelicals Endorsed Social Responsibility', *Transformation*, Vol. 2, No. 3, 1985, p. 32, n. 20.

[6]See, for example, Peter Gill, *A Year in the Death of Africa* (London: Paladin/ Collins, 1986), pp. 4–5 and Graham Hancock, *Ethiopia: The Challenge of Hunger* (London: Gollancz, 1985), p. 15.

[7]John Stott, 'The Biblical Basis of Evangelism' in J. D. Douglas (ed.), *Let the Earth Hear His Voice*, p. 65.

[8]Donald E. Hoke, 'Lausanne May be a Bomb', *Christianity Today*, Vol. 18, No. 12, March 1974.

[9]Since there was a Christian presence in nearly every *country* in the world it was

possible to think that the age of foreign mission was ending. Donald McGavran and Ralph Winter, however, from Fuller Seminary School of World Mission, formed after the Berlin Congress, drew attention to the fact that many *people groups* were still unreached. The Congress's steering committee commissioned World Vision and the Fuller School of World Mission to compile a handbook of unreached people. This showed that two billion people were without significant Christian witness. A follow-up book by Edward R. Dayton and David A. Fraser, *Planning Strategies for World Evangelization* (Grand Rapids: Eerdmans, 1980), made it clear, to Tom Houston at least, 'that you couldn't follow through that strategy for unreached people without getting into serious social analysis and social concern' (interview, 1 December 1992).

[10]See Athol Gill, 'Christian Social Responsibility', in C. René Padilla (ed.), *The New Face of Evangelicalism: An International Symposium on the Lausanne Covenant* (London: Hodder, 1975; Downers Grove, IL.: IVP, 1976), p. 89.

[11]Harold Lindsell, 'Lausanne '74: An Appraisal', *Christianity Today*, Vol. 18, No. 24, September 1974, p. 22.

[12]An expanded version of John Stott's Lausanne addresses, delivered as the 1975 Chavasse Lectures, Wycliffe Hall, Oxford, is included in John Stott, *Christian Mission in the Modern World* (Eastbourne: Kingsway, 1975, 1986). For Stott's comments on the place of evangelism and social action in mission see pp. 15–34, and especially p. 24.

[13]John Stott told me: 'Berlin is an embarrassment for me because I was invited to give Bible readings three days running and chose to take the great commission in its Matthean, Marcan and Lucan forms and . . . I said something to this effect: we note that the commission is the call to preach and not to engage in social work' (interview, 26 November 1992). See John Stott, 'The Great Commission', in Carl F. H. Henry and Stanley Mooneyham (eds.), *The Official Reference Volumes: One Race, One Gospel, One Task*, Vol. 1, p. 50–51.

[14]John Stott, *Christian Mission in the Modern World*, p. 23. Stott puts his shift in thinking between Berlin and Lausanne down to the Keele Congress (see chapter 1), his own reflection on the Scriptures and discussions with others. His influence on Keele is often noted; it is clear, however, that Keele also influenced his thinking (interview, 26 November 1992).

[15]*Ibid.*, p. 24.

[16]*Ibid.*, pp. 28–30.

[17]George Hoffman, 'The Social Responsibilities of Evangelization', in J. D. Douglas (ed.), *Let the Earth Hear His Voice*, pp. 698–709; Carl Henry, 'Christian Personal and Social Ethics in Relation to Racism, Poverty, War and Other Problems', *ibid.*, pp. 1163–1180; 'The Social Responsibilities of Evangelization Report', *ibid.*, pp. 710–712.

[18]John Stott, *International Review of Mission*, Vol. 64, No. 255, 1975, p. 289.

[19]Chris Sugden, 'Evangelicals and Wholistic Evangelism', Vinay Samuel and Albrecht Hauser (eds.), *Proclaiming Christ in Christ's Way* (Oxford: Regnum, 1991), p. 30.

[20]Samuel Escobar, 'Evangelism and Man's Search for Freedom, Justice and Fulfilment', in J. D. Douglas (ed.), *Let the Earth Hear His Voice*, p. 310.

[21]René Padilla, 'Evangelism and the World', in *ibid.*, pp. 116–146; also published in René Padilla, *Mission Between the Times* (Grand Rapids: Eerdmans, 1985), pp. 1–44.

[22]*Ibid.*, p. 117.

[23]Samuel Escobar, 'Evangelism and Man's Search for Freedom, Justice and Fulfilment', in *ibid.*, pp. 303–326; also published in G. H. Anderson and T. F. Stransky (eds.), *Mission Trends: Third World Theologies* (New York: Paulist Press, and Grand Rapids: Eerdmans, 1976), pp. 104–110.

[24]*Ibid.*, p. 310.

[25]*Ibid.*, p. 324.

[26]*Decision*, November 1971.

[27]René Padilla, *Mission Between the Times*, p. 37.

[28]*Ibid.*, p. 40.

[29]Although they were controversial in what they said, Padilla and Escobar were the most requested speakers to address the regional follow-up conferences after Lausanne (see Valdir Steuernagel, 'Social Responsibility within the Lausanne Movement', pp. 143–144).

[30]Interview with John Stott, 26 November 1992.

[31]See chapter 4.

[32]Samuel Escobar, 'The Return of Christ', in C. René Padilla (ed.), *The New Face of Evangelicalism*, p. 257.

[33]René Padilla, 'Spiritual Conflict', in *ibid.*, p. 207.

[34]Valdir Steuernagel suggests 'that Lausanne said what it said for a series of reasons: (1) the strong presence and participation of representatives of the Third World; (2) the openness that characterized the preparation period of the congress; (3) the ability of Billy Graham to perceive the importance, to many participants, of the social issue; (4) the posture of John Stott, who patiently incorporated suggestions and criticism but at the same time firmly maintained his own position; (5) the preceding regional congresses that had followed Berlin '66 and which dealt with the issue of social responsibility; (6) the pressure of, and the opposition to, the ecumenical movement and its process of articulating a contemporary theology of mission; (7) the evangelical development within the USA – e.g. Urbana 1970 and Chicago '73 Workshop – as well as the turmoil and the tension around Billy Graham's own former closeness to President Nixon (ICOWE took place two weeks before Nixon's resignation)' ('Social Responsibility within the Lausanne Movement', p. 169).

[35]In *Explaining the Lausanne Covenant* (Lausanne Occasional Papers, 1975), John Stott describes the drafting process. A short draft statement was drawn up on the basis of speakers' papers before the conference. This was then revised in the light of advisors' comments and then again at Lausanne itself by the drafting committee of John Stott (chairman), Hudson Armerding and Samuel Escobar with the assistance of Leighton Ford and Jim Douglas. This was distributed during the conference and a final statement written after all the conference delegates had had the opportunity to submit comments. Stott had two sleepless nights spent reading all the submissions! It was called a 'covenant' because it aimed to be a commitment as well as a declaration – something

suggested by Harold Lindsell from the earliest stages of planning. The Lausanne Covenant is printed in John Stott, *Explaining the Lausanne Covenant*; J. D. Douglas (ed.), *Let the Earth Hear His Voice*, pp. 3–9; *Christianity Today*, Vol. 18, No. 22, August 1974, pp. 22–24; *International Review of Mission*, Vol. 63, No. 252, October 1974, pp. 570–574; Arthur Johnston, *The Battle for World Evangelism* (Wheaton, IL: Tyndale House, 1978), pp. 369–378; Chris Sugden, *Radical Discipleship* (London: Marshall, Morgan and Scott, 1981), pp. 176–184; and in part in René Padilla and Chris Sugden (eds.), *Texts on Evangelical Social Ethics 1974–1983* (Bramcote, Nottingham: Grove Books, 1985), pp. 5–7.

[36]Valdir Steuernagel, 'Social Responsibility within the Lausanne Movement', p. 155.

[37]*Ibid.*

[38]From the Lausanne II press conference on evangelicals and racism, transcribed in *Transformation*, Vol. 7, No. 1, January 1990, p. 31.

[39]René Padilla, 'How Evangelicals Endorsed Social Responsibility', *Transformation*, Vol. 2, No. 3, 1985, p. 29. Likewise Chris Sugden says: 'The great thing about the Lausanne Covenant . . . was that it gave legitimacy to organizations like EFICOR as being evangelical, as saying that by being involved in social ministry we are not on a slippery slope to liberalism as defined by Western orthodox evangelicals; we are in fact centre stage, biblical and evangelical' (interview, 12 November 1992).

[40]Vinay Samuel and Chris Sugden, from the introduction to *idem* (eds.), *The Church in Response to Human Need* (Oxford: Regnum, 1987), p. ix. Likewise Tom Houston believes that while social action among evangelicals had been growing ever since 1950 when World Vision and Christian Aid were founded, it rose markedly after Lausanne (interview, 1 December 1992).

[41]*Third Way* 'aims to present biblical perspectives on a wide range of current issues. It is based on the Lausanne Covenant . . . which spells out (among other things) the Christian's responsibility to relate biblical faith to secular matters.' It was originally conceived in the offices of *Crusade* magazine (*Crusade* arose from Billy Graham's Harringay crusade) and launched in 1977 with Derek Williams as editor and John Capon as executive editor. Later in 1977 it merged with *Salt*, a quarterly broadsheet concerned to give a biblical perspective on the arts.

[42]Michael Saward, *Evangelicals on the Move* (Oxford: Mowbray, 1987), p. 64.

[43]See William Martin, *The Billy Graham Story*, pp. 453, 606–607.

[44]Martyn Eden says: 'Most people would get their Lausanne through Stott and Stott wrote Lausanne, so they don't see it as Lausanne [but] it's the same thing' (interview, 3 December 1992). Stott himself, while acknowledging that the actual documents of the major Lausanne conferences have received a disappointingly small amount of attention, suspects 'that the truth contained within them has filtered through' (interview, 26 December 1992).

Chapter 7: After Lausanne

[1]Interview with Vinay Samuel, 7 December 1992.

[2]Arthur de Moss was the founder of the Sunlife Insurance company. His brother,

Robert de Moss, worked with PIM and so PIM had plenty of financial support. When in April 1979 Arthur died while playing golf, his wife switched the trust money to Jerry Falwell just as PIM Asia, the Asian equivalent of the Latin American Theological Fraternity, was getting under way.

[3]Interview with Vinay Samuel, 7 December 1992.

[4]The Statement on Radical Discipleship is printed in J. D. Douglas (ed.), *Let the Earth Hear His Voice*, pp. 1294–1296; *International Review of Mission*, Vol. 63, No. 252, October 1974, pp. 574–576; Chris Sugden, *Radical Discipleship* (London: Marshall, Morgan and Scott, 1981), pp. 172–176; and René Padilla and Chris Sugden, *Texts on Evangelical Social Ethics 1974–1983* (Bramcote, Nottingham: Grove Books, 1985), pp. 7–11.

[5]Chris Sugden, *Social Gospel or No Gospel* (Bramcote, Nottingham: Grove Books, 1975).

[6]Interview with John Stott, 26 November 1992.

[7]René Padilla, 'How Evangelicals Endorsed Social Responsibility', *Transformation*, Vol. 2, No. 3, 1985, p. 29.

[8]See, for example, Peter Beyerhaus, cited by David Bosch, *Witness to the World* (London: Marshall, Morgan and Scott, 1980), pp. 30–31 and Arthur Johnston, *The Battle for World Evangelism* (Wheaton, IL: Tyndale House, 1978), p. 331.

[9]Chris Sugden, *Radical Discipleship* (Marshall, Morgan and Scott, 1981).

[10]On the origins of ECUM see chapter 15.

[11]Arthur P. Johnston, 'The Unanswered Prayer of Edinburgh', *Christianity Today*, Vol. 19, No. 4, pp. 10–14.

[12]Arthur Johnston, *The Battle for World Evangelism* (Wheaton, IL: Tyndale House, 1978).

[13]*Ibid.*, pp. 55, 60, 138.

[14]*Ibid.*, p. 19.

[15]*Ibid.*, p. 18.

[16]*Ibid.*, p. 329.

[17]John Stott, in his reply to Johnston's criticisms (see below), says: 'Supposing we go out exclusively to evangelize, and that under the blessing of God converts are won. Presumably they, being the "consequence" of our evangelism, are now free to become involved in social service. But then we ourselves are the consequences of other people's evangelism. Why then should we not also, on your own premise, engage in social action? I think the logic of your argument brings us closer to one another than you realize' ('The Battle for World Evangelism: An Open Response to Arthur Johnston', *Christianity Today*, 5 January 1979, p. 35).

[18]Arthur Johnston, *The Battle for World Evangelism*, pp. 302–303.

[19]*Ibid.*, p. 303.

[20]*Ibid.*, p. 331.

[21]*Ibid.*

[22]John Stott, 'The Battle for World Evangelism: An Open Response to Arthur Johnston', *Christianity Today*, 5 January 1979, pp. 34–35. See also John Stott, 'The Biblical Scope of the Christian Mission', *Christianity Today*, 4 January 1980, pp. 34–35.

[23]Peter Wagner, 'Lausanne Twelve Months Later', *Christianity Today*, Vol. 19, No. 20, 4 July 1975, p. 961.

[24]Peter Beyerhaus in his foreword to Arthur Johnston, *The Battle for World Evangelism*, p. 10.

[25]Letters deposited in the Billy Graham Archives, cited by Steuernagel, 'Social Responsibility within the Lausanne Movement', DTh Dissertation, Lutheran School of Theology, Chicago, 1988, pp. 167–168. At this time Harold Lindsell was editor of *Christianity Today*.

[26]See Andrew Kirk, *New World Coming* (Basingstoke: Marshall, Morgan and Scott, 1983), pp. 16–17. Kirk, referring to the title of Johnston's book, says: 'The battle is not so much for evangelism as for the biblical gospel. The struggle is to discover how personal evangelism, social involvement, personal integrity, growth in the knowledge of God and in Christian fellowship can all be related together as indispensable parts of a total Christian witness' (p. 16).

[27]Valdir Steuernagel, 'Social Responsibility within the Lausanne Movement', p. 78.

[28]This meeting decided on the organizational structure of the LCWE. It would be run by a General Secretary with an 11-person Executive Committee. The LCWE itself would meet annually and a consultative committee of 200 would meet every five years. In addition to this there would be regional gatherings to implement the Lausanne mandate.

[29]Interview with John Stott, 26 November 1992.

[30]See, for example, William Martin, *The Billy Graham Story* (London: Hutchinson, 1991), pp. 450–452 and Valdir Steuernagel, 'Social Responsibility within the Lausanne Movement', p. 174.

[31]Interview with John Stott, 26 November 1992.

[32]Cited in, for example, Arthur Johnston, *The Battle for World Evangelism*, pp. 343–344.

[33]*Ibid.*, p. 343.

[34]Peter Wagner, cited by Valdir Steuernagel, 'Social Responsibility within the Lausanne Movement', pp. 176–177.

[35]See William Martin, *The Billy Graham Story*, p. 452.

[36]Interview with Tom Houston, 1 December 1992.

[37]Valdir Steuernagel, 'Social Responsibility within the Lausanne Movement', p. 178.

[38]Interview with Tom Houston, 1 December 1992.

[39]Ronald Sider, *Rich Christians in an Age of Hunger* (London: Hodder, 1978). It is also summarized in the *Evangelical Review of Theology*, Vol. 4, No. 1, April 1980, pp. 70–83.

[40]*Ibid.*, p. 76.

[41]Donald Hay, *Economics Today: A Christian Critique* (Leicester: Apollos, 1989), p. 327, n. 1.

[42]See Tim Stafford, 'Ron Sider's Unsettling Crusade', *Christianity Today*, Vol. 36, No. 5, April 1992, p. 18.

[43]Brian Griffiths, *Morality and the Market Place* (London: Hodder, 1982), chapter 5. See also Michael Alison, 'World Poverty and Christian Responsibility',

Christian Graduate (now *Christian Arena*), December 1979. For the origins of the London Institute for Contemporary Christianity see chapter 8.

[44]David Watson, from the foreword to Ron Sider, *Rich Christians in an Age of Hunger*, p. 12.

Chapter 8: Theological developments

[1]See John Stott, *Issues Facing Christians Today* (Basingstoke: Marshall, Morgan and Scott, 1984), p. xii.

[2]Harry Blamires, *The Christian Mind* (London: SPCK, 1963).

[3]John Stott, *Your Mind Matters* (London: IVP, 1972). See also chapter 2 of John Stott, *Issues Facing Christians Today*, pp. 29–44.

[4]Sir Norman Anderson, *Issues of Life and Death* (London: Hodder, 1976).

[5]José Míguez Bonino, *Christians and Marxists: The Mutual Challenge to Revolution* (London: Hodder, 1975).

[6]John Stott, *Issues Facing Christians Today* (Basingstoke: Marshall, Morgan and Scott, 1984, revised and updated, 1990); John Stott, *The Contemporary Christian* (Leicester: IVP, 1992). See also Martyn Eden and David Wells (eds.), *The Gospel in the Modern World: A Tribute to John Stott* (Leicester and Downers Grove, IL: IVP, 1991).

[7]Interview with John Stott, 26 November 1992.

[8]Interview with Martyn Eden, 3 December 1992.

[9]Ronald Sider and John Stott, *Evangelism, Salvation and Social Justice* (Bramcote, Nottingham: Grove Books, 1977). Sider's article was published separately in the *International Review of Mission*, Vol. 64, No. 255, 1975, pp. 251–267 and the *Evangelical Review of Theology*, Vol. 2, No. 1, April 1978, pp. 70–88.

[10]*Ibid.*, p. 17.

[11]*Ibid.*, p. 24.

[12]*Ibid.*, p. 21.

[13]*Ibid.*, p. 9.

[14]Vinay Samuel and Chris Sugden employed it at both the Consultation on the Relationship between Evangelism and Social Responsibility (Grand Rapids '82) and at the Consultation on the Church in Response to Human Need (Wheaton '83). At the former they cite Ron Sider, but at Wheaton they cited David Bosch instead (*Witness to the World* [London: Marshall, Morgan and Scott, 1980], p. 209) – presumably because Sider repudiated it at Grand Rapids. See Vinay Samuel and Chris Sugden, 'Evangelism and Social Responsibility – A Biblical Study in Priorities', in Bruce Nicholls (ed.), *In Word and Deed* (Exeter: Paternoster, 1985), p. 210 and 'God's Intention for the World', in Vinay Samuel and Chris Sugden (eds.), *The Church in Response to Human Need* (Oxford: Regnum, 1987), p. 154.

[15]Ronald Sider and James Parker, 'How Broad is Salvation in Scripture?', in Bruce Nicholls (ed.), *In Word and Deed*, p. 104 and especially n. 32.

[16]Ronald Sider and John Stott, *Evangelism, Salvation and Social Justice*, p. 23.

[17]*Ibid.*; a similar phrase is used in *The Grand Rapids Report: Evangelism and Social Responsibility*, which Stott drafted (Exeter: Paternoster, 1980), p. 34.

[18]For a discussion of the way social action can be hindered by cultural assumptions see David Bosch, 'In Search of a New Evangelical Understanding', in Bruce Nicholls (ed.), *In Word and Deed*, pp. 63–83.

[19]Section 10 of the Lausanne Covenant: 'Evangelism and Culture'. In his foreword to the conference papers of the Willowbank Consultation, John Stott says: 'Only, I suspect, as a result of the Lausanne Congress on World Evangelization in 1974 has the evangelical community as a whole come to acknowledge the central importance of culture for the effective communication of the gospel.' He singles out as particularly influential Padilla's contribution to the Lausanne Congress and Section 10 of the Lausanne Covenant.

[20]The Consultation on Gospel and Culture was held 6–13 January 1978 at Willowbank, Bermuda. There were 33 participants from the six continents. The consultation was held under the auspices of the Theology and Education Group (LTEG) of the LCWE. The conference papers were published in John Stott and Robert Coote (eds.), *Down to Earth* (London: Hodder, 1980).

[21]Stephen Neill, 'Religion and Culture – An Historical Perspective', in *Down to Earth*, p. 6.

[22]The Willowbank Report, *Down to Earth*, p. 339.

[23]Over 100 participants gathered for five days in September 1978 for the National Evangelical Conference on Social Ethics. It was held at the High Leigh Conference Centre at Hoddesdon under the chairmanship of John Stott.

[24]David F. Wright (ed.), *Essays in Evangelical Social Ethics* (Exeter: Paternoster, 1979).

[25]Forty-one theologians and development workers met for the Consultation on the Theology of Development. It was held 10–14 March 1980 at the High Leigh Conference Centre, Hoddesdon, England, under the auspices of the Unit on Ethics and Society of the Theological Commission of the WEF. The conference papers are published in Ronald Sider (ed.), *Evangelicals and Development* (Exeter: Paternoster, 1981).

[26]Vinay Samuel and Chris Sugden, 'Toward a Theology of Social Change', in *ibid.*, pp. 45–68.

[27]The conference as a whole was sponsored by WEF and entitled 'I Will Build My Church'. The first two 'tracks', as they were called, were 'The Church in its Local Setting' and 'The Church in New Frontiers of Missions'. It was the third track, 'The Church in Response to Human Need', however, which, according to William Cook, was 'the most creative' ('Reflections on Wheaton '83', *Evangelical Review of Theology*, Vol. 9, No. 1, 1985, p. 29). The conference organizers made a deliberate decision to limit the size of the consultation to allow for true dialogue and to keep the costs down. Altogether 320 people took part, about 100 of whom were involved in the third track which was chaired by Vinay Samuel. The three tracks took place simultaneously 20 June–1 July 1983, although, apart from producing a collective letter to the churches, they effectively operated as separate conferences. The conference papers of the third track were published in Vinay Samuel and Chris Sugden (eds.), *The Church in Response to Human Need* (Oxford: Regnum, 1987).

[28]In addition to the collective letter to the churches the third track also pro-

duced a fuller statement: 'Transformation: The Church in Response to Human Need'. The drafting committee was René Padilla (chairman), Arthur Williamson, Andrew Kirk, Tito Paredes, Paul Schrotenboer, David Bosch and Max Chigwida. It was published in *Transformation*, Vol. 1, No. 1 (1984); in Vinay Samuel and Chris Sugden (eds.), *The Church in Response to Human Need*, pp. 254–265; and in *Transformation: The Church in Response to Human Need* (Bramcote, Nottingham: Grove Books, 1986).

[29]*Transformation* has included articles from both perspectives. Greg Bahnsen, 'Christ and the Role of Civil Government: The Theonomic Perspective', *Transformation*, in two parts, Part I, Vol. 5, No. 2, April 1988, pp. 24–31 and Part II, Vol. 5, No. 3, July 1988, pp. 24–28; and Norman L. Geisler, 'Dispensationalism and Ethics', *Transformation*, Vol. 6, No. 1, January 1989, pp. 7–14. On theonomism see also, for example, Rousas Rushdoony, *The Institutes of Biblical Law* (Philadelphia: Presbyterian and Reformed, 1973) and Greg Bahnsen, *Theonomy in Christian Ethics* (New Jersey: Craig Press, 1979).

[30]Christopher J. H. Wright, 'Biblical Ethics: A Survey of the Last Decade', *Themelios*, Vol. 18, No. 2, January 1993, p. 17.

[31]For a critique of theonomism see, for example, William S. Barker and W. Robert Godfrey (eds.), *Theonomy: A Reformed Critique* (Grand Rapids: Academie, 1990). Since it is a tendency of dispensationalism to say that we should only preach to the world and not try to transform it since the transformation of society belongs to a future dispensation, it has been widely criticized as evangelicals have endorsed social action. See, for example, Peter Kusmic, 'History and Eschatology: Evangelical Views', in Bruce Nicholls (ed.), *In Word and Deed* (Exeter: Paternoster, 1985), pp. 109–134.

[32]Christopher J. H. Wright, 'The Use of the Bible in Social Ethics', *Transformation*, Vol. 1, No. 1, January 1984, pp. 11–20. Also published as Christopher J. H. Wright, *The Use of the Bible in Social Ethics* (Bramcote, Nottingham: Grove Books, 1983). See also *idem*, 'The Ethical Relevance of Israel as a Society', *Transformation*, Vol. 1, No. 4, October 1984, pp. 11–21 and *idem*, 'The People of God and the State in the Old Testament', *Themelios*, Vol. 16, No. 1, 1990, pp. 4–10.

[33]Christopher J. H. Wright, *Living as the People of God: The Relevance of Old Testament Ethics* (Leicester: IVP, 1983); American edition: *An Eye for an Eye: The Place of Old Testament Ethics Today* (Downers Grove, IL: IVP, 1983).

[34]Stephen Charles Mott, 'The Use of the Bible in Social Ethics: The Use of the New Testament', *Transformation*, Vol. 1, No. 2, April 1984, pp. 21–26 and Vol. 1, No. 3, July 1984, pp. 19–26. Republished as Stephen Mott, *Jesus and Social Ethics* (Bramcote, Nottingham: Grove Books, 1984). See also Stephen Mott, 'The Contribution of the Bible to Economic Thought', *Transformation*, Vol. 4, No. 2, April 1987, pp. 25–34.

[35]Christopher J. H. Wright, 'Biblical Ethics', p. 15.

[36]See, for example, Michael Schluter and Roy Clements, 'Jubilee Institutional Norms: A Middle Way Between Creation Ethics and Kingdom Ethics as a Basis for Christian Political Action', *Evangelical Quarterly*, Vol. 62, No. 1, 1990, pp. 37–62.

[37]Michael Schluter and David Lee, *The R Factor* (London: Hodder, 1993).

Chapter 9: Living more simply and trading more fairly

[1]See William Martin, *The Billy Graham Story* (London: Hutchinson, 1991), pp. 449–450.

[2]Ronald Sider, *Rich Christians in an Age of Hunger* (London: Hodder, 1978), pp. 157–159. See also Ron Sider (ed.), *Living More Simply: Biblical Principles and Practical Models* (London: Hodder, 1980); Richard Foster, *Freedom of Simplicity* (London: Triangle, 1981); Doris Longacre (ed.), *Living More with Less* (London: Hodder, 1980) and Doris Longacre (ed.), *The More with Less Cookbook* (Tring: Lion, 1976) – the last two were commissioned by the Mennonite Central Committee and contain hundreds of practical suggestions, recipes and testimonies. See also Brian Hathaway's excellent chapter on 'Money, Materialism and the Kingdom of God', in *Beyond Renewal: The Kingdom of God* (Milton Keynes: Word Books, 1990), pp. 127–155.

[3]Oliver Barclay, for example, wrote (as A. N. Triton) in 1970: 'We need to combine a delight in God's good creation with frugality for the sake of others and for the sake of greater things than material goods.' *Whose World?* (London: IVP, 1970).

[4]Ronald Sider, *Rich Christians in an Age of Hunger*, p. 150.

[5]Cited by Ronald Sider in the introduction to *Living More Simply: Biblical Principles and Practical Models*, the papers of the US Consultation on Simple Lifestyle (April 1979), p. 11.

[6]Eighty-five participants from 27 countries gathered for the Consultation on Simple Lifestyle. It was held at Hoddesdon, England, 17–21 March 1980. The conference papers and the resulting statement are printed in Ronald Sider (ed.), *Lifestyle in the Eighties: An Evangelical Commitment to Simple Lifestyle* (Exeter: Paternoster, 1982).

[7]A fact acknowledged by John Stott, Leighton Ford and René Padilla, cited by Valdir Steuernagel, 'Social Responsibility within the Lausanne Movement', DTh Dissertation, Lutheran School of Theology, Chicago, 1988, p. 184.

[8]See John Stott and Ronald Sider in the preface to Ronald Sider (ed.), *Lifestyle in the Eighties*, p. 10.

[9]Stott defended the Statement in a letter to Leighton Ford (who was critical of it), cited by Valdir Steuernagel, 'Social Responsibility within the Lausanne Movement', pp. 184–185. Stott's comments on the lack of publicity given to the statement are from an interview with me, 26 November 1992.

[10]Ronald Sider (ed.), *Lifestyle in the Eighties*, pp. 167–173.

[11]*Ibid.*, pp. 203–209.

[12]*Ibid.*, pp. 195–202.

[13]*Ibid.*, pp. 210–218.

[14]David Watson, from the foreword to Ronald Sider, *Rich Christians in an Age of Hunger*, pp. 9–10.

[15]David Watson, 'Extended Households', in Ronald Sider (ed.), *Lifestyle in the Eighties*, pp. 183–187. See also David Watson, *You Are My God* (London: Hodder, 1983), pp. 114–126; and Teddy Saunders and Hugh Sansom, *David Watson: A Biography* (London: Hodder, 1992), pp. 151–160. David Watson's

thinking on this subject is also reflected in his books, *I Believe in the Church: The Revolutionary Potential of the Family of God* (London: Hodder, 1978) and *Discipleship* (London: Hodder, 1981).

[16]It would be wrong to judge any form of Christian community living which does not last as having 'failed'. Many have achieved much before being disbanded in order to adapt to new circumstances and ministries. Others, for example the Sojourners community in Washington, continue to flourish.

[17]David Watson, 'Extended Households', in Ronald Sider (ed.), *Lifestyle in the Eighties*, p. 185.

[18]Ronald Sider (ed.), *Living More Simply*, pp. 125–130.

[19]Vinay Samuel and Chris Sugden, 'A Just and Responsible Lifestyle: An Old Testament Perspective', in Ronald Sider (ed.), *Lifestyle in the Eighties*, pp. 42–53.

[20]See Arthur Simon, 'Bread for the World', *Transformation*, Vol. 1, No. 4, 1984, pp. 22–24.

[21]Figures and examples from the Christian Aid *Trade for Change* pack.

[22]Richard Adams, *Who Profits?* (Oxford: Lion, 1989), p. 74.

[23]*Ibid.*, p. 19.

[24]*Ibid.*, p. 38.

[25]*Ibid.*, p. 64.

[26]Stephen Rand, personal letter to the author, March 1993.

[27]Joe Remenyi, *Where Credit is Due: Income-Generating Programmes for the Poor in Developing Countries* (London: Intermediate Technology Publications, 1991); summarized in Joe Remenyi, 'Income Generation Programmes for Poverty Alleviation', *Transformation*, Vol. 7, No. 2, April 1990, pp. 12–13.

[28]Joe Remenyi, 'Income Generation', p. 12.

[29]See Vishal Mangalwadi, *Truth and Social Reform* (London: Spire, 1989), pp. 129–136, where Mangalwadi outlines a scheme in which readers can invest money, allowing it to be used to provide small loans for the poor.

[30]Norm Ewert, 'The Role of Business Enterprise in Christian Mission', *Transformation*, Vol. 9, No. 1, January 1992, pp. 7–14.

[31]The first Oxford Conference on Christian Faith and Economics was sponsored by the journal *Transformation*, the Oxford Centre for Mission Studies and Partnership in Mission. Thirty-six participants from around the world gathered on 6–9 January 1987. The findings report is published in *Transformation*, Vol. 4, No. 2, April 1987, pp. 22–24. The conference papers were published in a special double issue of *Transformation*, Vol. 4, Nos. 3 and 4, June/October 1987. In addition to the special study on small income-generation projects referred to above the conference instituted a process of study involving 17 regional groups.

[32]The second Oxford Conference on Christian Faith and Economics was held on 4–9 January 1990, and involved over 100 participants. Some of the papers were published in *Transformation*, Vol. 7, No. 2, April 1990.

[33]The Oxford Declaration on Faith and Economics is published with a list of signatories in *Transformation*, Vol 7, no. 2, April 1990, pp. 1–9. The document is divided into four main sections: A. Stewardship of Creation; B. Work and Leisure; C. Poverty and Justice; D. Freedom, Government and Economics.

[34]*Ibid.*, p. 5.

Chapter 10: Stirring voices from the Third World

[1] René Padilla, 'How Evangelicals Endorsed Social Responsibility', *Transformation*, Vol. 2, No. 3, 1985, p. 29. Paul Little in his post-Congress Program Director's Report, October 1974, likewise says: 'Half of the speakers, both plenary and small group, were from the Third World and this had a great impact' (cited by Valdir Steuernagel, 'Social Responsibility within the Lausanne Movement', DTh Dissertation, Lutheran School of Theology, Chicago, 1988, p. 139.

[2] René Padilla, 'How Evangelicals Endorsed Social Responsibility', p. 31.

[3] Interview with John Stott, 26 November 1992.

[4] Interview with Tom Houston, 1 December 1992.

[5] Michael Paget-Wilkes, *Poverty, Revolution and the Church* (Exeter: Paternoster, 1981).

[6] A total of 266 people met for the Second Latin American Congress on Evangelization (CLADE II), 31 October–7 November in Lima, Peru. (CLADE I was one of the regional conferences organized as a follow-up to the Berlin Congress.) The resultant *Lima Letter* is translated and reprinted in René Padilla and Chris Sugden, *Texts on Evangelical Social Ethics 1974–1983* (Bramcote, Nottingham: Grove Books, 1985), pp. 15–17. Social issues were not the only focus of the congress. The full involvement of the Pentecostals led to reflection on the relationship of Word and Spirit in evangelization. Another issue was relationships with the Roman Catholic Church, especially those sections of the Catholic Church experiencing charismatic renewal.

[7] CLADE III was convened by the Latin American Theological Fraternity and held on 24 August–4 September 1992, in Quito, Equador. It was attended by 1,080 people from 26 countries.

[8] Interview with Vinay Samuel, 7 December 1992.

[9] See, for example, 'Poorest of the Poor: an Interview with Chris Wigglesworth', *Third Way*, Vol. 2, No. 3, February 1978, pp. 3–5.

[10] The All India Conference on Evangelical Social Action was held on 2–5 October in Madras. The Madras Declaration was printed in the *All India Magazine*, Evangelical Fellowship of India, Delhi, November 1979; as an appendix to Chris Sugden, *Radical Discipleship* (London: Marshall, Morgan and Scott, 1981), pp. 184–189; and in René Padilla and Chris Sugden, *Texts on Evangelical Social Ethics*, pp. 11–15.

[11] Interview with Vinay Samuel, 7 December 1992.

[12] COWE involved 650 participants and 225 observers from 87 countries. They met in Pattaya, 17–27 June 1980, under the title How Shall They Hear?

[13] René Padilla, 'How Evangelicals Endorsed Social Responsibility', p. 30.

[14] Early in the planning stages a decision was made to exclude social issues, despite a complaint from John Stott. Valdir Steuernagel, 'Social Responsibility within the Lausanne Movement', p. 188.

[15] David Bosch and Peter Williams (editor of *The Churchman*) respectively, cited by Padilla, 'How Evangelicals Endorsed Social Responsibility'. Valdir Steuernagel says that in contrast to the openness of Lausanne, COWE had 'decided

beforehand what the task was and how to face it'. 'It was in this sense a pre-wrapped package that had to be accepted in its entirety.' 'Social Responsibility within the Lausanne Movement', pp. 195–196.

[16]See, for example, Kwame Bediako, 'World Evangelization, Institutional Evangelicalism and the Future of the Christian World Mission', in Vinay Samuel and Albrecht Hauser (eds.), *Proclaiming Christ in Christ's Way* (Oxford: Regnum, 1989), pp. 52–68. See also Orlando Costas' evaluation and critique of the church growth movement in *The Church and Its Mission* (Wheaton, IL: Tyndale, 1974), pp. 87–149. Costas himself argues for a holistic view of church growth; see, for example, pp. 310–311.

[17]*The Pasadena Consultation – Homogeneous Unit Principle*, Lausanne Occasional Papers No. 1 (Charlotte, NC: LCWE, 1978).

[18]This was specifically denied when a delegation of the drafters of the Statement of Concerns were invited to meet with the LCWE to elaborate their criticisms. See John Stott, 'Saving Souls and Serving Bread', *Christianity Today*, Vol. 26, No. 19, 7 November 1980, p. 1352.

[19]The Statement of Concerns on the Future of the LCWE is reprinted in Andrew Kirk, *New World Coming: A Fresh Look at the Gospel for Today* (Basingstoke: Marshall, Morgan and Scott, 1983), pp. 148–151; and René Padilla and Chris Sugden, *Texts on Evangelical Social Ethics*, pp. 22–25.

[20]The Statement of Concerns was accompanied with a covering letter signed by those who drew up the final draft: Orlando Costas, Bishop David Gitari, C. L. Hilliard, Andrew Kirk, Peter Kuzmic, Vinay Samuel and Ronald Sider.

[21]Tom Houston does not believe their criticisms were fair. 'My own personal feeling', he says, 'was that they were tilting at a windmill rather than really dealing with an issue that was substantial . . . I felt that they were posturing too much about things that from my point of view were already settled' (interview, 1 December 1992).

[22]The recommendations in full were:

1. That the LCWE reaffirm its commitment to all aspects of the Lausanne Covenant, and in particular provide new leadership to help evangelicals to implement its call to social responsibility as well as evangelism.

2. That the LCWE encourage and promote the formation of study groups at all levels, to deal with social, political and economic issues, and provide specific guidance on how evangelicals can effectively apply the Lausanne Covenant's affirmation of 'God's concern for justice and reconciliation throughout human society and liberation of men from every kind of oppression' (a reference to Paragraph 5 of the Lausanne Covenant).

3. That within the next three years the LCWE convene a World Congress on Social Responsibility and its implications for evangelization.

4. That the LCWE give guidelines on how evangelicals who support oppression and discrimination (thus hindering evangelism) can be reached by the gospel and challenged to repent and uphold biblical truth; and how to give encouragement and support to Christians of all races in situations of oppression as they are seeking to be faithful to the gospel at a great risk.

In responding the LCWE pointed out that the Thailand Statement had itself endorsed the Lausanne Covenant. Regarding the second and third recommendations it pointed to the plans for the Grand Rapids consultation (see chapter 12). This, however, was much smaller (about 50 participants) than what the framers of the Statement of Concerns envisaged. They had in mind a world congress on a par with COWE (with over 800 participants). Finally the LCWE declined to give the guidelines asked for in the fourth recommendation. Instead they referred the matter to the LTEG. See Orlando Costas, 'Proclaiming Christ in the Two Thirds World', in Vinay Samuel and Chris Sugden (eds.), *Sharing Jesus in the Two Thirds World* (Bangalore: PIM-Asia, 1983), pp. 1–15, especially p. 5, and Andrew Kirk, *New World Coming*, p. 15.

[23]Orlando Costas, 'Proclaiming Christ in the Two Thirds World', p. 6.

[24]See Chris Sugden, 'Evangelicals and Wholistic Evangelism', in Vinay Samuel and Albrecht Hauser (eds.), *Proclaiming Christ in Christ's Way* (Oxford: Regnum, 1989), p. 38. These concerns, it should be said, were not shared by all from the Third World. At Pattaya a group of Latin Americans created the Confraternity of Latin American Evangelicals (CONELA) which was officially launched in Panamá in 1982. Although conceived to offer an alternative forum to the ecumenical Latin American Council of Churches (CLAI) it also opposed the emphases of the LATF (see Valdir Steuernagel, 'Social Responsibility within the Lausanne Movement', p. 226).

[25]Chris Sugden, 'A Critical and Comparative Study of the Practice and Theology of Christian Social Witness in Indonesia and India between 1974 and 1983', PhD Thesis, Westminster College, Oxford, 1988, pp. 307–308.

[26]Altogether 25 people gathered, 22–25 March 1982. The conference papers are published in Vinay Samuel and Chris Sugden (eds.), *Sharing Jesus in the Two Thirds World*.

[27]Kwame Bediako, 'World Evangelization, Institutional Evangelicalism and the Future of the Christian World Mission', in Vinay Samuel and Albrecht Hauser (eds.), *Proclaiming Christ in Christ's Way*, pp. 52–68. See also, for example, Bryant L. Myers, 'A Funny Thing Happened on the Way to Evangelical-Ecumenical Co-operation', *International Review of Mission*, Vol. 81, No. 323, July 1992, pp. 397–407.

[28]John Stott, 'Seeking Theological Agreement', *Transformation*, Vol. 1, No. 1, 1984, p. 21.

[29]The conference papers and the Stuttgart Statement on Evangelism are printed in Vinay Samuel and Albrecht Hauser (eds.), *Proclaiming Christ in Christ's Way*.

[30]Namely Kwame Bediako, David Gitari, Michael Nazir-Ali, René Padilla, Vinay Samuel, Ron Sider and Chris Sugden.

[31]David Bosch, 'In Search of a New Evangelical Understanding', in Bruce Nicholls (ed.), *In Word and Deed* (Exeter: Paternoster, 1985), p. 67.

[32]John Stott, 'A Note about the Suttgart Statement on Evangelism', in Vinay Samuel and Albrecht Hauser (eds.), *Proclaiming Christ in Christ's Way*, p. 208.

Chapter 11: Converted to wholeness

[1]See David Bosch, *Mission to the World* (London: Marshall, Morgan and Scott, 1980), p. 204.

[2]See Valdir Steuernagel, 'Social Responsibility within the Lausanne Movement', DTh Dissertation, Lutheran School of Theology, Chicago, 1988, p. 201. Steuernagel gives a very full description of the tensions within the Lausanne movement in the run-up to the Grand Rapids Consultation.

[3]The Consultation on the Relationship between Evangelism and Social Responsibility (CRESR) was held in Grand Rapids, 19–25 June 1982, with 50 participants from 27 countries. John Stott chaired the drafting committee of the final report. In addition to Stott the drafting committee consisted of Gottfried Osei-Mensah, Bong Rin Ro, David Wells and Samuel Olson. The Grand Rapids Report was entitled *Evangelism and Social Responsbility: An Evangelical Commitment* (Exeter: Paternoster, 1982). The conference papers were published in Bruce Nicholls (ed.), *In Word and Deed* (Exeter: Paternoster, 1985).

[4]Interview with John Stott, 26 November 1992, and John Stott, 'Seeking Theological Agreement', *Transformation*, Vol. 1, No. 1, 1984, p. 22. 'Some of the papers', he explains, 'were really shrill to the point of rudeness and people were posturing' (interview, 26 November 1992).

[5]Tom Houston told me: 'the chairmanship of Gottfried Osei-Mensah was outstanding . . . it was masterly chairmanship that got them through' (interview, 1 December 1992).

[6]Bruce Nicholls (ed.), *In Word and Deed*, p. 7.

[7]John Stott, 'Seeking Theological Agreement' p. 22. Initially, explains John Stott, there was sharp disagreement and apparently no desire for a meeting of minds. After a couple of days, however, people 'get tired of shouting' and genuine listening begins. Then they begin listening to the concerns that lie behind what others say, and discover that they too want to safeguard those concerns (interview, 26 November 1992).

[8]See the Grand Rapids Report, *Evangelism and Social Responsibility*, pp. 21–24.

[9]*Ibid.*, p. 24.

[10]*Ibid.*

[11]*Ibid.*, p. 25.

[12]*Ibid.*

[13]*Ibid.*, p. 46.

[14]*Ibid.*, p. 24.

[15]*Ibid.*, p. 44.

[16]*Ibid.*, p. 24.

[17]*Ibid.*

[18]It is for this reason that Andrew Kirk, who welcomes the report as far as it goes, remains critical of it. 'It is regrettable, but given the present climate of opinion probably inevitable,' he says, 'that *The Grand Rapids Report* did not quite have sufficient courage to accept the full biblical position that evangelism – 'spreading the good news' – includes what the Report calls social responsibility, which is nothing else but the visual communication ('a demonstration and

commendation of the gospel') of what the Scriptures have to say about Jesus and the kingdom' (*New World Coming*, Basingstoke: Marshall, Morgan and Scott, 1983, p. 105). Given the constraints placed upon it by the LCWE, however, it was indeed inevitable that the Grand Rapids Consultation would not go as far as Kirk would have liked.

[19]René Padilla, 'How Evangelicals Endorsed Social Responsibility', *Transformation*, Vol. 2, No. 3, 1985, p. 30.

[20]Valdir Steuernagel, 'Social Responsibility within the Lausanne Movement', pp. 255–259, especially p. 256.

[21]See, for example, James W. Gustafson, *The Integration of Development and Evangelism*, Interchurch Relief and Development Alliance, Occasional Paper No. 2.

[22]The Wheaton conference papers and statement (see especially paragraphs 6–13) are published in Vinay Samuel and Chris Sugden (eds.), *The Church in Response to Human Need* (Oxford: Regnum, and Grand Rapids, MI: Eerdmans, 1987).

[23]Vinay Samuel and Chris Sugden, 'Evangelism and Social Responsibility: A Biblical Study on Priorities', in Bruce Nicholls (ed.), *In Word and Deed*, p. 211.

[24]'Converted to Wholeness' is printed in C. René Padilla, 'How Evangelicals Endorsed Social Responsibility' (Bramcote, Nottingham: Grove Ethical Booklets, 1985), pp. 20–22.

[25]Interview with John Stott, 26 November 1992.

[26]A fact evidenced by their insistence on being included in the MARC Europe *UK Christian Handbook* under 'Missionary Organisations' rather than under the category of 'Relief and Development Organisations'.

[27]The Villars Statement on Relief and Development is included in Marvin Olasky, Herbert Schlossberg, Pierre Berthoud and Clark H. Pinnock, *Freedom, Justice and Hope: Towards a Strategy for the Poor and the Oppressed* (Westchester, IL: Crossway Books, 1988), pp. 141–146.

[28]Cited by Alan Gibson, '"World Evangelical Issues", A Report on the 9th General Assembly of the WEF in Manila from the 21st to 26th June, 1992', *Foundations*, No. 29, Autumn 1992, p. 6.

[29]See, for example, 'Poorest of the Poor: an interview with Chris Wigglesworth', *Third Way*, Vol. 2, No. 3, 9 February 1978, pp. 3–5.

Chapter 12: Responding to the media

[1]Greg Philo and Robert Lamb, *Television and the Ethiopian Famine: From Buerk to Band Aid*, a report prepared for UNESCO on behalf of the Canadian Film Institute by the Glasgow University Media Group and the Television Trust for the Environment, p. 18. Philo and Lamb cite the *Economist* of November 1984: 'What put Ethiopia in the front page in October? Most cynically, competition between two television channels. This is the second time this year that a BBC news team has scooped a long-planned ITV programme on the famine (p.16).'

[2]Bob Geldof, *Is That It?* (Harmondsworth: Penguin, 1986), p. 270.

[3]Cited by Peter Gill, *A Year in the Death of Africa* (London: Paladin, 1986), p. 22.

For the story behind the Ethiopian famine and analysis of its causes and the reasons for the poor response to it see *ibid.*, and Graham Hancock, *Ethiopia: The Challenge of Hunger* (London: Gollancz, 1985).

[4]Peter Gill, *A Year in the Death of Africa*, p. 91.

[5]Mohamed Amin worked for Visnews and therefore the pictures belonged to them. The BBC showed them with Michael Buerk's report in order to pre-empt ITV's documentary, *Bitter Harvest*. When Visnews offered the pictures to NBC in the United States and Eurovision they both rejected them. Joe Angotti, head of NBC's London bureau, put a lot of pressure on NBC to take the pictures and eventually sent them over by satellite. NBC re-edited them and put them out as the last item of their evening news. Even so, the effect in America was electrifying. The next day Eurovision took the pictures as well. See Greg Philo and Robert Lamb, *Television and the Ethiopian Famine*, p. 9.

[6]Cited in *ibid.*, p. 14. As Philo and Lamb go on to point out, however, this does not in itself justify the lack of coverage. When news reports want to stress the potential impact of strikes they often use library footage of previous disputes to show the likely consequences. It would be equally possible to use library footage of previous famines to highlight the dangers of what might happen.

[7]Russell Johnston, 22 November 1984, cited in *ibid.*, p. 6.

[8]On 23 October, the day Buerk's report was shown, the BBC offered the *Sun* a full set of pictures. Its response: 'We're actually not interested in famine.' Five days later it ran with the two-inch headline: 'RACE TO SAVE THE BABIES'. Cited in *ibid.*, p. 29.

[9]Cited in *ibid.*, p. 7.

[10]Paddy Coulter, 'The Impact of Television Coverage of International Issues: The Third World', James Firebrace (ed.), *Losing the Picture: The Future for Television's Coverage of Global Issues*, a report for the Third World and Environmental Broadcasting Project (1990), p. 17.

[11]These figures, which vary according to different reports, are according to *The Times* of Monday, 15 July 1985. £2m and £5.5m were raised by ticket sales for the London and Philadelphia concerts respectively. In total Live Aid raised over £50m.

[12]Even with the Ethiopian famine, coverage tended not to question its underlying causes. Instead it chose to deal with the famine simply in terms of drought and crop failure. There was little attempt to grapple with the political and environmental problems which had been triggered by the drought into a major disaster.

[13]Mike Webb, *Behind the News*, a Tear Fund paper.

[14]Philip Schlesinger in *Putting 'Reality' Together: BBC News* (London: Constable, 1978, and Methuen, 1987) shows how news coverage is shaped by the factors we have described but goes on to point out that there is also a genuine sense of duty to inform the public despite high costs, perceived interest, or lack of pictures (see pp. 123–125).

[15]Tear Fund was able to give over £63,000 to rebuild homes and schools and support destitute Christians, many of whom faced discrimination in the government's relief distribution. It was Tear Fund's first grant to China. Many

Christians experienced discrimination in government relief distribution and yet it is estimated that as many as 10,000 people became Christians following the flooding.

[16]Mike Webb, *Behind the News*.

[17]Cameron Duodo, cited in *ibid*.

[18]Mike Webb, *Behind the News*.

[19]C. B. Samuel, 'Kingdom Partnerships', from *Good News to the Poor: The Gospel and Relief and Development*, a Tear Fund profile booklet. See also Vinay Samuel and Chris Sugden, *Partnership for Mission* (Bangalore: PIM-Asia, 1983).

[20]For a look at the relationship between the New Age movement and the green movement see Tim Cooper, *Green Christianity: Caring for the Whole Creation* (London: Spire, 1990), pp. 115–121.

[21]Chris Seaton and Lowell Sheppard, 'Environment and Youth', a paper presented to the WEF and Au Sable Forum on the Environment and Evangelical Christianity, p. 2.

[22]*Ibid.*, p. 5.

[23]*Ibid.*

[24]The WEF and Au Sable Forum on the Environment; see note 27 below.

[25]There were 2,300 people present, who set a new world record when they formed the largest ever human map of the world by congregating in the shape of the world. The organizers had hoped for over 5,000 people.

[26]See, for example, Lawrence Osborn, *Guardians of Creation: Nature in Theology and the Christian Life* (Leicester: Apollos, 1993), especially chapter 9, 'Christian environmentalism in practice', pp. 150–164.

[27]The forum, co-sponsored by WEF and the Au Sable Institute, Madison, Wisconsin, met on 26–31 August 1992. The forum report is published in *Transformation*, Vol. 9, No. 4, October 1992, and its conference papers in the *Evangelical Review of Theology*, Vol. 17, No. 2, April 1993.

Chapter 13: Renewal, restoration and social concern

[1]Interview with Gerald Coates, 27 November 1992.

[2]The story of the Ichthus Fellowship is told by Roger Forster (ed.) in *Ten New Churches* (MARC Europe and BCGA, 1986), pp. 48–71, and in Roger Forster, 'Wholistic Models of Evangelism and Social Concern: Ichthus Christian Fellowship, London', *Transformation*, Vol. 9, No. 2, April 1992, pp. 15–18.

[3]Roger Forster, *Ten New Churches*, p. 69.

[4]Roger Forster, 'Wholistic Models', p. 15.

[5]*Ibid.*

[6]Brian Hathaway, *Beyond Renewal: The Kingdom of God* (Milton Keynes: Word, 1990), see especially pp. 69–76.

[7]*Ibid.*, p. 58.

[8]In an appendix to *Beyond Renewal* (pp. 211–219) Brian Hathaway shares some of the projects the church has been involved in. They included adventure holidays, a shop, provision of Christian books to local libraries, providing a Christmas dinner for those living alone, a community newspaper, unemployment

projects, the provision of low-cost housing and emergency housing, tuition for exams, medical care and counselling, interest-free loans and financial advice, practical care from community workers, a playgroup and holiday play schemes, industrial chaplaincies, marriage counselling, ministry among homosexuals, the opening of Christian homes to those in need, prison visiting, settlement programmes for refugees, drug rehabilitation, visiting old people, food and vegetable co-ops, youth groups and a community care centre.

[9]Finding a convenient label for this group of churches is not easy. What distinguishes them from other charismatics is that they view the charismatic movement in terms of a restoration rather than a renewal of the church and so 'Restorationists' is the term preferred by Andrew Walker in *Restoring the Kingdom: The Radical Christianity of the House Church Movement* (London: Hodder, 1985) (see pp. 21–24) – the most comprehensive history of the house church movement to date. In practice, however, the term 'restoration' is usually applied only to those churches centred around Bryn Jones. The magazine *Restoration* – now a free quarterly broadsheet – was produced by his New Covenant Ministries team. The Restorationist were originally referred to as the 'house church movement'. Yet since many Restorationist churches no longer meet in houses and since there are many house churches which are not Restorationist – most notably the Ichthus Fellowship – the term 'house church movement' is no longer an accurate label. Likewise the term 'new churches' – which seems to be the most commonly used at the present – fails to distinguish them from other new churches planted by the traditional denominations or those which are non-aligned. In practice, as the separation between the new churches and other churches grows less and they themselves grow more diffuse, I suspect they will be increasingly known by the titles of their networks, *e.g.* Pioneer (Gerald Coates, John Noble), New Covenant Ministries (Bryn Jones), New Frontiers (Terry Virgo), *etc.*

To complicate matters, in 1976 the new churches split within themselves (see Walker, pp. 72–94). One group formed round the ministry of Bryn Jones in Bradford and, for example, the Dales Bible Week. The other group formed loosely round the ministries of Gerald Coates, John Noble, and others. These groups correspond to what Walker (pp. 24–25) refers to as R1 (now known as New Covenant Ministries) and R2 respectively. This, however, is something of a simplification. Some did not really fit into either category (Walker calls them R2 because they are more like the churches of Coates and Noble, although not formally associated with them). Others have left R1 for the R2 circle. Others, like Terry Virgo (Brighton) and Tony Morton (Southampton), were 'released' by Bryn Jones for a more independent ministry and now probably associate more with those in the R2 circle. In fact in practice there is now a loosely linked fellowship of different networks with the Bryn Jones network the most loosely linked.

[10]Andrew Walker, *Restoring the Kingdom*, p. 149.

[11]In fact the Festival of Light played an important part in the development of the Restoration movement. Many groups who had thought they were alone were put in touch with one another. Peter Hill, who initiated the Festival of

Light, eventually became part of the Barney Coombs network in Basingstoke.

[12]I owe these observations to John Corrie, 'Restoring the Kingdom', *Third Way*, Vol. 13, No. 3, April 1990, pp. 16–19.

[13]This is the assessment of Gerald Coates, interview, 27 November 1992.

[14]John Houghton, *Issues Facing Society* (Bradford: School of the Word, Harvestime, 1988). See also John Houghton, *Handling Your Money* (Milton Keynes: Word Books, 1986). This book of very practical advice includes a section in which God's concern for the poor is stressed with reference, for example, to Matthew 25:31–46 and the economic pattern of Israel's life. With the new birth, continues Houghton, comes 'a new impetus' and he illustrates this from the New Testament. 'The Gospel insists that only the new birth has the power to change our hearts sufficiently to make us love and care for the poor' (p. 79). 'Have you thought', he asks in conclusion, 'of helping the needy around you?' (p. 81).

[15]See John Corrie, 'Restoring the Kingdom', p. 19. Bryn Jones is also a director of the Institute of World Concerns, a research and educational institute based in Coventry, England, seeking to develop an inter-disciplinary approach to a variety of global issues.

[16]Interview with Gerald Coates, 27 November 1992.

[17]Larry Christenson, *A Charismatic Approach to Social Action* (London: Lakeland, 1974), pp. 12–13.

[18]Interview with Gerald Coates, 27 November 1992.

[19]Larry Christenson, *A Charismatic Approach to Social Action*, p. 113.

[20]Interview with Gerald Coates, 27 November 1992.

[21]Murray Robertson, 'Wholistic Models of Evangelism and Social Concern: Renewal Brings New Life', *Transformation*, Vol. 8, No. 4, October 1991, pp. 19–22.

[22]*Ibid.*, p. 21.

Chapter 14: Words, works and wonders

[1]The Grand Rapids Report, *Evangelism and Social Responsibility: An Evangelical Commitment* (Exeter: Paternoster, 1982), p. 31.

[2]On signs and wonders see John Wimber, *Power Evangelism: Signs and Wonders Today* (London: Hodder, 1985) and John Wimber, 'Power Evangelism: Definitions and Directions', in C. Peter Wagner and F. Douglas Pennoyer (eds.), *Wrestling with Dark Angels* (Ventura, CA: Regal Books, and Eastbourne: Monarch, 1990), pp. 19–56. On spiritual warfare also see *Wrestling with Dark Angels*. The book collects the papers of a symposium hosted by Fuller Seminary in December 1988 involving 40 scholars from North America which was entitled 'Academic Symposium on Power Evangelism'.

[3]See, for example, C. Peter Wagner, 'Territorial Spirits', in *Wrestling with Dark Angels*, pp. 83–110.

[4]*Ibid.*, pp. 88, 91.

[5]Interview with Gerald Coates, 27 November 1992.

[6]See John Stott, *The Message of Acts*, The Bible Speaks Today series (Leicester:

IVP, 1990), pp. 100–104.

[7]The Manila Manifesto is published in J. D. Douglas (ed.), *Proclaim Christ Until He Comes* (Minneapolis: World Wide Publications, 1990), pp. 25–38; this citation from p. 31.

[8]Paul Hiebert, 'Spiritual Warfare: Biblical Perspectives', *Mission Focus*, Vol. 20, No. 3, September 1992, pp. 41–46.

[9]Interview with Vinay Samuel, 7 December 1992.

[10]*Ibid.*

[11]See *Transformation*, Vol. 5, No. 4, October 1988.

[12]The conference was entitled 'Spirit, Kingdom, Church and Creation'. See *Transformation*, Vol. 7, No. 3, July 1990.

[13]See *Transformation*, Vol. 8, No. 4, October 1991.

[14]The Kingdom Manifesto is printed in *Transformation*, Vol. 7, No. 3, July 1990, pp. 6–10 and in Brian Hathaway, *Beyond Renewal: The Kingdom of God* (Milton Keynes: Word, 1990), pp. 193–205.

[15]Michael Harper, *A New Way of Living: How the Church of the Redeemer, Houston, Found a New Lifestyle* (London: Hodder, 1973).

[16]See, for example, David Prior, *The Church in the Home* (Basingstoke: Marshall, Morgan and Scott, 1983).

[17]John Wimber, *Power Evangelism*, p. 126.

[18]See D. W. Bebbington, *Evangelism in Modern Britain* (London: Unwin Hyman, 1989), pp. 245–247.

[19]Stuart Murray, 'Good News to the Poor', *Prophecy Today* (1992), p. 29.

[20]Cited by Ron Sider in his report on the conference in *Transformation*, Vol. 8, No. 4, October 1991. See also Brian Hathaway, *Beyond Renewal*, p. 128, and Viv Grigg who also speaks of 'the demon of affluence' (*Companion to the Poor*, Sutherland, NSW, Australia: Albatross Books, and Tring: Lion, 1984), p. 197. The International Charismatic Consultation on World Evangelization, held in Brighton, 8–14 July 1991, brought together 1,500 charismatics including Catholics, Anglicans, Pentecostals and those with no denominational affiliation.

[21]*Finding Faith Today*, Bible Society. Report in *The Times*, 3 October 1992. Only 4% of adults are converted through rallies according to the report.

[22]Viv Grigg, *Companion to the Poor*, p. 26; see also p. 13.

[23]*Ibid.*, p. 118; see also p. 115.

Chapter 15: Salt and light

[1]There were 316 participants at the Salt and Light conference, 31 October–4 November 1988.

[2]See Jim Smith, *A Heart for the Poor* (Eastbourne: Kingsway, 1988).

[3]See Colin Moreton's profile of Steve Chalke in *Church Times*, 11 December 1992, p. 7.

[4]See John Martin, 'When it comes to the needs of the mentally ill, do we need another Wilberforce?', *Church of England Newspaper*, 8 January 1993.

[5]David Potter, 'Back to the Future in '93?', *Evangelicals Now*, Vol. 8, No. 1, January 1993, pp. 1–2.

[6]Local authorities are legally obliged to set out their plans for community care including the use they intend to make of voluntary bodies. The EA co-ordinates the Evangelical Coalition in Community Care (Whitefield House, 186 Kennington Park Road, London, SE11 4BT). The Shaftesbury Society (18 Kingston Road, London, SW19 1ZJ) have also produced *Love in Action*, a church resource for practical community involvement.

[7]Interview with Tom Houston, 1 December 1992.

[8]The Mayflower Family Centre began in 1957 under the leadership of David Sheppard as a response to rising unemployment in the East End of London.

[9]David Sheppard, *Built as a City* (London: Hodder, 1974).

[10]See Maurice Hobbs, *Better Will Come: A Pastoral Response to Institutional Racism in British Churches* (Bramcote, Nottingham: Grove Books, 1991).

[11]The original partners were Frontier Youth Trust, the Evangelical Race Relations Group (now Evangelical Christians for Racial Justice), the Shaftesbury Project (now Christian Impact), the Evangelical Urban Training Project, *Christians in Industrial Areas* (relaunched in 1983 as *City Cries*, the journal of ECUM) and the London Consultative Group on Urban Mission. The present supporting partners are Christian Impact, the Enigma Trust, the Evangelical Urban Training Project, Frontier Youth Trust, Ministry Among Asians in Britain, Scripture Union's Urban Ministries, World Vision of Britain, and Evangelical Christians for Racial Justice.

[12]See, for example, Michael Paget-Wilkes, *Poverty, Revolution and the Church* (Exeter: Paternoster, 1981); Roy Joslin, *Urban Harvest* (Welwyn: Evangelical Press, 1982); David Sheppard, *Bias to the Poor* (London: Hodder, 1985); Colin Marchant, *Signs in the City* (London: Hodder, 1985).

Chapter 16: Continuing tensions

[1]Around 4,300 participants gathered from 173 countries for the second International Congress on World Evangelization, Lausanne II, in Manila. They met under the title 'Proclaim Christ Until He Comes' and produced the Manila Manifesto, again with John Stott chairing the drafting committee. The Congress papers and the Manifesto are printed in J. D. Douglas (ed.), *Proclaim Christ Until He Comes: Calling the Whole Church to Take the Whole Gospel to the Whole World* (Minneapolis: World Wide Publications, 1990). A number of the papers dealing with social action were published in *Transformation*, Vol. 7, No. 1, January 1990.

[2]Caesar Molebatsi, 'Reaching the Oppressed', in J. D. Douglas (ed.), *Proclaim Christ*, pp. 294–297. Caesar Molebatsi has been a key figure in evangelical opposition to apartheid in South Africa. He is Executive Director of Youth Alive Ministries and has been involved in evangelism, community development and reconciliation; see Caesar Molebatsi with David Virtue, *A Flame for Justice* (Oxford: Lion, 1991).

[3]Interview with Tom Houston, 1 December 1992.

[4]Brian Hathaway believes that just as Lausanne I confronted the evangelical world with the importance of social action in mission, so Lausanne II confronted it with the importance of the miraculous. As such Lausanne II linked signs

to words and deeds as the three dimensions needed to present the whole gospel (*Beyond Renewal*, p. 74). Others, however, did not feel the charismatic issue had been dealt with quite so successfully (see, for example, the comments of Bishop John Reid reported in the *Church of England Newspaper*, 28 July 1989, p. 5, and Alan Gibson, 'Evangelism in Tension', *Evangelicals Now*, Vol. 4, No. 9, September 1989, p. 20). At the Congress differences of opinion were represented by the balancing of speakers, Jim Packer and Jack Hayford, in the plenary session 'The Power and Work of the Holy Spirit'. The Manifesto itself held these emphases in tension: 'Although the miracles of Jesus were special, being signs of his Messiahship and anticipations of his perfect kingdom when all nature will be subject to him, we have no liberty to place limits on the power of the living Creator today. We reject both the skepticism which denies miracles and the presumption which demands them, both the timidity which shrinks from the fullness of the Spirit and the triumphalism which shrinks from the weakness in which Christ's power is made perfect.'

[5]See, for example, the Congress reports of Alan Gibson ('Evangelism in Tension') and Chris Sugden (*Church of England Newspaper*, 28 July 1989, p. 5).

[6]The Great Commission Congress was held in January 1989 in Singapore. There were 314 participants gathered from 50 countries. The resulting commitment, the Great Commission Manifesto, is printed in Luis Bush (ed.), *AD 2000 and Beyond: Handbook*, 2nd edition, p. 72.

[7]The Singapore Congress was the first Global Congress on World Evangelization. The second GCOWE is due to take place June 1994 in Seoul. At the same time, on 25 June, a world day of prayer is to be held including 'marches for Jesus' in every capital of the world. The third GCOWE is scheduled for 1999.

[8]*AD 2000 and Beyond: Handbook*, p. 10. There is also a good deal of co-operation between AD 2000 and WEF with a number of joint consultations planned and WEF officers involved in the organization of AD 2000. AD 2000 is an associate member of WEF and has adopted its doctrinal statement.

[9]*Ibid.*, p. 33.

[10]John Woodhouse, 'Evangelism and Social Responsibility', in B. G. Webb (ed.), *Christians in Society* (Homebush West, NSW, Australia: Lancer Books, 1988), p. 18.

[11]*Ibid.*, p. 20.

[12]*Ibid.*, p. 23.

[13]The emphasis on the lordship of Christ in all areas of life and the many examples from church history mean that some measure of social action is usually accepted as legitimate by those from the Reformed tradition. Groups such as A Cause for Concern (working with mentally handicapped people) and Caring for Life in Leeds (working with homeless youngsters) come from and are influenced by this tradition. See also, for example, Ian Shaw (ed.), *Social Issues and the Local Church* (Bryntirion, Bridgend: Evangelical Press of Wales, 1988). Also O. R. Johnston, the then director of the Nationwide Festival of Light, made an influential contribution to the 1975 Banner of Truth Leicester Ministers' Conference, later published as *Christianity in a Collapsing Culture* (Exeter: Paternoster, 1976).

[14]The discussion is in part a question of semantics. Legg criticizes Tear Fund material for saying, 'Social action is an essential component of the proclamation of the gospel', while he himself says, 'There should be no doubt that the preaching of the gospel *must* be accompanied by good works' (my emphasis). The problem is that certain words and phrases evoke fears of a social gospel – a proper concern but one which is not borne out by the facts.

[15]George Hoffman, Tear Fund Annual Report, 1982/3.

[16]*Christian Witness to the Urban Poor*, the report of the Mini-Consultation on Reaching the Urban Poor, Thailand, Lausanne Occasional Papers, No. 22 (1980), p. 9.

[17]Colin Marchant, *Signs in the City* (London: Hodder, 1985), p. 118.

Chapter 17: Getting into politics

[1]Donald Macleod, 'Can We Afford Political Hibernation?', *Evangelicals Now*, Vol. 7, No. 7, July 1992, p. 11.

[2]See, for example, Stephen Williams, 'Structural Change', *Third Way*, Vol. 13, No. 5, June 1990, pp. 8–9.

[3]Interview with Martyn Eden, 3 December 1992. At CLADE III Bishop David Gitari told of a group of Christians who provided an ambulance to ferry injured workers from a local factory to hospital. Then they began to ask why there were so many accidents at this factory and called in government officials to check its working conditions. As a result workers stopped being injured and the ambulance was no longer used and had to be sold. (Recounted to me by Dewi Hughes.)

[4]The story of evangelical involvement in Peruvian politics is told in Victor Arroyo and Tito Paredes, 'Evangelicals and "The Fujimori Phenomenon"', *Transformation*, Vol. 9, No. 3, July 1992, pp. 15–19. The whole of this issue of *Transformation* is given over to evangelicals and politics in Latin America.

[5]The story of evangelical involvement in Nicaraguan politics is told in 'Nicaragua: Evangelicals, Sandinistas and the Elections – an interview with Gustavo Parajón', *Transformation*, Vol. 2, No. 1, January 1985, pp. 4–6 and Adolfo Miranda Saenz, 'The Political Metamorphosis of Evangelicals in Nicaragua', *Transformation*, Vol. 9, No. 3, July 1992, pp. 20–25.

[6]Cited by Paul Gifford, *The New Crusaders: Christianity and the New Right in Southern Africa* (London and Concord, Mass.: Pluto Press, 1991), p. 30.

[7]Adolfo Miranda Saenz, 'The Political Metamorphosis of Evangelicals in Nicaragua', pp. 23–24.

[8]See 'Evangelical Witness in South Africa', *Transformation*, Vol. 4, No. 1, January 1987, pp. 16–30.

[9]See David Gitari, *Let the Bishop Speak* (Nairobi: Uzima, 1988) and 'Church and Politics in Kenya', *Transformation*, Vol. 8, No. 3, July 1991, pp. 7–19.

[10]See, for example, Roy McCloughry, *Taking Action* (Leicester: Frameworks, 1990), Kathy Keay, *How to Make the World Less Hungry* (Leicester: Frameworks, 1990), and Richard Bauckham, *The Bible in Politics: How to Read the Bible Politically*, a *Third Way* book (London: SPCK, 1989).

[11]The members of Christian Election Forum 1992 were CARE, Christian Caring for Life, Credit Action, Evangelical Coalition for Urban Mission, Keep Sunday Special Campaign, Knights of Saint Columba, Tear Fund and the Union of Catholic Mothers. The Jubilee Centre acted as its secretariat.

[12]Michael Schluter with David Lee, *Keeping Sunday Special: The Fight Against the Shops Bill* (Basingstoke: Marshall Pickering, 1988), pp. 111–112.

[13]Ronald Sider and others, *Completely Pro-Life* (Downers Grove, IL: IVP, 1987).

[14]Stephen Rand, personal letter to the author, March 1993.

[15]Charles Elliott, *Comfortable Compassion? Poverty, Power and the Church* (London: Hodder, 1987).

[16]See, for example, Michael Cromartie, 'Fixing the World: From Non-players to Radicals to New Right Conservatives: The Saga of Evangelicals and Social Action', *Christianity Today*, Vol. 36, No. 5, April 1992, pp. 23–25; Frances Fitzgerald, *Cities on a Hill: A Journey through Contemporary American Cultures* (London: Picador, 1987), pp. 121–201; Jim Skillen, 'Morality Politics or Public Justice?', *Third Way*, Vol. 13, No. 1, February 1990, pp. 28–31; and Clyde Wilcox, *God's Warriors: The Christian Right in Twentieth-Century America* (Baltimore, Maryland: Johns Hopkins University Press, 1992).

[17]Charles Colson, *Kingdoms in Conflict: An Insider's Challenging View of Politics, Power and the Pulpit* (London: Hodder, 1987), p. 45.

[18]At the same time the sister organizations Religious Roundtable and Christian Voice were established. New Christian Right is an umbrella term for these and other organizations and their leaders.

[19]Charles Colson, *Kingdoms in Conflict*, p. 45.

[20]See further, Paul Gifford, *The New Crusaders*, pp. 15–17.

[21]Clive Calver, 'Voting for God at the US Ballot-box', *The Independent*, 31 October 1992, p. 37.

[22]Donald Macleod, 'Can We Afford Political Hibernation?', *Evangelicals Now*, Vol. 7, No. 7, July 1992, pp. 11–12.

[23]Interview with Martyn Eden, 3 December 1992.

[24]Clive Calver, 'Voting for God at the US Ballot-box', p. 37.

[25]Although not overtly partisan there are those who believe that evangelicals, particularly in England, are innately conservative (and Conservative) – at least outside of the inner cities. Donald Macleod believes 'there is little doubt that the evangelical vote in Britain is anti-Labour'. Labour, he argues, is perceived by most evangelicals to be 'ungodly' – as if the other parties were more godly! See Donald Macleod, 'Can We Afford Political Hibernation?'

[26]For Abraham Kuyper's political thought see, for example, Abraham Kuyper, *The Problem of Poverty*, 1891, ed. James W. Skillen (Grand Rapids: Baker, 1991) and Abraham Kuyper, *Lectures on Calvinism*, 1898 (Grand Rapids: Eerdmans, 1961).

[27]See, for example, Alan Kreider, *Journey Towards Holiness: A Way of Living for God's Nation* (Basingstoke: Marshall Pickering, 1986).

[28]For a summary of both sides of the argument see Oliver Barclay and Chris Sugden, 'Biblical Social Ethics in a Mixed Society', *Evangelical Quarterly*, Vol. 62, No. 1, 1990, pp. 5–18. This edition of the *Evangelical Quarterly* is devoted to a

symposium on the subject of creation and kingdom ethics. See also Oliver Barclay and Chris Sugden, *Kingdom and Creation in Social Ethics* (Bramcote, Nottingham: Grove Books, 1992). See also A. N. Triton, *Whose World?* (London: IVP, 1970), especially p. 13.

[29]Vinay Samuel and Chris Sugden, 'God's Intention for the World', in *idem* (eds.), *The Church in Response to Human Need* (Oxford: Regnum, 1987), p. 146.

[30]See Oliver Barclay and Chris Sugden, 'Biblical Social Ethics', p. 17.

[31]See Christopher J. H. Wright, 'The Use of the Bible in Social Ethics', *Transformation*, Vol. 1, No. 1, January 1984, pp. 11–20, especially pp. 19–20, and Michael Schluter and Roy Clements, 'Jubilee Institutional Norms: A Middle Way between Creation Ethics and Kingdom Ethics as the Basis for Christian Political Action', *Evangelical Quarterly*, Vol. 62, No. 1, 1990, pp. 37–62.

[32]Oliver O'Donovan, 'The Natural Ethic', in David F. Wright (ed.), *Essays in Evangelical Social Ethics* (Exeter: Paternoster, 1979), pp. 19–35.

[33]Oliver O'Donovan, *Resurrection and Moral Order: An Outline for Evangelical Ethics* (Leicester: IVP, and Grand Rapids: Eerdmans, 1986, 1993), p. 15.

[34]Ron Sider, 'A Plea for More Radical Conservatives and More Conserving Radicals', *Transformation*, Vol. 4, No. 1, January 1987, pp. 11–16.

Conclusion: a personal reflection on faith, hope and love

[1]Jim Wallis, *A Call to Conversion* (New York: Harper and Row, and Tring: Lion, 1981), pp. 19–20, 29.

[2]Theo Donner, 'Some Thoughts on the Theology of Liberation', unpublished paper, p. 17.

[3]See, for example, Martin Luther, *The Heidelberg Disputation*, 1518, paragraphs XIX–XXII, in James Atkinson (ed.), *Luther's Early Theological Works*, Library of Christian Classics, Vol. 16 (London: SCM. 1962).

[4]The phrase is borrowed from Jürgen Moltmann, *Theology of Hope* (London: SCM, 1967), pp. 154–165.

Index